I HATE YOU JIMMY

Jeff,

Thanks for the support!

Eddie + Jimmy

[handwritten signature]

Jimmy Curran

Published 2018 in Philadelphia, Pennsylvania, by Prince Street Publishing, LLC.

This book may be purchased for educational, business, or sales promotional use.

Editing contributions by:
Laura Mae Isaacman at Clyde Editing
Stephanie Heilman

This book is printed on acid free paper by DiggyPOD, Inc., a small business located in Tecumseh Michigan.

The text type used in the body of the book is Garamond.

ISBN : 978-1-7320713-9-1

Author's Note/Disclaimer: This is a work of creative nonfiction that I did not plan on writing until I started writing it. I have scoured photographs, videos, my personal journals and notebooks, and interviewed some of the people in this book, in order to ensure that the events are portrayed accurately to the very best of my ability. While all the stories in this book are true, all names have been changed, other than my own, Jimmy's, and those of celebrities/public figures. Furthermore, a very few identifying details may have been changed in order to protect the privacy of the people involved.

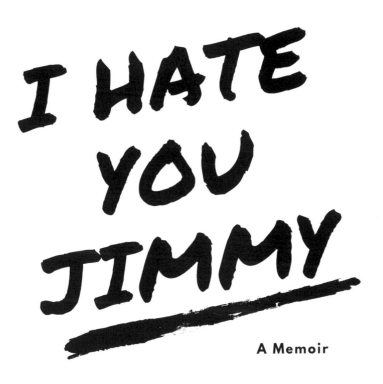

I HATE YOU JIMMY

A Memoir

EDDIE DOYLE

Prince Street Publishing

PHILADELPHIA

Table of Contents

Table of Contents

Introduction

For me, it was his hands. It's not that I couldn't stop looking at them . . . it was all I wanted to look at. It was the visual I let my eyes hang on as I acted like I was looking around, like a perfectly filled bikini top, or your best friend's cold sore. It was what I fixated on when he was looking away and I knew he wouldn't catch me. It was what struck me as most abnormal . . . disfigured . . . different.

Maybe it was because they were crippled, bent at the wrist, barely moveable. Long, skinny fingers that looked like sharpened-down pencils with a matching thumb tucked underneath. Maybe it was because he was able to use that deformed body part for so many things—handling his chair's joystick, using his phone, and, to my surprise, to sign his name or feed himself if necessary. Maybe, actually, most likely, his hands stood out to me because I had been teased for my own short, stubby fingers and I focused on his as a result of my own insecurity. In time, I would find out that this 63-pound man, who is barely four feet tall when measured in his permanent knees-bent position, has the same sized hands as me. I would also find he would mention this embarrassing fact whenever he had the chance.

Regardless of the reason, it was his hands that stuck out to me. For you, it might be his normal-sized head, which, when placed on a miniature body with arms and legs being barely anything more than bone and skin, somewhat resembles a golf ball on a tee. Or it might be the way his head nods when he is chewing, using the momentum of that heavy golf ball to help his weaker jaw. When he pulls his hands close to his chest while eating, I still sometimes think of a Tyrannosaurs Rex. Maybe it is when you see the wheelchair at the after-hours bar, or the five-star restaurant, or the professional sporting event—the hopeless and heartbroken expectation of disability is met with crisp Gucci shoes, a button-down Burberry shirt, the scent of sophistication, and a scarf meticulously wrapped around his neck, the logo positioned to make sure the world sees the little guy on the horse. Maybe Jimmy stands—err, sits—out when your bus is held up for the five-minutes it takes for the ramp to lower down, load him up, and strap him in. Or maybe it's when he's throwing back shots at the party, and suddenly you find an exception to the rule about never drinking and operating a motor vehicle. Maybe the disconnect comes when you see this handsome young man courtside at an NBA game chatting it up with the players, or smooching with the *Sports Illustrated* swimsuit model in the middle of the bar . . . settling for a prolonged kiss only because his condition does not give him the strength needed for a frencher.

Even more interesting than the way Jimmy interacts with the world is the way the world interacts with him. The waitress who asks *me* what Jimmy is going to have, even as he is sitting there reading the menu. Or the impatient bathroom line, making rude comments and banging on the door, until it swings open and everyone quietly adjusts their attitude as they clear a path for the wheelchair. The girl who is left speechless when this cute, innocent little man she spent the evening talking to invites her back to his apartment as the bar is closing. Or the visible shift from an expression of anger to apology after a guy's been nailed in the back of the leg with an unknown object and turns around to find he's been struck by muscular dystrophy. Jimmy has a special power to hit someone—and hit them hard—and have the victim say "sorry." For what they are apologizing, I still don't know.

Most revealing, however, is the uncontaminated reaction from children. It's not uncommon for a child walking past Jimmy to continue moving forward while his head turns and turns and turns like an owl, perplexed and cemented on this person who is similar in size but looks so dissimilar to themselves. It is a raw look of confusion—a look that says, *You are different than me.* Usually this is followed by a guilt-ridden, hushed scolding from a nearby parent who's telling the kid not to stare. I don't know if the child gets scared of how Jimmy looks, or upset that this happened to someone, or bewildered as to why it would happen.

What I do know is that it is a pure reaction, one not masked or inhibited by years of trying to make sense of the world.

And, no matter if you are young or old, seeing, meeting, or interacting with Jimmy threatens to change the bubble of the world you have created for yourself.

For me, it was in a common area of our college dorm, with a group of us playing PlayStation 2. Jimmy said he would play the winner of the next game. There was an uncomfortable pause in the room, with everybody—well, every "able" body—thinking, *How the hell is this kid going to do that?* When the time came, he instructed me on how to set him up to play like a seasoned mechanic helping a teen put on a spare tire.

"Turn my chair off so it doesn't move . . . swing my joystick out . . . move my hips to the left . . . head forward . . . controller in the lap . . . now put my hands [*Oh, god, his hands*] on top of the controller . . . put my pointer finger on the gas . . ." He looked at me and smiled. "I don't need the brakes."

It was not an issue to be skirted anymore. It was not a stolen glance. It wasn't a thought of confusion or disgust or fear. It was real. I touched them. And they didn't shatter into a million pieces like I thought they might. Though small, and skinny, and limited, they belonged to a man. A man like me.

1

Meeting Hot Wheelz

Friendship is so weird . . . you just pick a human you've met and you're like, "Yup I like this one," and you just do stuff with them.

—Bill Murray

It was the first week of my sophomore year and all I wanted to do was head back to the spot I missed the most: the Lobby. The size of a city block, 1300 was my X-shaped, five-story dorm at Temple University. Its only entrance was in front, the courtyard was in the back, and the Lobby was located between the two, with a study and TV lounge on either side. There were couches and chairs, vending machines, and even a small cafeteria within half a flight of steps. Add those amenities to the fact it was impossible to enter or exit the building without going through the Lobby, and that made it the perfect spot to post-up and hang out—not just on campus, but probably in the entire world.

Though we had lost a lot of the Lobby roster to graduation, transfers, and a few who wanted to venture out to the free agency of off-campus housing, my friend Stephanie and I knew that the magnetic powers of that hallowed entryway would shine through. It was only a few days into the fall semester, and we had been spending the majority of our time in and around our usual hangout, seeing old friends and meeting new ones. We were still waiting for that clincher though—that X-factor that could make the Lobby great again.

On nice days, the Lobby hangout sessions extended to the walkway leading up to the dorm, as those of us in Philly needed to soak in those few weeks of the fall semester where the weather doesn't make you hate life. Stephanie and I were sitting on a bench when I noticed Jimmy rolling by. I hadn't met him yet, but being that he was the only person in a wheelchair in the dorm at the time, I definitely recognized him. As he came closer, I was trying to discreetly look at those hands. Then I realized he was coming right towards me.

Shit. Did he catch me staring?

"What's up?" he said.

The feeling that overcame me was only comparable to when the most beautiful woman—the one that everyone notices the moment she walks in the room—completely and totally unsolicited, approaches and says, "Hello." I was nervous—I had never seen up close, let alone spoken to, someone who looked like that. And why was he talking to me? Was I that obvious in staring? As I gathered myself and tried to give a smooth and calm reply—

"What's up, Jimmy?" Stephanie said. Just like when the extremely attractive woman says hello, I had been mistaken in thinking the greeting was directed at me.

Stephanie was involved in any and every student organization she could get her hands on, and had met Jimmy while volunteering at the welcome week for new freshman. She introduced us, and that was that. There was no crazy, interesting, or disability-related start to our friendship. I met Jimmy the way most people meet friends in college: we lived in the same dorm and a mutual friend introduced us.

Being part of the Lobby required two things: sitting and conversing. Jimmy had a lifetime of experience with the former, and turned out to be a natural at the latter. The group that formed that year was made up of individuals who were as diverse as you could get, and I don't mean in appearance, either. Sure, we had the qualities of a bad sitcom—different colors, sexual orientation, style of dress, even physical abilities (Division 1 athletes to . . . well, Jimmy). But I mean that beyond those superficial things, we were diverse in our values. From a libertarian to a real-life American-born communist, from chauvinists to feminists, atheists to Christians, what separated sides in our in-depth discussions (ranging from global politics to the age old question of "boobs or butt?"), I found, had less to do with appearance and more to do with our values.

I wish I could say we had a grand scheme behind the time spent there, a sort of secret society with ties to conspiracy theories, one with a fancy name like The Illuminati or The Order of Skull and Bones. I'd even settle for name that gave us an air of intellectualism that predetermined a ridiculous amount of success for all its members, like the Inklings. But that's just not how it goes up there on North Broad Street. Fact is, we were just a group of kids who loved to procrastinate and meet new people. The Lobby was open to everyone, and whenever someone passed through, they were sure to stick around for a little a bit.

And that's the exact reason Jimmy was rookie of the year in the Lobby. The spot had a natural gravitational pull to it, and Jimmy only magnified it. It seemed like everyone who walked by wanted to talk to him, and if they didn't initiate a conversation, he would. There were more than one thousand people living in 1300, and I'll be damned if not every single one of them knew Jimmy. When I first noticed this, I thought it must have been some sort of liberal arts, millennial, *Look how accepting I am of all kinds of people* bullshit. But then I had an experience with him that made me start to look at him just a little bit differently.

In the Lobby one day, I had mentioned to everyone my current anxiety over an assignment to make a radio commercial. In addition to my tendency of imagining a task to be bigger than it actually is, I was specifically irked by the idea of having to use the audio editing software. I wasn't really paying attention in class when the professor went over it, and I was dreading having to trek all the way across campus, in the cold, to the library, only to frustrate myself with a program I knew nothing about. Like all great procrastinators, I was thinking if I just put it off as long as possible it may never become real.

"Just a thirty-second commercial?" Jimmy asked.

"Yeah. I may just eat the grade."

He laughed, shaking his head. "Come to my room. I want to show you something."

I followed Jimmy to his room, and he pushed a button on his lap that swung his door open. I had never been in a wheelchair-accessible dorm room. It was a lot bigger, with a huge bathroom, a full kitchen, and two twin beds. On his desk, next to his laptop, was a separate computer, complete with speakers, a mixing board, noise-cancelling headphones, and a stand-up microphone that even had a pop filter—one of those circular screens in front of the microphone that I've always seen but had no idea as to its purpose.

"Is this your room or a music studio?"

"I got everything you could possibly need. We could do it now if you want."

Skip going to the library and have Jimmy walk me through it? Sounded good to me. As he started setting up the computer, I asked him why he had all this stuff.

"I used to rap," he said.

"Nice," I replied . . . politely. I took that with a grain of salt. Every white suburban kid who grew up in the era of Eminem wanted to rap, myself included. I just figured him having this equipment meant his parents spoiled him.

"Yeah, now I use it to charge other rappers who want to record their own music."

"So, I was right. This is a music studio."

"It's the dorm room of a business man, is what it is."

"Fair enough."

After he walked me through the step-by-step instructions to start and stop the recording, I read the transcript. Then only thing he wanted from me was a title for the project. Other than that, he basically did the rest on his own, adding the edits, effects, and other bells and whistles the project required, without me even asking. I was starting to like this guy.

Looking around the room as he worked on my project, I figured I should contribute something. "You know, you can have campus services remove the one bed so you can have even more space," I said, proud that my sophomoric knowledge would help the new freshman.

"The second bed is for the overnight nurse."

"Oh." It was moments like these that I dreaded. Innocent questions or comments that turn into an extremely awkward situation. *What have I just done? I didn't just point out how different his life was than mine, I pointed out my ignorance too! He must be so offended. And mad. And embarrassed. And uncomfortable.* As he continued to work on my project, my stupid comment only grew louder in my head, and my insides cringed with discomfort. *I have to say something to break this awkward silence. I need to redeem myself. I need to tell him "I'm sorry," and I didn't mean anything by it, and that I think it's ok he's in a wheelchair. I mean, not ok, like good, but like, I accept it. I mean, not like I need to accept it, I mean like I accept him, I mean—*

"Done." Jimmy cut the silence he didn't even seem to notice. "Want to hear some of my songs?"

"Songs?"

"Yeah, I told you, I used to rap."

Jimmy opened a file titled "Hot Wheelz" and played a handful of songs that he wrote and produced. Up until that point, I thought "Hot Wheelz" was just his AIM* screen name—I didn't know it was his rap persona.

The songs weren't bad . . . in fact, I kind of liked them. He sounded tough, aggressive, explosive.

"This is you?!" I asked.

"Yeah."

"It doesn't sound like you. You sound really . . ." *Shit. I caught myself. I was going to say tough. But I don't want him to think he's not tough. I was going to say strong, but I don't want him to think he has a weak voice. I was going to say adult—but I don't want him to think he sounded young.*

"Yeah, so my voice sounds thicker, I layered the vocal track. It's a common thing, actually, but I used it all the time."

I wasn't sure how I was supposed to react. I was surprised he knew what I was thinking, and how well he knew music, and especially at how self-aware he was. Mostly, I was surprised at how comfortable he was in talking about these things, and how comfortable it was making me.

After listening to a handful of songs, and with my project complete, there was only one thing left to do: head back down to the Lobby.

---

* To put a time stamp on my college years, AOL Instant Messenger was still in common use and Facebook was only for those with school email addresses. Such simpler times.

2

A Professional and Informative Interview

I never let my schooling interfere with my education.

—Mark Twain

It was another night in the Lobby and I once again found myself procrastinating on an assignment. This time, however, completely avoiding it until the day it was due would be impossible. I was tasked to conduct a live, professional interview in class, and I had to find a person with a "newsworthy" story to interview. Not only did this extra effort burden me, I was scared that my "who had the wildest Saturday night?" idea of newsworthy wasn't what the professor, a former news anchor himself, was looking for.

When I offered this predicament up to the Lobby crew, I thought maybe someone on the school's basketball or football team would do it. Even though they were really just regular people, because they played a sport the campus ground they walked on was damn near worshipped. At the very least, the sports fans and the girls in my class would find it interesting, for sure. Unfortunately, when it came to school, these athletes tried even harder at not trying than I did. They passed.

"It can be anyone?" Jimmy asked.

"Yup."

"Why not me?"

Hmmm. There was an idea. It didn't take long to learn that when you are in the presence of Jimmy, you are in the shadow of Jimmy. It was impossible to go anywhere without him seeing someone he knew or running into a friendly stranger who sparked a conversation. He obviously had some sort of magnetic pull, and there's nothing that screams *newsworthy* like a disability. People like talking about it, exploring it, and, most of all, showing that they support those with it. And Jimmy was cool with coming to my class—he loves meeting new people and talking about himself. I told him when and where the class was, and boom, my interview prep was complete. I figured Jimmy basically had a PhD via his life experiences concerning his own condition, and was proud for finding a story that pretty much wrote itself.

On the day of the interview, I met Jimmy outside of my class.

"I didn't know you owned anything other than sweatpants and t-shirts," Jimmy said, commenting on my suit.

"Don't be jealous because my entire wardrobe costs less than your outfit."

"It's not jealousy, Eddie. It's definitely not jealousy."

After we watched a couple of my classmates go through their interviews, it was our turn. As I sat down on the set, I thought of how my roommate recently pointed out the slight thinning of my hair, making me feel like I was the next Matt Lauer[*], ready to crush this interview. After the scripted introduction, I turned to him, thinking the hard part was done and he would carry it from there.

"I understand you have been in a wheelchair all of your life. Could you tell us more about that?"

"I have spinal muscular atrophy, it's a form of muscular dystrophy. It's a progressive disease, but other than that I don't really know the science behind it."

Pause.

Then some more pause.

I looked him like, *Damnit Jimmy, I wasn't supposed to have to work for this.* "Anything else?" I asked.

---

[*] For the record, I am referencing the Matt Lauer America knew and loved back when I was in college. Not the button under the desk sex villain Matt Lauer that was discovered literally during the final stages of editing this book. Ain't it crazy how a couple pieces of new information can shift your perspective on someone so drastically?

"Well, I've been in a wheelchair since I was two. And my muscles are pretty weak."

Surprised was an understatement. If I get a bad cough and a stuffy nose, I'm on *WebMD* for three hours coming to the conclusion that I'm most certainly going to die. Here's a kid who has never been able to walk because of his condition and he's telling me he doesn't know anything about it? I was expecting him to carry the interview, and instead he throws me a curveball like this? I attempted to get him to elaborate—to get him talking about treatments, doctors—anything.

"Well, when I was younger, I was offered the chance to be a part of medication trial studies."

"Did you do it?"

"No way. I'm not a freakin' lab rat."

Hm. I guess that made sense. Never thought of his situation like that before. Though it had nothing to do with the assignment, that fresh perspective satisfied my learning quota for the day. That was it for my effort in conducting a professional, interesting, and informative interview. The ensuing three minutes were full of nonsense and fluff, Jimmy and I trying to contain our own laughter as we talked about silly things like what he does for fun and his favorite part of campus.

When the camera stopped rolling and we came off set, it seemed like everyone, the professor included, made it a point to tell Jimmy what a good job he did. We looked at each other like, *Are these people messing with us?* Not only did none of the other interviewees receive that kind of praise, but we were literally just two friends sitting and talking about how there is no such thing as too much cheese on a cheesesteak. Groundbreaking stuff, I know.

I got an A on that assignment. Having had that professor before, and being very familiar with how he grades, I couldn't believe it. Maybe he didn't realize Jimmy and I were friends, and gave me the grade because he thought I approached a stranger with an uncomfortable topic. Maybe it was a typo. You've got to figure that happens once in a while. I wouldn't be surprised, though, if part of the reason I got that A was because the professor didn't want Jimmy to think he did a bad job.

3

What We Saw from the Cheap Seats

I have discovered in 20 years of moving around a
ballpark, that the knowledge of the game is usually in
inverse proportion to the price of the seats.

—Bill Veeck

Embarrassingly, I had based my college search on the
schools I would root for during the NCAA March Madness
Basketball Tournament. When touchdown Jesus didn't answer
my Hail Mary application to Notre Dame, I decided on what is
known—by me and very few others—as the Harvard of North
Philadelphia: Temple University.

I lived for basketball season, and freshman year
Stephanie and I were two of the five students from the entire
student body to log perfect attendance to the home games.
Sophomore year, the two of us picked up right where we left off,
when a couple of weeks into the season Jimmy confronted us
with an overwhelming predicament: he asked the two of us to go
to a game with him. On its surface, that may not seem like a big
deal, but superstition dictated that Stephanie and I sit in the same
exact seats in the same exact row of the same exact section every
single game. We needed to be in those specific seats to sing the
Temple fight song and will every foul shot into the basket by
holding up our hands and waving our spirit fingers. But where we

sat was not wheelchair accessible— we knew we would have to move to wherever it was that Jimmy sat, bringing bad luck to the team and most likely throwing away the game.

Ok, I am being dramatic and don't actually believe any of that, but being a sucker for sentimental routine, I will admit I was reluctant to break tradition. Regardless, Stephanie and I felt it would have been a little messed up to leave Jimmy hanging, especially because it would have been due to his disability. We threw away over a year of commitment to go with him.

Once we were in the building, Jimmy said, "Follow me." *Here we go*, I thought, *time to find an elevator or backway ramp up to a wheelchair accessible balcony, or some other bullshit seating*. It's not like I'm too good for cheap seats, it's just frustrating when you know you could have the better seats that you've sat in for an entire year, and are instead settling for less. Sure enough, Jimmy rolls right up to a roped-off, guarded entrance and tells the ushers that Stephanie and I are with him. As we walk past the ticket and administrative offices in a carpeted hallway, I notice that they're adorned with all sorts of Temple sports memorabilia. *Pretty cool*, I thought. The usher brings us to the elevator, and as we step inside, he hits the button and tells us to enjoy the game. *This sure is a fancy way to get to the nosebleeds*. Then I feel that momentary weightlessness of an elevator dropping. *Are we going down?*

The door opens and we follow Jimmy past the press conference room, trainer's room, visitor locker room—all the behind-the-scenes places I've never seen in person. Jimmy says hello to another usher standing by a large black curtain, who returns the greeting by name. We continue through the curtain and into the arena, and I realize we are coming out of the same tunnel the players go through when they run on and off the court.

We follow Jimmy to an open spot on the baseline, right next to where the cheerleaders were sitting. He tells the staff he needs two fold-out chairs, and they move as if it was a request from Temple Head Coach (and Philly legend) Fran Dunphy himself. Jimmy slides forward, square to the court until he is just about inbounds, and then reverses his chair straight back a couple of feet into the space right next to me.

This.

Is.

Awesome.

Stephanie and I looked at each other like, *Did this really just happen?* And to think, we had thought we were doing Jimmy a favor.

"How the hell did you get these seats?"

"You saw the way we came."

"No, but like how did you get them?"

"*Eddie*," he said, as if to hush me. "You *saw* the way we came."

"You mean . . ." I realized at no point in our trek to courtside did Jimmy show any sort of ticket or pass to anyone.

"Yeah," he laughed. "It works every time."

We were so close that I could see the beads of sweat on the players and hear everything—the trash talking, the grunts, the constant squeaking of their sneakers on the court. Every Temple game I ever attended, when an opposing player was at the foul line and the stadium grew quiet between the first and second shot, I would pay homage to the classic art film known as *Happy Gilmore* and yell, "YOU WILL NOT MAKE THIS SHOT . . . JACKASS!" At every other game, I could hear those around me chuckle, but this time, I could see the players trying to contain a grin. I even had a loose ball come my way, which I caught and threw back to the ref.

That ball got me thinking about all those highlights you see, the ones of players running or falling or diving into the stands. *How awesome would that be?* Then it got me thinking about Jimmy . . . *What if they were heading towards him? He has no way to defend himself.* That got me thinking, *I am the one next to him . . . it would be on me to step in and protect him. Could I do that?* Like every guy who retired from sports after he graduated high school, my idea of my strength and athleticism was much higher than my actual strength and athleticism. Every time the ball was on our half of the court, I was not only ready, but hoping for an opposing player to come Jimmy's way. I could already see the *SportsCenter* highlight in slow motion: me springing from my chair, reaching out a hand to knock the ball away, and, the moment before he crashed into Jimmy, I would meet the player, shoulder to hip, leveling him with perfect tackling form and sending him the opposite direction. I would then get up and glare at the opponent laying there, for just a moment, before I step over him, pick up the ball, and without even looking toss it towards the hoop as the entire stadium watches in silence, until the ball swishes through the net and the crowd goes wild!

Unfortunately, that didn't happen that night, nor at any other point during our college career. What did happen, though, was a change in the way we supported our team. Gone were the days of the measly student section—we wanted to sit courtside. Stephanie and I were hell-bent on making sure we got that invite from Jimmy to each game, and we would get super salty when he took anyone else.

Whenever we did get the privilege to go with him, we were there on that baseline, singing the Temple fight song at the top of our lungs. And when it came time for spirit fingers, Stephanie and I were on either side of Jimmy, lifting his arms above his head as the three of us waved Temple along to victory.

4

Jimmy's First Drink

A person's a person, no matter how small.

—Dr. Seuss

Jimmy was a hit on campus. Despite Temple's 40,000 student and staff body being described as one of the nation's most diverse, if you are a 63-pound man in a wheelchair, you are going to stand out. He wasn't but one semester into college and it seemed like everyone knew Jimmy, and if there were someone who didn't, they sure as hell knew *of* him. Even when I wasn't with Jimmy, more times than I could count, someone would approach me—at a party, before class, in the cafeteria, wherever—with the sole intent to ask about him. "Hey, don't you know that kid in a wheelchair?" they would say. "I see him all the time!" They would ask me how I knew him, what his name was, and other things of that nature. As someone who loves to meet new people, I didn't mind it—but I do remember every now and then someone would ask a question like, "Can I say 'hi' to him the next time I see him?" The first time I was asked a question like that, I was so taken off guard, I could only respond with a simple, "Yeah, sure." As time went on, I couldn't help but answer such ridiculous questions sarcastically with responses like, "It's a free country," or "As long as it's not a Tuesday." I had no idea why they hell they were asking me for permission. It had a "Can I pet your dog?" feel to it that made me really uncomfortable.

The way I see it—and to be honest, the way I sometimes felt—is that there was a line drawn that Jimmy couldn't cross. Even for those of us who hung out with him all the time in the Lobby, it was like there was an invisible boundary. We could get over our fear of talking to him and introduce ourselves to the wheelchair. We could hang out with the wheelchair in our free time, and kick it in the Lobby . . . maybe grab a bite or go to a basketball game. But when it came time for our real social lives— the weekends (and certain weeknights)—we couldn't let the wheelchair get in the way. That invisible line said Jimmy had no part in our partying.

Even after meeting him, and realizing he was just like me in a different body—Jimmy was still in a wheelchair. A chair that couldn't climb up the stoop and into the house party. And even if we carried Jimmy inside, we couldn't leave an expensive wheelchair outside on the streets in North Philadelphia. If we did, how would Jimmy operate without it?

We couldn't see him as capable, even after he explained the homework that no one else understood. We couldn't ignore his handicap, even after he opened and held the door for us with his protruding back wheels. We couldn't see him as independent, even after seeing him eating out by himself, slowly but surely lifting the fork into his mouth. I remember a mutual friend explaining to me, in private, that he happened to be walking by a pizza place and saw Jimmy sitting there by himself, waiting for a meal.

"I mean, I couldn't just leave him there by himself, you know?" he started.

I nodded in appeasement, because that's how most conversations go. But in my head, I didn't understand.

"So then I fed him his lunch," he continued, "and I'm just thinking like, if I wasn't there, what would have happened, you know?"

"Yeah, man, I hear you." *If Jimmy went there by himself . . . I am sure he would have been fine to stay there by himself. What am I missing here?*

"It's like, almost kind of messed up that he would put someone in that situation," my friend continued.

I couldn't even bullshit a nod at that point—I had to change the subject. As we talked, my mind wandered. *Did this guy really get frustrated with Jimmy because he chose to help Jimmy with something he didn't ask for? What don't I see here?*

In one way or another, we couldn't get past the disability because, though no one ever asked him, we just *knew* he was too handicapped . . . too dependent . . . too sick. He wasn't like us. He can't go out with us. He can't party with us. He most certainly can't drink.

He had no business being around a bunch of kids still trying to figure out how to drink as irresponsibly as possible. The nerves and worries of a bunch of underage students partying couldn't handle the added pressure of giving alcohol to a wheelchair. There were many times when we drank around Jimmy, whether in the Lobby or a dorm room, passing around a concoction of well liquor and diet soda and trying to pretend it wasn't the grossest fucking thing we have ever tasted. And as people tried to convince themselves and others that this high quality libation is "*sooo* good, you have to try it," the bottle always seemed to quietly and uncomfortably skip past Jimmy, with an offer to partake in it never coming his way. And because Jimmy never asked, nobody was really jumping at the chance to pour poison down his throat.

It's not as if he didn't have a social life on the weekends—it's just that it was stopped short. Before heading to a grimy party in a musty row home basement, someone would host a pregame party in a dorm room. Jimmy would get the invite to that—it was accessible, he could operate in the dorms, and it was just like hanging at any other spot, except that some people were drinking. But when it came time to leave, "Later, Jimmy," awkwardly came out of everyone's mouth in some way, shape, or form—everybody *knowing* it was impossible for him to tag along.

Then Tommy O'Connell happened.

Tommy O'Connell was one of those rare individuals who could connect with anyone. Transferring in at the start of the spring semester, this teddy bear of a man was instantly friends with the All Conference quarterback and on a first-name basis with the homeless guy in fatigues in front of the 7-Eleven. It didn't matter who you were, what you did, or how you looked, Tommy just wanted to have a good time and for you to have it with him. So late one night—just a regular school night in our go-to spot—Tommy was drinking some cheap liquor out of a Nantucket Nectar bottle, when he looked over at Jimmy.

"You ever drink before?" he asked.

"No."

"You want to?"

I had left the Lobby by that point, and when I found out about it the next day, I have to admit that initially, I was glad I wasn't there. *It was wrong. It had to have been. To give alcohol to a guy in a wheelchair?! I can't really put my finger on why, but I just know it is. It must be. He should have been more careful. He should have made sure it was ok! He should have done something—I don't know what, but he should have . . . uh. . . just not given alcohol to the underage kid in the wheelchair!*

But I have to admit that I gained a certain amount of respect for Tommy. His question to Jimmy wasn't, "Can you?"—it was "*Do you want to?*" Despite the chair, and the small frame, and all the other differences Jimmy had, Tommy saw an independent young man capable of making his own bad life decisions, just like the rest of us. Did Tommy know that alcohol affects someone with SMA no different than it does someone without it? I doubt it. But did he feel the need to baby someone just because he looked different—because he was reliant on other things? No. Tommy was the first person to offer Jimmy a drink—the first to offer him the choice.

It is an extremely rare occurrence for Jimmy to turn down the opportunity to try something new, and this sure as hell was not going to be one of them. As the snow began to fall on that cold January night, a couple days after Jimmy's eighteenth birthday, in his freshman year of college, for the first time, Jimmy had a drink.

After some time carrying on in the Lobby, looking out the window at the now freshly covered, white courtyard, Jimmy told Tommy to take him out of his chair and put him in the untouched snow. Without hesitation, Tommy O'Connell picked him up, brought him outside, and laid him down on the fresh powder. He spread out Jimmy's arms for him, and then set down a short distance away. Jimmy used all the strength he could muster to generate some movement, and the two of them lay in the middle of the empty, white, untouched courtyard, at the end of a single set of footprints, making snow angels as the flakes fell out of the cold, dark night sky.

5

Innocence on Wheels

I think innocence is something that adults project upon children that's not really there.

—Donna Tartt

Temple University was located in the heart of North Philadelphia. It would be an understatement to describe it as a rough neighborhood. Because of that, every dorm on campus was on lock down. One way in, one way out, security cameras, and desk guards on duty around the clock. Just to get into the building, everyone had to hand their student ID to the guard, who would not only verify it was actually you, but swipe you into the computer system as well. The ID was only good for entrance to the dorm you lived in—none of the others. Residents had to sign in and sign out every guest, remain with their guests at all times, and succumb to the "random selection" for bag checks . . . which was reserved mostly for people staying over, shopping bags, and pretty much any time after dinner Thursday until Sunday morning. There was even an entire week, every year during Spring Fling, where we weren't allowed to bring any open containers into the dorm. Nothing like spending two bucks on a soda and having to throw it out in order to get into your own residence.

Now, Temple students may not have exerted the most energy in the classroom, but we sure as hell weren't going to be deterred from partying. While the library would only get full during finals week, we didn't hesitate to take the necessary planning required for smuggling alcohol into the dorms. That meant a Monday or Tuesday lunch time trip to one of the many off-campus corner stores that didn't seem to know there were such things as fake IDs, sometimes not even bothering to ask for one. Throw the drinks in a backpack or shopping bag, and as long as we came into the dorms during normal class hours, there was a decent shot of clearing the security desk. Though with so much to lose—suspension from school, getting kicked out of the dorms, and most importantly, the drinks for the party—it took a brave soul to take the risk.

One weekend in the Lobby, we were contemplating how to start the night off. The group was dry.

"What happened to the handle I gave you?" I asked Tommy.

"You mean the half empty handle of Banker's you hustled me for?"

Just a week ago I had given him the last of my liquor for $30. I learned more about supply and demand from the university alcohol rules than in Economics 101. "It wasn't a hustle—that was just the only amount I was willing to part with it for."

"You could buy it full at a liquor store for $12.99."

I pointed to the security guards in the midst of checking every bag that came through the door. "If it was as easy as that, we wouldn't be in the predicament we're in now."

"Wait . . . it's the security guards you guys are worried about?" Jimmy chimed in.

"Yeah, I know where I can get it. I'm just not trying to risk bringing it in on a Friday," Tommy said.

"If you can get the booze, I can get it in," Jimmy said.

At this, Tommy and Jimmy left the Lobby and headed to a corner store. When Tommy came back to the Lobby, Jimmy was nowhere in sight.

"He literally just told me to put it in his bag," Tommy said to us.

"The one hanging from the back of his chair?" I asked.

"Yeah. I wanted no part in that. I told him he's doing this 'hide in plain sight' operation on his own." Tommy sat back down, and we all waited to see what would happen when Jimmy came rolling through the automatic doors.

I wish there was some sort of event that went with this. Some crazy build up that led to Jimmy almost getting caught. But the fact is, the only drama that occurred took place in our own heads as we waited. Jimmy came right up to the door, through the gate, saying hi to the guards as he always does. And that was that. I think he may have wanted to show off a little bit, because he wasn't even in a rush to get up to the room. We kicked it in the Lobby for a little while longer, where Jimmy sat in the most public part of the residence hall with a bag full of contraband hanging on his chair, and not a worry in the world.

6

The First Party

First you take a drink. Then the drink takes a drink. Then the drink takes you.

—F. Scott Fitzgerald

It was a Friday night and the Relay for Life was taking place—an overnight walkathon to raise money for cancer. Well not *for* cancer, but you know what I mean. Jimmy and I decided to check it out before the evening festivities began.

At the walkathon, there was a giant track roped off around the student pavilion. Multiple basketball courts were covered with all sorts of events, activities, vendors, and games. As usual, we weren't half way around the track before Jimmy was stopped a handful of times by friends, leaving me feeling like a sidekick to a celebrity. As we made our way around the track, I saw that there was a basketball court still open, and a handful of kids were shooting around. One kid in particular stood out—he was showing off, beating up on kids smaller and slower than him, and talking trash to go with it.

"What an asshole," Jimmy said, noticing him too. Don't get me wrong, I'm a competitive person, and I don't mind (even sometimes enjoy) people talking a little smack and having some flash to their game. It's all in fun. But I can't stand when people do that to those who are obviously not equipped to meet the competition—when it's not an even playing field. Like, you know that guy who was good enough to play in college but probably didn't get much playing time, and once he realized that his athletic career peaked in high school he compensated by spending his nights and weekends showboating and talking mad shit to every average Joe in the local rec league? Well, I fucking hate that guy.

Now, I'm not a great basketball player, but I am good enough to know when I am better than someone else. And I wanted to shut this dickhead up. I was about to take to the court, but then I remembered Jimmy couldn't join. *Would that be rude?* I thought. *He obviously can't play. Am I exploiting his handicap, doing something he can't? Will he feel left out? Is it almost like an insult if I go out there?* As I just about convinced myself I shouldn't go out there, Showboat blocked a kid a whole head shorter than him and flexed his scrawny little arms over him. That did it. "Jimmy. I'll be right back."

The loose shoot-around quickly turned into one-on-one, and it was like all the pent-up anger and aggression I ever had for any sort of bully came out that night on the basketball court. I crissed and I crossed, dribbling around, under, and through Showboat, beating him every which way. As we were playing, I would glance over at Jimmy who was watching, cracking up whenever I made Showboat look stupid.

Afterwards, Jimmy and I resumed the walk around the track. When we got back to court, Showboat was back out there, engaging in the same ridiculousness he was before. To my surprise, Jimmy encouraged me to go back out there again. At that point, however, I felt vindicated, and I wasn't trying to break a sweat before the party. As trivial as it may sound, though— Jimmy encouraging me to do the very thing I thought might be rude if I do in front him—got me thinking . . . *was Jimmy sensitive to his disability? Or was it just me?*

*　　*　　*

Afterwards, Jimmy and I headed to the party. This set into motion a course of events that would change everything.

I wasn't really sure what to expect—I knew Jimmy had gone to a couple of little house gatherings by then, courageously leaving his $30,000 chair on the sidewalks of North Philadelphia. He'd be carried in and set on a couch, where he would be served a drink and given attention, as if he was a prince. But where we were headed that night was no little house gathering. This was one of the notorious Temple house parties where the entire first floor would be cleared of furniture, there would be a five-dollar charge for a red solo cup, and most appealing, a fifteen-minute line to fill it up with warm, shitty keg beer. Knowing there would be no place for Jimmy to sit, and stairs to prevent him from riding in, I figured we would just kick it outside on the stoop for the night, talking with people as they came and went.

Jimmy thought otherwise. When we walked up to the crowd of students waiting to get in, the pseudo bouncer (aka the roommate who drew the short straw and had to work the door) asked Jimmy, "You coming in?"

Before I could even register the question, Jimmy said "Yeah, let's do it," and in the blink of an eye, Bouncer Boy was behind Jimmy's chair, ready to lift. Jimmy started screaming, "WAIT, STOP!" but he didn't really need to. Within moments, Bouncer Boy realized it was impossible to lift on his own and let go.

As he looked at the chair, trying to make sense of its weight, a handful of guys who were overeager to help (and I think, to show off to the ladies in line) gathered around the chair. Jimmy explained to the group that there were four handles on the chair that were used to lift it, and that there should be four people to do the job—one for each spot. Over the years, I learned three strong men could do it, and once even saw it done by two . . . but with 250 pounds to lift and awkward positioning, it makes a hell of a task.

Four guys of the bunch who won out the chance to help bent down ready to lift when Jimmy started throwing a fit. It was an incomprehensible sound of panic that caused the four guys to jump away from the chair as if it was on fire.

"You can't lift the chair with me in it!" he yelled. There was a pause of reflection on that obvious fact we all missed. As I was unbuckling his seatbelt, he told me that there was something behind him I needed to grab before I lifted him out of his chair. Tucked just under his arm and hidden by his body was a brown paper bag. Unbeknownst to me, the underage Jimmy had gone to the school-organized, on-campus, charity event with a little bottle of grey goose sitting right next to him the entire time. I grabbed the bottle and put it in my back pocket. As I held Jimmy, he supervised the guys struggling to get the chair up the stoop, turn on the landing, and into the house. I followed them in, and as they caught their breath, rubbed their hands, and stretched their backs, I set Jimmy in his chair.

The house was wall to wall packed, the music blaring, and everyone was drinking way more than they should . . . and Jimmy took to this environment like a duck to water. And while he was thrilled to finally be inside a real party, I was thrilled that I didn't get charged the five-dollar cover.

As they say, sober thoughts are drunken actions . . . well, it would seem that the sober actions of excessive kindness and friendliness towards Jimmy were only magnified with alcohol. It seemed like every guy in there wanted to drink with Jimmy, and being that he weighed only a little more than sixty pounds, this was a recipe for disaster. Jimmy wasn't worried about that though—he was more concerned with the way the women were treating him. After a couple kisses, a couple shots, a lap dance, a couple more shots, and a very busty woman taking Jimmy's big head into her very big chest for what was probably only a couple of seconds, but for him, seemed like an eternity, Jimmy found his bliss. Then, someone even delivered him an actual glass with ice and Sprite to mix with his Grey Goose. I had never seen such a luxury at the kind of sweatbox house party where new shoes go to die.

With Jimmy six sheets to the wind and loving life, the party started to wind down. We had to reverse the entrance process to get his chair back outside. As we walked toward the door, the crowd of people parted as if Jimmy was Moses entering the Red Sea, and he got to the door faster than I ever could have on my own. I held him as people carried the chair out. When it was placed on the ground I set Jimmy back into his seat, and the moment I snapped his seatbelt on he took off like it was a Talladega night. He was chasing this girl we called "Bird's Nest"—a beautiful cheerleader who earned that nickname due to her spectacular head of curly hair. I am not sure if Jimmy had been talking to her earlier, or if she was just something pretty who happened to be leaving at the same time and caught his eye. Either way, at this point, he was running on pure instinct.

Jimmy had his chair in fifth gear, trying to catch up to her on a North Philadelphia sidewalk, full of cracks, bumps, holes, and a general unevenness that would jerk and jolt his chair like a car speeding on a road of potholes. This would send his giant head bouncing like a paddle ball and knock his hand off of his joystick, stopping him in his tracks. He would then gather himself, shift his weight back to balance, and reach for the joystick, only to repeat the process all over again: zero to a hundred for three yards, hit a bump, jerk, jolt, stop, reset, and repeat.

Stephanie and Darren left the party with us, and being the good friends we are, we thoroughly enjoyed watching, from a couple yards behind, Jimmy in this difficult pursuit before the three of us convinced him to let Bird's Nest go. We decided to head home to 1300, and this turned out to be quite the task.

We were in the street to avoid the bumpy sidewalk, and Jimmy turned his chair into a one-man ride at an amusement park. He was veering into the middle of the road, jetting out into intersections, and started playing chicken with oncoming cars. We kept trying to calm him down, but he was on cloud nine. We realized there was no stopping him when he almost broadsided a car stopped at a light. We had no other option but to retract his driving privileges.

I hit the power button on his chair, and like a cat fighting to avoid a bath, Jimmy was using all his might and volume to make the process of getting him out of his chair as difficult as possible. Though he weighs far on the lighter side of the average college-aged male, he is still a decent amount of weight to carry for prolonged period of time. After a little more than a minute, my forearms started burning. I had to pass him to Darren. For the next couple of blocks, the two of us were sending Jimmy back and forth between us, as Stephanie sat in Jimmy's chair, cruising down the street beside us. All the while, Jimmy was verbally assaulting us with a never-ending barrage of insults and threats and demands to "PUT ME BACK IN MY CHAIR!"

Our route home led us right past the Relay for Life, where our night had started. There were a handful of cops out front. Being that Temple is a city school, and is in one of the worst neighborhoods in Philly at that, it's not a bad thing to see a cop, even when you've been drinking underage. They've got more important things to worry about. As long as you're not a total jackass, you're probably not going to get an underage. Unfortunately, I think two guys taking turns carrying someone who is screaming, "HELP! I'm being kidnapped!" as a girl next to them is riding a small, motorized wheelchair that obviously isn't hers, definitely fits in the category of total jackass.

With Jimmy screaming bloody murder, we thought an about face at the sight of the cops would not look good. We told him we would put him back in his chair if he stopped yelling, and when he agreed, the three of us begged him to hold it together for a couple minutes. We were walking past the policeman with no problem. Jimmy seemed oblivious, and Stephanie, Darren and I were looking straight ahead, holding our breath, hoping he wouldn't do anything crazy.

It was my own stupidity for not adhering to the idea to let sleeping dogs lie. For some reason, just as we were about to clear the cops, I thought to encourage Jimmy, under my breath, "That's it . . . keep going . . . almost there." This only reminded him of the situation.

"THEY ARE TRYING TO STEAL MY CHAIR!" Jimmy yelled, as he punched it to full speed as if to make a getaway.

Simultaneously, Steph, Darren and I yelled, "Jimmy!"

"HELP! HELP!" Jimmy said, trying to make a call of distress over his own laughter at his own joke.

The cops turned when Jimmy yelled, but I think the sight they saw—Jimmy in front, barreling down the street hysterically laughing, me in a half jog trying to keep up, and Stephanie and Darren taking up the rear, trying to hide their face, fear, and laughter—was just weird enough for them to decide they did not want to deal with whatever the hell was going on.

As soon as we were out of sight, we cut down an uncommon pathway between the tennis courts and the old basketball stadium. Halfway on this block-long path, and still a good ways from the dorm, given the pace we were moving, our relationship was taken to another level. What would happen next would solidify a friendship in perhaps the strangest way a friendship has ever been solidified.

"Guys," Jimmy stopped in his tracks. "I need to pee."

Steph, Darren, and I paused and looked at each other, eyebrows raised and eyes wide. The encouragement for Jimmy to hold it immediately followed.

"No, I need to go now. I'll piss myself."

As our encouragement turned to pleading, the back of the mechanical chair slowly started reclining, Jimmy putting himself in more of a laying position. Finally, when he was as far back as he could go, he yelled, "Steph, pull my pants down! I need to go!"

"Are you nuts? No way!" Steph said.

"Jimmy, do you really need to go that bad? You can't hold it?" I didn't know what the peeing process entailed, but I didn't want to find out.

"No! I have to goooo. SO. BAD!"

If you ever wondered how many idiots it takes to undress a handicapped kid for the first time, the answer is three. For what felt like twenty minutes, the three of us attacked the situation as if we were performing brain surgery with no instruction—one person lifted his hips, one was tugging his pants down before another realized we should unbutton his pants, another moved his legs, and all three of us were trying to make sure he didn't fall to the ground.

Finally, we got Jimmy to a position where he was secure in the chair, pants at his ankles, and hips at the edge of his seat, and pointing in a way that gave him a clear shot.

"Alright, Jimmy, go. Hurry up."

"I can't yet. You gotta aim it." He paused. "Stephanie . . . you do it." He had a shit-eating grin on his face and chuckled a little as he asked her.

"Jimmy you're being weird!" Stephanie shrieked.

"Yeah man, you're getting creepy dude," Darren said.

"Jimmy I swear, if you don't even have to go, I'm going to kick your ass," I assured him with an empty threat.

"No, I really can't! I'll piss myself! Look!"

Up until that point, we were all just trying our best to avoid making eye contact with everyone, and most importantly, everything. But as we looked down, we were confronted with something we never expected.

"Holy shit, look at that monster!"

"Hurry, I'm about to blow!"

"How is that big thing on that little body?"

"Steph, aim it! Please!"

"No. I am not touching that thing."

"Well I can't go yet!"

Then the truth hit us. Not that Jimmy probably had the biggest dick I have ever seen in my life, but that it was laying up on his stomach, and someone was going to need to grab it and point it so that Jimmy didn't piss all over himself.

"I. Need. To. Goooooo," Jimmy said, making one last desperate plea as his voice trailed off to silence and he closed his eyes, trying to find the inner peace needed to hold his bladder.

Though it could not have been earlier than 3 a.m., the campus was so well lit that it seemed as though we were standing in broad daylight, huddled around the chair in a standstill. For what seemed like an eternity, we stood there frozen, playing out in our heads the different ways this scenario could go. I was praying someone else would step up to the plate, and in my head started to justify letting Jimmy piss on himself. I didn't go out that night looking to touch another man's dick.

Finally, Darren looked at me, looked at Steph, and then at that cartoonish thing between Jimmy's thighs. He pulled up one sleeve, took a deep breath, and said, "Fuck it." And with a scrunched face, he reached down, with his hand as far away from his own body as possible, as if he was about to touch the very last thing in the world he wanted to. He grabbed hold of the rope, aimed, and told Jimmy, "Fire away."

Jimmy did so immediately, letting out a sigh of relief as his stream hit the ground and started flowing toward me, forcing me to straddle the river of piss coming my way. We went through the process in silence—me holding his legs, Steph securing his body, and Darren on the hose.

What seemed like six gallons and an hour later, we got his pants back up, and right after we finished, another group of students walked by. I remember thinking that would have been one weird scene for them to stumble upon.

When we finally got to our dorm building, Jimmy was still exhibiting his party self to the world, talking all sorts of nonsense and veering back and forth across the wide walkways. Fears were realized when we noticed who was working the desk that night: Patrice Jones, the meanest, strictest, guard Temple had. She was the type that enjoyed barring drunk students from entering the dorm, and wouldn't hesitate to call the campus police. I gave Jimmy a sort of pep talk, telling him that he needed to focus hard for just a few minutes to get to the elevator, and then we'd be in the clear. As we came inside, P-Jones immediately asked, not with a tone of caring but with a tone of suspicion, "Is he ok? He looks really drunk."

"Oh no, he's fine, it's just allergies."

"Well, he wasn't like that when he went out."

"Seasons sure do change quickly, don't they?" I said.

At this, Jimmy took off. He wanted nothing to do with this confrontation and knowing he didn't need to show ID, he floored it through the gate.

Way to have my back, asshole, I thought, as I continued the exchange at the security desk. I figured he was making his getaway to the elevators to get to his room. For some reason, though, he blew full speed past the elevator and was heading directly towards the Lobby's fire place. The conversation with P-Jones lost all importance and I start walking, then jogging, then running after him, yelling his name. He was moving as fast as his chair allowed, looking like a four wheeled projectile homed in to the brick face. It was one of those things where you don't really believe you are seeing what you are seeing, and Patrice Jones' shouts of, "Come back here!" and "I am not finished with you yet, young man!" faded the closer and closer Jimmy got to impact.

Please, Jimmy, stop. Just stop. Please stop, I prayed, realizing he wasn't listening to my yelling. Time was going so slow, it felt like a century as the distance from Jimmy's chair to the wall to change from yards . . .to feet . . . to inches . . . and then . . . , BOOM! From where I was, directly behind him, I could see his chair wheels briefly lift off of the ground, as his entire body was jolted, violently flinging his big head forward, directly toward the cement. He was stopped in that position—the front of his chair up against the wall, body slumped forward, his head over his knees.

I caught up to him with my heart in my stomach. I was fully expecting to see blood pouring out of his skull, or at the very least, my friend unconscious after hitting his head so violently. I looked down, and noticed that in between Jimmy's thick hair and the cement was the smallest, tiniest space imaginable. I'll be damned if there weren't even a couple of stray hairs that were actually touching the fireplace.

"Jimmy?" I asked, afraid there would be no answer.

"Could you lift my head up for me?" I heard him say into his lap. I pushed up on his forehead to bring his head back to its normal position, only to reveal a man with a huge smile on his face.

"My hand was stuck," he said, cracking up.

By some miracle, there was a cement lip in front of the fireplace. We figured that when his wheel hit the lip, it must have knocked his hand off the joystick. This stopped the chair dead in its tracks, and sent his body forward, his head just grazing the cement wall that could have done some serious damage.

Patrice Jones was still yelling from the front entrance as I cursed at Jimmy under my breath. He was too busy laughing to feel any sense of urgency, so I grabbed his joystick, and clumsily steered and jerked his chair over to the elevator. As the doors were closing, P-Jones was threatening to call the cops and I kept reassuring her that once he got his allergy medicine, he would be just fine.

The next morning I got a text from Jimmy that would pretty much be a precursor for the next decade: "Eddie. We GOT to do that again."

7

Expectations Are Everything

Your assumptions are your windows to the world. Scrub them off every once in a while, or the light won't come in.

—Alan Alda

One day I made the long trek down an entire flight of stairs to Jimmy's room to see if he wanted to hang out. To my surprise, he was sitting in the hallway outside of his room, all by himself.

"I am trying to read this article for class and I just couldn't concentrate in there," he said, "all that noise is giving me a headache."

He shook his head when I asked for an explanation, and my curiosity led me to investigate. One foot in the door and I had an inkling of what was bothering him, and it was confirmed when I stepped all the way in. Total chaos: bed squeaking, floor shaking, screaming, moaning—someone could have told me a NASA engineered space drill was running in the dorm room above, and I would have believed it.

The speculation of that noise ran rampant for a long time. Did Temple have a swinger's club that met in the room above? Was it a pornography studio? Some weird sex-aerobics . . . it sounded like the kind of workout that would put to waste even an Olympian. Maybe, just maybe, a rhinoceros had gotten stuck in the fourth floor room and was throwing a fit to get out. We did consider the fact that each floor was laid out similarly, and being that it was directly above Jimmy's meant it was a handicap-accessible room. The notion of someone in a wheelchair being up there was quickly dispelled, for whatever they were doing up there definitely required the four limbs of each participant to be fully functional. Whatever it was, it was getting on Jimmy's last nerve. The noises would wake him up in the morning, keep him up at night, and was no afternoon delight.

Other than that, his dorm room in 1300 was perfect for him. Built after the American's with Disabilities Act, which required all buildings to meet a certain level of accessibility, living at school was never an issue for Jimmy. To get in the building, Jimmy had a remote, which opened the outside door, and once inside, a motion sensor slid the second set of glass doors open. It may seem counterintuitive for an accessible dorm room to be on the third floor, but with one thousand other students in the dorm, and a security guard always at the desk, it was at most a one- or two-minute wait to find a passerby to push the elevator button for him. That being said, there were a few times people would help Jimmy onto the elevator, make sure to hold the door as he got on it, and then walk away without pushing the button for the third floor. Jimmy would turn around to see no one standing there and the door closing, leaving him high and dry. He would sit and wait until it opened again, sometimes taking a ride up to another floor. I always thought it would have been funny to see someone call the elevator, and the doors open to Jimmy sitting there, relieved someone was there to help him out of that jam. When Jimmy did get to his floor, the same remote for the outside door also opened his room.

Despite the maximum-security type entrance for the average student—ID verification, guest check-ins, etc.—those rules didn't apply to Jimmy. After the first week, the guards were fine with him rolling through the gate without showing anything. They even let him put a handful of guests on a list he left at the desk so he didn't have to go downstairs to check his nurses in.

To be fair, it was for good measure the security was extremely strict. I don't know a single person who went to Temple and didn't know someone who got robbed or held at gunpoint, or had it happen to them. It was just part of the college experience of being an Owl. Temple did everything it could to make sure that kind of stuff stayed off campus, and that carried over to the way security was handled in the dorms. Most guards were friendly, but strict. Policies like residents having to walk a guest to the bathroom could technically be enforced, but like rolling through a stop sign, most guards were more reasonable than to bother with things like that.

Everyone, that is… except Patrice Jones.

Patrice Jones was a mean old lady who started working at Temple halfway through the year. Being that us Lobby members considered ourselves the de facto power of the dorm, we were a little slighted when she acted like she knew more about the place than we did. We learned how tight of a ship she ran when, early on, I walked into Jimmy's room to find his round and wayward nurse, Barbara, sitting on his bed with a towel wrapped around her waist. To my left, hanging in the shower, were her pants.

Apparently, Barbara had been rushing to 1300 after it took her forever to find parking. She had to pee because she is in her sixties and always has to pee, and in the haste of getting out of her car and to the dorm, she had forgotten her wallet. Halfway there, she realized her ID was in the car, but there was no turning back at this point. She needed a bathroom.

When she got to the door, she immediately explained that she was there for Jimmy, that she was his nurse, and that she really needed to use the bathroom but had forgotten her ID.

P-Jones wasn't having it. "No ID, no entrance."

"But I was just here the other night. We met! I am in the logbook for Monday, Tuesday, and Thursday. You can look. Don't you remember me?"

"I can't let you in."

"I know you remember me." Barbara had a point; she was probably the only sixty-year-old with dyed, flaming red hair and well-worn scrubs that had ever been in 1300. But P-Jones wouldn't budge.

"Can't I just use the bathroom?" Barbara asked, pointing to a door ten feet away. "I'll leave my purse here as collateral."

"If you walk through that gate I am calling the police."

"If you don't let me use the bathroom . . . you don't understand . . . I am going to wet myself. "

"If you use that bathroom without giving me an ID, I am calling the police," P-Jones repeated.

"You know me! You know I was here! Why are you like this? If you don't let me in I'm going to have to pee right here!"

"If you go in, I am calling the cops."

Barbara clenched her jaw, looked her dead in the eye . . . and let go. "Well," she said, "now you can call the janitor."

Barbara then turned, walked five blocks in the cold with soaking wet pants to get her ID. When she came back, she saw a look of disgust on Patrice Jones' face as she was directing foot traffic around the puddle of piss stinking up the entranceway.

That's what you call poetic justice.

*   *   *

Not only did the university hope the guards would prevent alcohol from coming into the dorms, they encouraged the guards to prevent drunk students from entering as well. In one of those rules that sound great to the parents who are school shopping for their kids, Temple boasted that they would never allow intoxicated individuals in the dorm. Realistically, though, that meant many students were denied access to their own living space and were left to drunkenly wander around North Philadelphia for a couple of hours at night until they sobered up. That's the part of the sales pitch the campus tour guide leaves out.

Along with having immunity from the ID process, coming in drunk was usually never an issue for Jimmy. This usually had a very convenient "innocent by association" effect on those who came home with him. And that was good, too, because Jimmy took every chance he got to lure me or any other unsuspecting victim to Maxi's, a bar that, until they got slammed with crazy fines, never really felt the need to check IDs. He would offer to buy me a cheesesteak for the last day of semester classes, or tell me it was too nice to stay in, or I'd receive a text at 2 p.m. on a Thursday saying that spring break had officially started. What would be presented as an innocent lunch or a single afternoon drink would end at 2 a.m., with neither of us coherent.

Being economical (broke) college students, all we ever drank at Maxi's were Long Island Iced Teas—easily the most bang for our buck. Though it may have been the responsible financial decision, it was reckless in every other aspect. Time and time again it would only ensure Jimmy rumbling and me stumbling back home. We never really worried about getting back into our dorm, unless we saw Patrice at the desk. Then all bets were off.

We were winning battle after battle—from Jimmy arguing with her about checking in guests, to the "allergies" situation, to Barbara marking her territory animal kingdom style. But those battles aside . . . P-Jones wanted to win the war. The next Thursday night we came stumbling in at 2 a.m., she was ready.

The crazy thing was, this time around Jimmy was fine . . . relatively speaking. The most reliable metric for Jimmy's drunkenness is his ability to cart home, and that night he wasn't just driving himself home, he was shepherding my hammered ass the whole way. I got so drunk that, earlier at the bar, when Jimmy asked me to take him to the bathroom, I stood up, tripped over my own feet and dropped my glass. He quickly changed his mind and decided to wait until he got home. In my current state, I was not the kind of person he wanted to hold him over a toilet.

Maybe it was because she had a chip on her shoulder from before, or because we were getting home around the time bars let out. Maybe it had to do with me loudly asking Jimmy how his allergies were holding up as we passed by. Who knows. But when I left Jimmy in the lobby, talking to someone he knew, I would not have in a million years guessed how the rest of his night was going to go.

At about 2:45 in the morning, there was a knock at Jimmy's bedroom door. Barbara got up to open it and there stood an EMT unit, with an open stretcher. They had gotten a report of a visibly intoxicated individual who couldn't walk, and that per campus rules they were required to take him to the emergency room.

Jimmy, who was listening to the EMTs at the door, yelled from his bed, "I can't even walk when I am sober!"

But the EMTs were persistent. If he didn't go with them, he wouldn't be able to live on campus and could potentially be kicked out of school. He finally agreed, but only if he could use his chair. The EMT's said this wasn't an option—after all, they were there under the impression that it was for someone who couldn't operate under his own recognizance. Jimmy persisted, saying that he needed his chair at the hospital—otherwise when he was discharged, he wouldn't be able to get home.

Jimmy thought he had them with this one, but the EMTs didn't budge. Jimmy realized he had no choice, and told Barbara to put him on the stretcher. She scooped him up, bed sheet and all, and put him on the stretcher. Laying on his back, he couldn't see if P-Jones was still at the desk as he was carried to the ambulance, but he imagined that she was sitting there, trying hard to refrain from a smile as she basked in her victory.

As per usual, no matter the situation, Jimmy actually ended up having a good time. In the emergency room, he was the life of party, cracking the nurses up by responding to questions like, "What did you have to drink tonight?" by answering, "Everything," and telling the staff to move things along because he wanted to get back to campus and hit up some parties. He was having a ball, not thinking about the implication of not having his wheelchair—meaning that his Mom was awakened in the wee hours of the morning by a call from Barbara, only to be informed that her son was in the emergency room and needed a ride home. She told Barbara that she could leave, and she brought along Jimmy's younger brother, who would then stay over in the dorm. He didn't mind . . . what high school kid wouldn't love the chance to skip a school day and hang out at college with his brother?

After the discharge papers were signed, his mom went to carry Jimmy to his van. "Geez, Jimmy," she said, removing the sheet that was covering him. "Where are your pants?"

"Huh?"

"You're not wearing any pants."

"I'm not?"

Then his memory came rushing back. Since I had been too unreliable to take him to the bathroom, just before he got to his room, he couldn't take it anymore. He had no choice but to relieve his bladder a bit in the elevator. When he got to his room, Barbara took off his wet clothes, and after washing him, put him in bed, where he fell asleep with nothing but a t-shirt on. In all the commotion—being woken up in the middle of the night, the ambulance ride, and the emergency room party—Jimmy realized that at no point did he even put boxers, let alone pants, back on.

I would like to say that being sent to the emergency room made Jimmy realize the gravity of alcohol, but it didn't. I could blame the fact that he was totally fine when the EMTs were called, and say that unwarranted punishments only encourage the action. In reality, it was just that Jimmy does what he wants to do.

So the very next week, Jimmy told me to meet him, Tommy O'Connell, and Darren out at Maxi's for dinner. He knew I wasn't trying to party that night, and he told me that they were just grabbing a quick bite. But when the three of them ordered drinks and I refrained, the insults started coming. I am a sucker for peer pressure, especially when one of the people telling you to "stop being a little bitch" shops at Gap Kids. So I gave in, and I ordered a beer. Sure enough, as we were sitting there eating, big ol' fat snowflakes start pouring down.

"I think it's a sign, Eddie."

"A sign for what."

"That we need to stay."

"How the hell is snow related to that?"

"Because I said so! Look, how many times are you going to get the chance to do this?" Jimmy knew he struck a chord by the look on my face. "One day, we're going to graduate, and then it's all done. Sure, we can visit. But it won't be the same. One day we'll move on to other things, but for now, we got this, and we got a limited amount of time with it. Don't let this beautiful thing go to waste!"

Damnit, Jimmy. You do know how to tug on my heartstrings. "Alright, fine. But only if you get next round." And just like that, another night of partying began.

We all had classes the next day, and when the snow let up around midnight, we decided to make moves home. The problem, however, was that it had snowed nearly half a foot—about two inches too much for Jimmy to maneuver his go-cart through.

With Darren behind the chair pushing, Tommy and I set in front like a pair of sled dogs—not pulling, but plowing a path for each wheel. Fifteen minutes of dragging my legs to move the snow, laughing, and throwing snowballs made for one of the best walks home in my entire life. As we approached the dorm in the highest of spirits, we saw her. Patrice Jones was sitting at the desk.

Darren and Tommy decided they weren't ready to deal with her yet, so they went to get greasy, cheap food from the 7-Eleven. As for me, aided by liquid courage, I decided right then and there that I was not going to run. I was not going to shy away from her. Sure, she might deny my access for the rest of the cold, wintry night, but I decided I wasn't going to continue the ongoing war with Patrice Jones. Drunk Eddie was sure he could charm a truce between us.

"You coming with me, Jimmy?"

"Let's rock." Jimmy wasn't changing his plans for anyone, and he was planning on getting his ass in bed.

I walked in and addressed her as kindly as possible. "Miss Jones. This all needs to stop. We can't go on like this."

"Can't go on like what?"

"The tension between us! It's palpable! You know it, I know it, we all know it! Can't we just get along?" I smiled, finding entertainment in my melodramatic speech.

"There's no tension here."

"Then why did you call the EMTs last week?"

"I was concerned—"

"For what?"

"That he needed help. I was watching him and he seemed like he had drank way too much."

"Patrice—"

"Don't call me Patrice."

"Look, I just don't want to worry every time I come home from a party."

"What's there to worry about?"

"You know what I am talking about."

"Should you be worried?"

"No." I could feel the situation slipping from my grasp.

"It seems like maybe you drank a little bit too much tonight."

"No, I really didn't." The threat of her not letting me in was becoming more of a possibility. As for Jimmy—he was in the clear. At some point in our back and forth, he decided to slide over to the elevator, undetected. I didn't even realize it until I saw him asking a passerby to hit the button for him.

"I'm not sure I should let you in, considering your current state."

"This is what I am talking about! Why do you got to jump to that?" I said, as the elevator doors closed on Jimmy. She started into some speech about university alcohol rules state blah, blah, blah . . . I had given up, and nodded in appeasement in hopes of not pissing her off anymore. As I pretended to listen to her drone on, I noticed the digital numbers above the elevator started to turn: 1... 2... 3... 4. I didn't know if Jimmy had not been clear about which floor he lived on, or the volunteer pushing the button made a mistake . . . but I did know that Jimmy lived on 3.

I interrupted the lecture as politely as I could. "I totally see what you're saying. I get it. I'm sorry. You are right." She seemed shocked—I don't think she believed me, but was just happy to hear me apologize. "So, can I have my ID back now. Uh, please?" She thought for a second, and then slid it over. I picked it up and bee-lined it to the elevators. I got on and punched the button to go up, and when the doors finally opened on the fourth floor, Jimmy was there, eyes wide in disbelief.

"Eddie." Dramatic pause. "I think I just got shocked sober."

With each floor having the same exact layout, and each floor decorated and coordinated in the same way, Jimmy didn't realize he was on the wrong one. When he rounded the corner and pushed his remote, the door didn't open. He thought maybe there was a malfunction, as there sometimes was, and so he rammed into it with his chair. This was the signal for his nurse to open the door for him.

The door opened, but it wasn't his nurse. Jimmy realized where he was. He was at the room directly above his, facing the maker of the moaning, of the screaming, of the floor creaking that distracted him around the clock.

The source of the noises, he would tell me, was a morbidly obese female, who answered the door wearing nothing but a robe. And just past her, from a large bed in the corner of the room, a half-naked man called out hello.

The reason this woman had the room right above Jimmy—the corresponding handicap room on the floor above—was because she was so heavy that she qualified for disability. She needed a bigger bathroom, wider hallway, and a bigger sized bed. And apparently she had managed to fit a partner in there as well.

Speaking in the hushed tone of revelation, Jimmy looked up at me as we got back on the elevator. "Eddie . . . you really can't assume anything about anybody."

8

The First Sleepover

I am like any other man. All I do is supply a demand.

—Al Capone

During my junior year I lived off campus, and Jimmy was still in the dorms. One night, during the first couple weeks of the semester, he called me.

"What are you doing tonight?"

"Probably just hitting the racetrack." In college, Mario Kart was life.

"Wanna have a slumber party? The overnight nurse called out and they can't find a replacement."

"Really? Or is this just a ploy because you miss me?"

"It isn't a ploy, but I did ask a handful of women before you. So don't feel special."

I volunteered without thinking—a friend needed help. Immediately after I hung up, though, a bit of anxiety came over me. *What the hell did I just sign up for?*

When I got to 1300, I saw Jimmy exactly where he was meant to be—the Lobby, talking to passersby as if he was the mayor. He checked me in, and we posted up. That's when I saw him: Other Wheelchair Guy. He didn't look like Jimmy and didn't operate like him either. Other Wheelchair Guy had full use of his arms. In fact, he kind of looked like me, except he was in chair.

"Oh shit, there's another dude in a chair here now? You two gonna be best buds?"

"Fuck that."

"Seriously?"

"Yeah man. He is stealing my show. Funny thing though . . . big weed dealer."

I had to take a moment to digest all of that before I made my confession. "So, I kind of have no idea what I am supposed to do tonight. I'm not really skilled in the healthcare department."

"You'll be fine. You know how you move in your sleep?" I nodded. "Well, I can't do that on my own, but I still need to. Otherwise I get super uncomfortable. Like, bed sores and stuff. Every couple of hours I am going to call out, and then you'll just flip me. And that's that."

"That's it? Doesn't sound too bad."

"Oh shit," Jimmy said, checking his phone. "Gotta make a booze run." Jimmy had taken it upon himself to smuggle alcohol in for the new residents. Not only did he enjoy meeting new people, he liked the power that came with being *that guy*. I don't want to make it out like he was the dorm version of Al Capone in prohibition Chicago, but starting that year, it wasn't uncommon for Jimmy to have to run outside to meet a friend in need. He had a free pass, and he knew it. The guards never thought that the duffel bag hanging on the back of his chair was full of 40s, did not suspect that there was a bottle behind his back, and never considered that the adult sized sweatshirt laying on this tiny man's lap on a warm spring day was covering a couple Four Lokos.

"It's like a public service," he would say.

Jimmy went outside to get the goods, and I sat in the Lobby waiting. After a while, the weight of my responsibility hit me. *I am going to be Jimmy's call for help tonight. What if I don't wake up when he calls? I'm a deep sleeper. What would happen? Could he get hurt? Sick? Could he die? Could I kill Jimmy?*

By the time I convinced myself that a mistake tonight would most certainly lead to my friend's demise, Jimmy came rolling back in with a shopping bag that wasn't on his chair when he went out. Coincidentally, Other Wheelchair Guy crossed the

Lobby, and in my mind, it couldn't have been for anything other than a drug sale. I watched the two students, who can't even walk, scooting back and forth with the weed and alcohol market of 1300 cornered. I smiled as I thought they couldn't be any further from suspicion if they tried.

When the residents of 1300 had their booze delivered and the foot traffic in the Lobby was all but dead, it was time to hit the sack.

"Eddie," Jimmy said when we got into his room. "Take me to bed or lose me forever." There was something about him being so comfortable in this routine that made stripping my friend down to his Polo underwear somehow feel heterosexual.

I assumed my position in the nurse's bed. We laid awake, fighting sleep, talking like two middle schoolers at their first slumber party. Finally, I couldn't fight it anymore and drifted off into a peaceful dream world.

The next thing I know, the death calls of Jimmy jolt me awake. I popped out of bed as Jimmy is sreaming, "HEEELLLP HEEELLLP! AHHHH AHHHH." *Shit! I slept through his yelling,* I thought as I raced to his bed in a panic. *You really fucked up this time, Ed!*

He continued to yell painful cries for help until I slid my hands under his head and legs. I turned him over, scared that if I wasn't careful I would make whatever was hurting him, worse. When Jimmy was completely on his other side, he made a sigh of relief that reminded me of stepping out of a car after a long ride.

I couldn't fall asleep after that. I lay in bed thinking about how badly I had messed up and how I wasn't going to let him down the next time. Sure enough, a couple hours later he started calling out again. To my surprise, however, I heard, "Barbara! Barbara!"

"No, Jimmy . . . it's me." He didn't even acknowledge me—except for another sigh of relief when I turned him over.

I was still awake the next morning when his alarm went off. As soon as he was awake, I started to apologize profusely for what happened. "Dude, are you okay? I am so sorry, man, I totally blew it."

"What are you talking about?"

"I didn't wake up when you called. It sounded like you were in a lot of pain. . . are you ok?"

"Eddie," he sounded sympathetic. "Relax. I'm fine. I have been doing this all my life. I was asleep the whole time."

9

A Chair Malfunction

It was the first week of my senior year, and my six roommates and I decided to start the year off at our favorite spot—Mill Creek Tavern. Though it was on the other side of the city, the Monday special of $12 all you can eat wings and all you can drink beer made it worth the trek. Jimmy wasn't 21 yet, so he didn't come along.

Sitting along the bar, despite the unlimited beer, my genius roommates decided it would be a good idea for everyone to buy a round of shots. One by one, someone picked their poison and ordered a round for the group. By the time it got down to the end of the bar Poker Josh and I were sitting at, we were hurting. Neither one of us are good drinkers.

We called the bartender over, out of earshot of the rest of our house, and told him we were each going to order a round of vodka—the shittiest vodka he has—for the five of them . . . but to pour us two shots of water. As our roommates took down the first round with a lot of complaints and groans, Poker Josh and I played along in our display of discomfort. I'll never forget the look on their faces, though, when a second round of Banker's was immediately presented to them. They looked so discouraged and disgusted that Poker Josh and I looked at each other and just knew we could never tell them what we just did, out of fear of repercussions.* Believe me, the show we put on when we downed that second shot of water, you would have thought we were drinking gasoline.

When the special was over and the karaoke was crushed, we decided to head to Center City. It's a hike back to the subway, and we felt as though luck was on our side when we spotted a taxi. The alcohol told us that if we were quiet and slick and quick in getting into the cab, the driver might not notice that there were seven of us.

The alcohol lied.

As quickly as we piled in the taxi, the driver told us he couldn't take us all. I don't know what it was—the liquor, the beer, the confidence I had from the prank I just pulled—but I went into a rallying speech that my roommates still talk about today.

"Kind sir," I addressed the driver. "I believe in you. We believe in you. This is America! This is the land where if you put your mind to something, anything is possible! You can't believe in 'can't!' You can do it! I know you can! We know you can!"

The driver turned to look at me in the backseat, as my friends and I fell silent, waiting for his decision. I don't know if he thought I was crazy, or inspiring, or simply wanted the fare. After a pause, he shrugged . . .

"Where to?" he asked, causing us all to let out a victory cheer. The driver smiled as he put the car in gear, and moments after we started moving we could hear the rear bumper scratching against the uneven Philly pavement.

"Alright," the driver slammed on the brakes. "Get out."

Damn. We tried.

So we walked all the way to the subway and headed downtown. When we got there, being the twenty-one-year-old college kids we were, we had no idea where to go on a Monday

---

* The only reason I am even sharing this story now is because one night, a good five years after the incident, Poker Josh took too many actual vodka shots, and texted the group the truth. I'm still pissed he did that.

night in the city. As we aimlessly wandered around, I looked down the block and saw a man with a toolbox kneeling next to a wheelchair. I thought to myself, *Man that looks like Jimmy's chair.* As I got closer, I thought, *Man, that looks like Jimmy's big ol' head.* And when I was close enough, I realized, *Oh shit, that's Jimmy!*

Jimmy had been at dinner with a friend downtown, and was making his way home. On that particular evening, however, as he was rolling along the wide, empty city sidewalk, the back of his chair gave out. The back of the chair has a mechanism that allows him to recline almost all the way flat, but the piece that controlled that movement got loose and the back of the chair dropped. Though jolted at first, Jimmy wasn't injured, but he was totally fucked in every other sense of the matter. He started yelling for help as loud as he could, to no avail, as that part of the city was lifeless at that time of night. He had no other choice but to take matters into his own hands.

Fortunately, even lying flat on his back, he was able to reach the joystick, and he remembered where he was on the sidewalk when the back gave out. He was approaching a cross street, but he was in line with the curb cutout so that by driving straight, he could get off into the street, cross it, and then get back onto the sidewalk. Jimmy plowed forward, slowly but surely. As he got off the curb, he knew that there was the possibility of a car coming, and he could do nothing but hope the driver would see him and stop and help, rather than run him over.

He made it across the street, and recognized the good and the bad strokes of luck for there to be no cars—none to hit him, but none to help him either. He had no choice but to move forward, praying he would run into a helpful stranger before an inanimate object, sidewalk crater, or open storage cellar that would surprise him with the ride of his life. Lying flat on his back, looking straight up at the buildings and their skyline for reference as to where he was on the wide, concrete walkway, he started yelling, "HELP" as loud as he could. After a little more than half a block, he came upon a hotel with a bellboy standing out front. Hearing Jimmy's shouts, he asked, "Hey Buddy, you alright?"

"NO! I need HELP!"

Under Jimmy's guidance, the bellboy helped sit him up, and Jimmy called his Dad, who came down to fix the chair.

Later that week, I relayed that story of finding Jimmy in the middle of the city, and the circumstances that had him stuck there, to my Dad.

"See, I know I am old-fashioned," he said, "but I believe that if someone goes out with someone like Jimmy they need to make sure he gets home alright."

"The thing is," I replied, "is that the person Jimmy met for dinner that night was also in a wheelchair."

"Hmm." My dad thought for a second. "I guess that means they would be in a never-ending cycle of walking each other home, wouldn't they?"

10

To Push or Not to Push

The world worries about disability more than disabled people do.

—Warwick Davis

As I stood on the corner waiting for the light to turn, I saw impending doom come rolling across the street. A very attractive woman was turning onto 15th Street, directly ahead of me. The tragedy of this situation laid in the fact that this woman was in a wheelchair.

My mind immediately started racing. The trek on 15th Street is slightly uphill, and this woman was moving much slower than I was walking. It wouldn't be long before I would overtake her. The sidewalk wasn't wide enough to go around her, and walking in the busy one-way street wasn't a viable option. I considered crossing to the other side, but I would have had to cross back over and in front of her to get to my house. I could have walked slowly and uncomfortably behind her. I justified avoiding that inconvenience, however, by thinking I wouldn't do that for someone that wasn't in a wheelchair, so why would I give her special treatment? Then again, someone who wasn't in a wheelchair wouldn't take up the whole sidewalk, and I wouldn't have had to climb over tree roots and bushes to scurry by.

The closer I got, I realized she wasn't having the easiest time getting up the hill. It would be a lot easier for the both of us if I just pushed her up the hill. But would that be rude? If I saw a heavy person struggling up a hill, I wouldn't ask if they wanted a piggyback. Then again, if I saw my grandmother laboring up the hill carrying grocery bags, I would feel like a jackass if I didn't offer to carry them. But then even again, I don't think this young woman would want to be compared to a grandmother.

It was a manual wheelchair, and she looked kind of fit—athletic outfit, sneakers, and, to be blunt, her legs looked *normal*. If she were sitting on a couch, I wouldn't have known she used a wheelchair. Was she permanently confined to the chair, or was it just a temporary injury? If the injury is only temporary, should I assume that this person is frustrated and would gladly welcome help? But did that mean I expect people who are permanently confined to chairs to have a higher tolerance of frustration, or greater level of patience?

I can't tell you that I did the right thing, but I am pretty sure I can tell you I did the wrong thing. Like most college boys, as I approached the pretty girl and her long, wavy blond hair, the want and intimidation of starting a conversation became the only troubling aspect of the scene. And, like most college boys, I was absolutely terrible at accomplishing this. Figuring that trying to squeeze by was my best chance at sparking a conversation, I damn near took a bush out of the ground as the only sentence my dumbass was able to utter was, "That is sure one hell of an arm workout." As I heard the stupidity coming out of my mouth, I picked up my pace and as best as I could, concealed a sprint into my house, never to see her again.

After brushing the dust off my worst pick-up attempt of all-time, I asked a handful of people what they would have done—offer to push or not offer to push. Now this wasn't a large sample size and it wasn't approached scientifically, but what I found interesting with my To Push or Not To Push survey was the clear split. Everyone less familiar with people with disabilities thought it was very rude that I didn't ask, while those close to someone with a disability was adamant that I should never ever undermine someone's ability by offering to push.

Jimmy, especially, as serious as he had ever been, looked me dead in the eye, and started with "Eddie," in a tone of condemnation before letting out a little laugh at how ridiculous I was being. "Don't. EVER. Offer to push someone."

I was beginning to think maybe I was looking at this disability thing all wrong.

11

Jimmy's 21ˢᵗ

'Twas the night before Jimmy's 21ˢᵗ birthday and I was in the Lobby with him, reminiscing about the way I celebrated mine a few months prior. On a whim, a roommate of mine drove with me to Atlantic City, picking up a friend on the way and arriving minutes after the clock struck midnight, making me of age to legally drink and gamble. As I told Jimmy the story, it was as if I saw the bulb light up above his head.

"Eddie . . ." He didn't even need to finish the sentence.

Jimmy would not be satisfied in turning twenty-one and thinking his celebration was outdone, and, more importantly, thinking he couldn't do something someone else did. As for me, it didn't take any convincing to get me on the road to Atlantic City. A text was sent out, and in retrospect, I don't know if I am proud or ashamed of the response—all of our closest friends were ready to take an impromptu late night ride to Atlantic City on a school night. It wasn't like they were just coming along just because it was Jimmy's birthday, either. Tommy O'Connell and Darren were throwing Jimmy a surprise party that Friday, so they were in for the AC trip on their own degenerate accord. Stephanie was never one to say no to, well, anything, and Poker Josh had recently taking a liking to playing cards online and wanted the chance to play live.

We piled into Jimmy's accessible 1990 Ford conversion van. It had a mechanical lift to get Jimmy's heavy chair in, and we called it The Limo because it was missing the middle bench. This forced everyone to sit on the floor, around the walls of the spacious back. We could have fit twenty people in there if we tried.

As I drove, everyone was drinking, and by the time we arrived the group had a nice buzz going. This would only add to Jimmy's already inhibited demeanor, and I would see firsthand the true extent of that chair's effect.

With all the booze, drugs, hookers, and money being thrown around, Atlantic City is a no-bullshit type town. Being that I had learned the hard way—multiple times—how one is expected to act in Atlantic City, and being that I was the only sober one in the group, I felt somewhat responsible for making sure we didn't get kicked out of anywhere . . . prematurely, at least.

That task would have been impossible if it weren't for that chair. Jimmy was being as belligerent as one could be playing blackjack, displaying a passionate and profanity-laced reaction to every hand, good or bad. I have seen (and experienced) this kind of behavior quickly shut down with a stern warning multiple times in the past—but with Jimmy, the dealer was just laughing. Meanwhile, the floor managers were constantly checking on his needs, and the waitresses made sure his drink was always full.

When the time came to leave, as fate would have it, the birthday boy turned out to be the only one up money on the night. It was the wee hours of a weekday morning, and Jimmy felt like he was on top of the world. The only thing missing was a pretty woman for some birthday action. The problem was that the only women around were working women. Jimmy didn't realize this as we were heading back to the Limo and crossed paths with an attractive, young, blonde and busty woman wearing the exact outfit that grabs every guy's attention.

"Hey beautiful, where you going? You should come with us," Jimmy said.

"Oh, yeah? Where you going to take me?"

I don't know if it was the liquor, the lucky streak, or just the surprise of the receptive response from this very attractive, half naked chick who looked like she could have very well been a college student like us. Jimmy paused for a second and then adamantly replied, "To the moon!"

"That would be one expensive trip," she said. It didn't take long for Jimmy to realize what she meant.

The rest of us decided in that very moment, without even saying a word to each other, that we would never let Jimmy live this down. "Let's, go Jimmy!" Darren called from ahead. "The space ship is set to launch!"

"Shut the fuck up," Jimmy said, as we started to the van in laughter. Walking in the rear of the group, I felt a tug on my sleeve. It was the hooker. She slipped me a card that read nothing but "Cinnamon" on one side, and a phone number on the other.

Without drawing attention to the exchange, she spoke to me in the thickest southern drawl ever spoken in New Jersey, "Y'all gimme a cawl if y'all wanna play a lil' touch footbawl, with no clothes on, if ya know what I mean . . ." Then, nodding towards Jimmy, "I can even throw the astronaut a freebie . . . he's lookin' like he could use it."

Shocked was an understatement. On so many levels, too. The exchange. The accent. But mostly, her attitude toward Jimmy. Not only was she talking as if she knew that Jimmy had a life of hardship and troubles, but that a night with her would make it all better. And was "the freebie" some sort of sales pitch, trying to offer us a group discount? Or was it that she was willing to knock her cowboy boots with Jimmy for free just because he was handicapped?

We drove back to Philly, and after we took advantage of the short-lived McDonalds 100 McNuggets for $20 deal, we dropped everyone off at their respective residences. Now it was only Jimmy and I, driving the Limo back to 1300, where the night had started.

"You sure you want head home, birthday boy?"

"It's almost 4 in the morning! Where else could we go?"

"We could always head to the moon."

I don't know if Jimmy was more disappointed in how much I enjoyed my corny joke, or that he rolled right into it. Regardless, we were still a good bit off campus when we spotted a girl stumbling down the street in a short skirt, with a handbag glimmering in the night. It was obvious she was not from the neighborhood. Maybe she was getting back from an after-hours bar, or leaving a party, or skipping out on a new boyfriend before the sunrise—I don't know. What I do know is that she seemed very lost.

Jimmy and I looked at each other like, *What the* . . .

"We should do something," Jimmy said.

"I know, but what?" Though we called the van The Limo, that old, creepy looking thing—at that hour, in that neighborhood—could easily be taken for a rape-mobile.

Being that I was slowly riding next to her as she walked down the sidewalk, I realized with every second, we seemed more and more like stalkers. Jimmy encouraged me again to act. I rolled the window down, and asked, "You ok?"

She didn't respond. She looked desperate and defeated, and a little scared. I don't know if it was a fear of us, or the neighborhood, or both.

"You know where you're heading?"

Her silence answered the question.

"If you want, we can drive you home."

She was just standing there looking at us, confused and unsure of how to respond.

"We have to take her home," Jimmy said to me, low enough so that she couldn't hear. "We can't have a robbery or rape or murder on our hands!" All of those things very plausible in that neighborhood.

"I know man . . . but we can't kidnap her either."

She was still frozen, not wanting to walk any further in that area alone, but also not wanting to get into a van with two strangers. Jimmy and I were going back and forth as to what to do.

"Dude, show her your student ID," Jimmy said.

Solid idea. I pulled it out of my wallet and displayed it out of the window.

"Look, you can either take your chances on the streets of North Philly at 4 a.m., or you could take your chance with two fellow students, one of them being in a wheelchair," I said, pointing my thumb toward Jimmy.

She titled her head so she could see around me and into the passenger side of the van. She thought for another second, before she said, "Okay. I'll come with you guys."

She climbed in and told us where she lived. It was in the complete opposite direction of where she was walking. We spent the ride talking about those trivial, filler things—like our majors and meal plans and roommates—topics no one actually cares about at 4 in the morning in a van with strangers, but do a great job of showing people you aren't a psychopath. When we got to her place, we waited until she was inside before we went on our way.

"That was wild!" Jimmy said after her door closed.

"Dude! She was walking the wrong way!"

"I wonder what she was doing out so late."

"That was a good idea with the student IDs."

"We had to take her home. That could have been real bad."

"I know this is purely speculation . . . but, even with the IDs, I don't know if she would have gotten in the van if she didn't see you in a wheelchair."

"Who knows. I'm just happy she trusted us."

*   *   *

I am sure a lot of people thought the idea for Jimmy's surprise party came from some sentimental place—something like, "That's a nice thing to do for a guy with a disability," or that it was some sort of recognition that he made it to age 21.

As Mr. West would say: That shit cray. I think back over my college career and recount numerous surprise parties. I don't know if that is common, or if our group just had a unique liking to startling each other. What I do know is that the compliments and kindness that came with the surprise party for Jimmy was different than any I ever encountered before. It was as if we were donating an arm and a leg to Jimmy, the way we were lauded. Truth is, if we weren't throwing a surprise for Jimmy that night, we still would have been drinking at the same house, with most of the same people, and going to the same bar after.

The only way the wheelchair actually had any bearing on the surprise party was in the logistics. Tommy and Darren had the idea, and offered up their house as the locale. I would be the decoy, and the day of the party, I told Jimmy we would grab pizza before we headed over to their house for the pregame—a typical night. Like with any surprise, timing needed to be considered. For one, it was a hike to get to Tommy and Darren's place, which was way off-campus. Two, Jimmy tends to take a little longer to eat, as the food needs to be cut up real small and he doesn't have the strength in his jaw or throat to chew quickly or swallow big things. Finally, who knew if Jimmy was going need to go the bathroom or to change clothes after we ate. That could have meant another 10 minutes if he peed at the pizza place, or up to an hour if he wanted to go back to his dorm and subject me to the excruciating process of waiting for him to choose something "better" to wear.

As things go, of course, the day of his surprise he decided to eat quickly. It also turned out to be the one time he didn't give into his metrosexual tendencies and was fine with the outfit he wore to class. In no time at all, he was ready to head to Tommy and Darren's and get the night started, and I was forced to pull every stall tactic in the book. I ordered another slice of pizza, told boring stories, and insulted his outfit hoping it would get him to change. Being that Jimmy has no respect for my fashion sense (and rightly so), that didn't work. With no other options, I told him I needed to poop and stood around texting in the bathroom for a while, figuring out the status of the party.

I finally got the green light to head to Tommy and Darren's house. Like most houses in North Philly, it has a stoop. Going to parties every weekend, we had fallen into a nice little routine to overcome the obstacle the stoop presented. I would take Jimmy out of his chair and carry him inside, every time shouting, "The party's here!" to no one in particular. I would set him down on a couch, and every time, tell him, "Don't you go nowhere," laughing at my own joke, because someone had to do it. Then I would go back outside, and I would instruct the guys who boxed out the other volunteers for their chance to show off their strength and kindness by carrying in the wheelchair.* With the chair inside, I would grab Jimmy from the couch, put him back in his chair, and then it was time to party.

---

* Don't get me wrong, I usually think it is super nice when people want to help. But if there are seven people around a wheelchair taking care of the situation, when that eighth guy comes up and makes it a point to insert himself (usually being very vocal about it, too)—I can't help but think . . . does he actually want to help fill a need? Or does he just want people to know he is helping?

The thing is, with that routine, Jimmy would have entered his own party, out of his chair, by someone carrying him in. As if that wouldn't be awkward enough, after that, he would have to be set down on a couch and wait for his chair, as everyone watched. Plus, none of us wanted to be the one holding Jimmy as everyone shouted "SURPRISE," looking like Rafiki presenting Simba to the Pride Lands. So we had a plan.

When Jimmy and I got to the stoop, Tommy, Darren and their roommates who were helping us carry the chair, offered a bullshit excuse about trying to carry the chair in backwards, claiming it would be easier. I suggested Jimmy and I stay outside to watch and make sure they did it alright.

In reality, the way the chair is designed, it makes absolutely no sense to carry it backwards, but Jimmy bought it. I held Jimmy and we watched the four of them struggle (more so than usual) to get it up the steps. Eventually, they made it. The chair was in, and the seat was facing out into the street, away from the crowd of people silently waiting behind it.

The last leg of the plan was all on me, and I was really hoping I didn't screw it up. I had to carry Jimmy inside, making sure his line of sight stayed facing the street. If I did that successfully, then all I'd have to do was place him in his chair and put his seatbelt on. Then he could turn to see the place packed with our friends, waiting to give the surprise.

Holding Jimmy with his back to the crowd, my arms were stiff as boards as I carried him in, not wanting to turn his head in slightest. When they carried the chair in, however, they forgot to turn the power off. So as I'm lowering Jimmy down, my jacket catches the joystick, and with the whole crowd watching, I run the chair into myself, while trying to hold onto Jimmy who is not yet strapped in. All the while, I started yelling and cursing at him as if it was his fault and he could do something about it. Thankfully, when the chair nailed me in the leg, it jolted my sleeve off the joystick, and though it hurt, it didn't turn Jimmy towards the crowd with the impact. Up the steps, into the house, and back in his chair, his eyes never left 18th Street. Once he was buckled in, Jimmy turned his chair around to get a surprise that left him speechless. Eyes wide and smiling as he scanned the friendly faces that were there, he started to tear up a little. "This is one of the nicest things anyone has ever done for me," he said, when he could finally form a sentence, to no one in particular.

During the party, Jimmy struck up a conversation with a girl who recently landed herself a spot in *Playboy*'s college edition. Sometimes I wonder if Jimmy so easily attracts beautiful women because, like him, they are used to being stared at—so much weight placed simply on the way they look. This girl was indeed good looking, but when I saw the magazine photo a couple days later, I was beyond shocked. It was almost unbelievable that it was the same person. I couldn't imagine exposing myself like that, only to have some guy on a computer photoshop the normal things magazines consider to be flaws.

At the party, the two were really hitting it off when *Playboy* Model came to tell me Jimmy wanted something. I found him in the kitchen with a drink on his armrest, and his eyebrows shot up to the sky the moment he saw me.

"Eddie," he said when I leaned down, so that only I could hear. "She said she wants to be alone with me. I'm going to park my chair the hallway, and I need you to put me in the bedroom."

"Are you going to be able to fit in the hallway?"

"We'll find out. If not, we are leaving the chair in the kitchen."

"Whose bedroom?"

"I don't care! Tommy's. He won't care. I just don't want her to be the one that picks me up!"

Playboy Model followed me as I followed Jimmy as he zoomed his chair down the narrow hallway. He couldn't make the turn at the end of it, so he stopped. "Ok, Eddie. Let's go." As I picked him up out of his chair, he was silent and focused, centering himself as if he was about to attempt the game winning shot in Game 7 of the NBA finals. I laid him in the middle of the bed, and *Playboy* Model sat down next to him. I stepped back into the hallway, closing the door behind me at her request.

I wasn't really sure what to do next. I didn't want to go back to the party too quickly. He would eventually need to be carried out, and I knew there was a fifty-fifty chance that Jimmy would say some asinine shit that would have her out of that room within the first few minutes. That's just how Jimmy rolls. See, for most guys, it is almost impossible to start a conversation with a female without her thinking he has certain intentions. For Jimmy, it's almost impossible to start a conversation with a female and make her think he *does* have certain intentions. Jimmy once told me he had learned he has to take a proactive approach in order to be treated like the sex object he wants to be. Lucky for him, his forward remarks are usually well received, and if not, quickly forgiven.

As I was debating how long it would take until I knew Jimmy's explicit approach to love wouldn't give *Playboy* Model reason to leave him stranded, some girl came rushing up to me, frantic. She heard that *Playboy* Model was in a room with a guy, and this girl was oh so worried. "Is she ok? Oh, my god. This is so like her. It always goes like this. I am always the one that has to take care of her. I need to check on her."

"Woah, woah, woah. Slow down. Please don't go in there." It's not every day that one of my friends has a *Playboy* model in a bedroom—never mind the fact that a cramped college house party is typically a logistical nightmare for a guy in a wheelchair trying to get laid. Jimmy somehow made it this far, and I didn't want Frantic Friend to wreck it.

"You don't understand. I'm her *person*. I need to make sure she is not getting taken advantage of."

"Holy smokes! Easy there. Look," I said, pointing to the wheelchair down the hall. "The guy in there can't even sit up on his own. Your friend is totally safe." When she realized my point, she settled down a bit. Plus, I think she was more concerned with showing she was there to help *Playboy* Model than in actually helping *Playboy* Model. At that point, I figured if Jimmy was going to scare *Playboy* Model out of the room, he would have done it by now. I told Frantic Friend that I was going back into the party, and that I hope she doesn't interrupt them. "And if for some unknown reason you feel like you absolutely must," I begged, "just please try not to ruin everything."

Turns out, she took my advice to heart—though not how I expected. About twenty minutes later, I noticed Frantic Friend was back out in the party. *That's good. I hope she didn't bother them.*

A little while after that, I noticed Jimmy rolling back in, with *Playboy* Model at his side. He spotted me across the room, and gave me two quick eyebrow raises to go with a look on his face that said, *Have I got a story for you.* When our paths finally crossed during the party, I leaned down partially to talk to him, but mostly to block anyone else out of the conversation. The height of Jimmy's chair allows for private conversations in crowded places, all without being seen as rude.

"Eddie," he started with his dramatic pause. "You won't believe what happened."

"Did her friend go in there?"

"Yeah . . ."

"Shit! Sorry, man, I tried to talk her out of it."

"I'm glad you didn't. Me and the model were in there, laying on the bed, talking all about sex, and then her friend comes in. I don't know how it happened, but the next thing I know, my pants are down, they both have their shirts off, and they're pushing their boobs in my face. It was awesome."

"What?!"

"Yeah. And then after a little bit the friend left, and I was trying to have sex, but she would only stroke the monster . . . and didn't even finish. So that sucked."

Typical Jimmy. Never satisfied.

"She did say it was big, though," he said with a smile.

12

Officer Voorhees

On and around Temple's campus, students learn very quickly that police officers are our friends. Charged with patrolling the streets of North Philly, with one of the most dangerous corners in the city being close to campus, cops couldn't care less about underage drinking. When I visited friends at other schools, I thought they were kidding when they worried about the campus police while they were out drinking. At Temple, we were happy when we saw police coming down the street.

All except for one, that is. Officer Voorhees was a real ballbuster who believed that campus was a warzone, the students were terrorists, and he was Temple's last line of defense. He had a shaved head, looked like he was pumped full of steroids, and folded his sleeves purposefully, just enough to show he had one of those tribal tattoos running down his arm.

Usually, when a party was broken up, an officer would knock on the door, ask for the people who lived in the house, and kindly tell them a neighbor complained—that it was getting a little loud or out of control or whatever—and that people had to leave. That was it.

Voorhees went about it a bit differently. He approached a noise complaint like a high-stakes drug raid. Being that the police had to conduct actual drug raids somewhat regularly around Temple's campus, no arrests or charges really ever came of Voorhees' charades. It was more the intimidation and appearance that Voorhees was going act on his authority that would freak people out.

Despite being of age to go to a bar, Jimmy and I still preferred to soak up our college years in the filthy campus house parties. We always knew that it wouldn't be long until we were too old for those shenanigans, and wanted to enjoy those moments while it was still acceptable. So one night, we were at a party when Voorhees came busting through the door. He was so intense with his entrance you would have thought they used a battering ram and had a swat team ready to follow him in. He had his nightstick out as if he was going to use it, and was screaming, "EVERYONE WHO LIVES HERE, UP AGAINST THE WALL! EVERYONE ELSE, GET THE FUCK OUT!"

I was near the front, by the door. I watched as most of the people in the room jetted out the back door, to the patio, and climbed over or squeezed through a rusted cyclone fence, as if they were actual criminals. The room cleared out enough for me to catch a glimpse of Jimmy, who was near the back. He was frozen—not out of fear, but because earlier in the party he had someone turn off his chair. He learned the hard way that this was a necessity in crowded parties, so as to avoid the sensitive joystick being jerked around by passersby, or the lap dance the chair so wonderfully lends itself to. He didn't bother asking anyone to turn the chair on during the frantic exodus, because he knew he wasn't getting out of the house on his own—it had steps at both entrances.

A handful of other police came through the door like teenagers forced to do chores on Saturday. They were more concerned with talking and laughing amongst themselves than with the task at hand, and I never knew if they hated being associated with Voorhees or were amused by his extreme antics. They started to shuffle out the handful of people who had the sense to know they didn't need to flee like outlaws. Being that I was near the door, I was in that group. I was repeatedly asking the officers to let me stay in the house to help my friend in a wheelchair get out, but they didn't want to listen to a word I said.

Outside of the house, the police were still ignoring my request. The house was completely emptied except for the people who lived there, some officers, and Jimmy. When the cop at the door finally noticed Jimmy inside and realized I wasn't making my story up, he let me back in. I felt kind of untouchable as I headed back to Jimmy to turn his chair on, walking right passed Voorhees, who had the housemates lined up against the wall— only to turn around and walk back through his stupid lecture about how reckless it is to throw a party, with Jimmy at my side.

He was still going on his stupid rant, which had a subtext to it that screamed, *I was never invited to parties so I hate other people having fun*, when Jimmy and I got to the door and lined his chair up for the exit.

"Excuse me, Officer," I said in a polite tone to Vorhees—though I'll admit, it was no accident I interrupted him mid-sentence. "I'm going to need them to come and help move this chair out," pointing to the guys who lived in the house.

His eyebrows dropped with his jaw as he turned to look at me. He was pissed I would address him at all, especially while he was on his soapbox—let alone with a demand.

I saw he was about to blow, and before he could speak, I added, "Look, it is either they help," pointing to the roommates, "or you guys help," pointing to the cops. Voorhees hated this dilemma. He didn't want to heed my request, but he also didn't want to reduce himself to actually helping someone and carrying out a wheelchair. He quickly put a punctuation on his speech with some finger-waving, a warning and a threat, and then stormed out, ready to go ruin someone else's fun.

After we got Jimmy's chair out, the night was still young and we weren't going to let it go to waste. We hit the corner store, where I bought a couple of 40s and Jimmy treated himself to a six-pack of Blue Moon—quite an upgrade from the usual watered-down beer or malt liquor typical of our college days. We headed to our friend's house for one of our favorite past times: sitting on the stoop. It was like the Lobby of the outside world.

We had been brown-bagging it for over an hour when a patrol car zoomed up and onto the opposite curb, slamming on the brakes and stopping with half the car on the sidewalk, directly across from us. Voorhees flew out of the driver side like his pants were on fire, and sprinted across the street, coming right at us. He got to us before the other officer could even close his car door.

To be fair, I have no idea what the actual law is. I don't know if putting a brown bag over an open container is enough concealment to prohibit a cop from searching, or how close to the stoop one needs to be in order to be considered at a private residence. I would bet that it is against the law for us to have been drinking out there, but also illegal for the cops to search and cite us for it. It seems like one of those things where innocence is only determined by the quality of lawyer one can afford. Regardless, I do know what happened next was nothing short of asinine.

"You guys know you're not supposed to be out here drinking."

Being that we were both twenty-one, I was being honest when I told him I thought it was okay because the bottle was in a brown bag and we were on the steps of a private residence. He rolled his eyes and said that it wasn't.

"Sorry about that officer, we will take it inside." I wasn't trying to cause a stink, even if the officer was an asshole. If we were in the wrong, we were in the wrong. That wasn't enough, though, for Officer Voorhees.

"I'm going to need to confiscate that beer."

"Can't we just take it inside?"

"Not a shot. I cannot let you walk away with that."

"Walk away? We are two steps from the steps!"

We went back a forth for a little, but being that the Hurricane 40s I had purchased were two dollars, I gave it up with only a little resistance.

Jimmy, only the other hand, wasn't budging. He had treated himself to his favorite beer, spending what felt like a fortune to a college student, and most importantly, just cracked a brand new one. He kept asking the officers if he could just take it inside. Voorhees must have been holding on to his embarrassment from earlier, because he wasn't going to succumb to us again.

It was a circle, Jimmy telling Voorhees he is just going to take it inside, and Voorhees saying he can't. The two were getting testy, and the more frustrated Jimmy got, the more I am telling him to let it go—that it's not worth it. Finally, seeing that there was no chance of winning against a douchebag with authority, Jimmy gave up. He told me to dump his open beer into the trashcan.

As I did that, Voorhees went to reach for the rest of the six-pack, which was on the ground next to Jimmy's chair. Like an NFL lineman protecting his quarterback, Jimmy quickly moved into the officer's path, using his chair to shield his beer.

"Whoa, what are you doing?" Jimmy demanded, his testicles damn near bulging out of his pants.

"You need to give me that beer," Voorhees said, obviously unhappy. This was the second time that night Jimmy was taking away from the officer's control of a situation.

"No, I don't. It is mine and it's not open. You have no right."

"Because it is not a full six-pack and it is involved in a possible citation it is now police property," Voorhees said, most likely making that up on the spot.

"No, that's bullshit. I am keeping it."

Voorhees hit the peak of his frustration. He knew he was one hundred percent wrong, and didn't know what to do since he couldn't resort to his usual method of physical intimidation (up against the wall, handcuffs, etc.) with Jimmy. So he decided to take it in another direction.

"You give me that beer or you are getting a D.U.I."

If there were music playing, it would have scratched. It was one of those moments where everyone there, even the other officer, just kind of froze and looked at Voorhees, like, "Dude, are you for real?"

Jimmy was the first to speak. "Are you kidding me?"

"No, I'm not fucking kidding you. You're operating a motor vehicle under the influence. You want a DUI or what?"

"I had one sip. The beer was still full." The sound of defeat was creeping over Jimmy's voice.

"There is no way he is anywhere close to the limit," I added, as our friends around us agreed.

"It doesn't fucking matter! He is operating a motor vehicle with an open container."

At this point, Jimmy saw that there was no point and gave it up. Voorhees took his beer, and as his car sped away, we sat there with Jimmy in disbelief. I had been with Jimmy in other situations where people were disrespectful, rude, or just plain ignorant towards him, and had seen him roll with even the hardest of punches like it was nothing. There was something about this exchange, however, that really struck a cord.

"I'm just going to head back," Jimmy said, as everyone else took the party inside.

"I'll walk with you." On the way back, I tried to cheer him up, and kept talking in hopes of either distracting him or saying something that helped . . . but he just stared at the sidewalk ahead, in complete silence. I had never seen Jimmy this upset before.

I guess he really wanted that beer.

13

The Penn State Trip

After I graduated, I worked about twenty minutes away from campus. For the year that Jimmy was still at Temple, we had a set date night every Thursday. I would meet him at our pizza spot, and ramble on about my trivial post-college trials and tribulations and Jimmy would share his most recent shenanigans. One night, in between the forkfuls of his staple meal—cheesesteak, with cheese fries cut up and mixed in, with extra, extra, extra cheese and ketchup—he proposed we go to Penn State for the weekend. He had visited when he was looking at schools, and though he didn't really like its location, he needed to party there at least once to get it off his bucket list. He said he would get the hotel, and we could take his van. As much as I hate* that cult of a school, it was the weekend of the St. Patty's Day celebration they used to throw in State College called State Patty's Day. I think they still do it today, but last I heard, in an effort to discourage drinking, bars weren't allowed to open on that day. It's so funny to me—a

---

* Part of being a Temple Owl is hating Penn State

school that revolves around drinking and partying will put on the facade that they care about preventing that stuff. What a joke.

I am never one to say no to travel, so Jimmy and I geared up for a trip to the middle-of-nowhere Pennsylvania. Again, it was one of those things that I mindlessly said "yes" to, and then got kind of nervous after realizing what it meant. I had just signed up to be Jimmy's lone "caretaker" for the next thirty-six hours. I had never done it before for that long—or after a night out drinking. But I wasn't worried about it enough to mention it to him. If Jimmy wasn't making it an issue, why would I? I figured if there was something I couldn't do, it was going to affect him a lot more than it would affect me, right?

Nevertheless, on a cold Saturday morning, we climbed into the Limo and set out on the trek to Happy Valley. When we got there, I asked Jimmy what hotel he made a reservation in. This was the first time I witnessed Jimmy's notorious planning skills. Notorious for not having any.

"I didn't. Pick one," he said.

"What?"

"I figured we would just get it now."

The first two hotels we stopped at had no rooms available. None. I didn't even get the chance to ask about accessibility. So here we were tasked with not only finding a hotel with open rooms on one of the school's busiest weekends, but in an accessible hotel.

"Didn't you think to figure this out beforehand?" I asked, as we aimlessly drove around, seeing NO VACANCY on sign after sign.

"We'll figure it out. We can always sleep in the van. I've done it before." Classic Jimmy. Deciding on what he wants to do, and letting the details, even the major ones, figure themselves out.

Finally, we found a spot a little ways away from the downtown area, but a lot more comfortable than the Limo. Checked in, we grabbed a late lunch, and then went to find a place to party. Not really knowing what the bar scene was like in State College, our plan was to wander around until we found a spot that looked busy, figuring a crowd had to count for something. We were walking in the middle of a downtown backstreet when Jimmy spoke up.

"Just so you know, I am going to have to pee at some point. It's your call—we can either do it at the bar or before." He said it so matter of fact, it kind of caught me by surprise. Was he really letting me decide on when he pees?

"You tell me. What's easier for you?"

"Doesn't matter." His ambivalence to the situation was oddly reassuring.

"Well, now that I think about it, wherever we go will probably be crowded, and who knows what the bathroom situation will be like."

"Alright. Then let's do it now."

"Sounds good. Where though?"

"Here works."

I looked around. Though we were next to a long, blank, brick wall, which was probably the back of a store, and at the moment, no one else was in sight, we were still downtown on a busy Saturday.

"Dude, there's driveways on this block. And I think that's a store on the corner."

"Stop being such a pussy," Jimmy said, as he moved next to a bush that was guarding a parking lot. "You know how many drunk college kids piss in these bushes every night?"

"Yeah, but it's daytime. And we aren't drunk!"

"What's the difference?" he said, reclining his chair.

"Alright, but it's on you if any sort of fines come from this."

"Yeah, yeah." I think Jimmy and I both knew that we would be hard-pressed to find an officer that would give either one of us a citation if Jimmy said he couldn't help it. As he started to pee, though, a small group turned the corner.

"Oh shit." I said. Dressed in all green, they were carrying on, making the kind of ruckus drunk college kids make . . . until they saw us—a small man lying on his fully reclined wheelchair with his pants at his ankles, with another man holding his knees up and standing in an awkward position to avoid the stream of piss shooting into the mulch. One by one, they fell silent.

"Are they coming this way?" Jimmy laughed, unable to see anywhere but up.

"Yeah, just shut the fuck up and finish." I felt like I was supposed to be uncomfortable with the situation, but with Jimmy laughing, I guess it kind of allowed me to recognize the humor in it. As the group passed by, I figured it was time to make light of it all.

"Nothing to see here, folks."

"Yeah, except the biggest dick you've ever seen!" Jimmy snapped, so quickly I couldn't help but laugh out loud. Neither joke landed with the passersby, though. They all put their head down with uncomfortable smiles and kept walking, without saying a word.

After Jimmy finished, it was time to get weird. We found a bar that was not only known for their Long Island Iced Teas (our go-to drink), but they were only a dollar. Inside, I even found some people I knew through friends, and I was pumped to finally make Jimmy feel like I was the social connection of our duo. This group we partied with went pretty hard, and one of them even managed to get himself kicked out without ever leaving his seat.

"That's something to aspire to," Jimmy remarked, as we watched our new hero plead with the bouncers for an explanation that never came. Between the cheap drinks, party atmosphere, and the group we were with, it was game over for me. I was toasted. As for Jimmy, on the scale of one to too-drunk-to-drive, he was at about a four. When we started to make the journey back to the hotel, the only thing he was struggling with was the freezing weather. While I was wearing a hoodie, a coat, and a very comfortable liquor blanket, Jimmy couldn't put his ice-cold hands in his pockets in his sitting and driving position. Gloves have always been too bulky or too thin to be of any practicality because he needed to man the chair's joystick, and as usual, he wasn't wearing a jacket, as he values his look more than his comfort. So there he was, trying to keep up with me as I stumbled home, freezing cold without damn-near any feeling in his hands. He persevered without complaint, however, making it slowly but surely back to the hotel, stopping every now and again to gather himself, and then throw his body forward, giving his arm some momentum to push the joystick as far as it would go. Noticing him struggling, I offered to steer the chair for him—an offer that was firmly denied. Jimmy was determined to get himself home, garnering every last bit of strength in his freezing arms and hands to make it there.

When we got back into the room, as I crossed his arms onto his chest before I lifted him out of the chair, I felt his hands.

"Holy shit, Jimmy." They were ice. "Can you still feel them?"

"Not really. It was worse outside though."

His lack of concern didn't make me feel any better. As I sandwiched his hands in mine hoping to warm them, I began to get nervous. *Shit. Why aren't they getting warmer? Does he have frostbite? What if his hands don't work anymore? Is Jimmy going to lose his fingers? Would he still be able to work his chair? I should have known not to come up here. This is all my fault. What the hell was I thinking!*

After what seemed like forever, his hands finally started to feel as if they belonged to a living human being. But by then, it was too late. I already let my mind go back to the uncertainty I had before the trip, and it hit me that Jimmy was a little drunk, and cold, and I was really drunk, and I was supposed to be his caretaker, and I didn't know how to handle myself. I felt like there was something I was supposed to be doing, and was scared. I asked him a million questions, to which he responded that he was fine, I checked on his every possible need, which he said he didn't have any, and even after he was asleep, I laid awake, feeling like I did something wrong. Replaying the night in my head, I realized nothing really changed about the situation to prompt my freak-out, except my own attitude towards it.

The next day, I asked Jimmy if he was ok, and what I should have done different, or better. It was obvious to Jimmy that I was nervous.

"Eddie. You're being ridiculous," he said. "You wouldn't worry like this over anyone else being a little drunk."

14

The Job Hunt

Dean's list, Honors College, double major college graduate.

Numerous clubs and organizations headed, created, or participated in on campus.

Recommendation letters from professors, work managers, and Fran Dunphy, head basketball coach at Temple and kind of a legend in Philadelphia.

Internship at a finance company on Wall Street.

Internship for a United States Congresswoman at the Capital Building in Washington DC.

Most people would kill to have a resume like this during their job search senior year of college. But for some reason it just wasn't cutting it for Jimmy. He had no problem getting interviews, and if the first interview was over the phone he would get second interviews in person. He had gone on over thirty . . . yes, THIRTY interviews and received no offers. He practiced, said everything he was supposed to say, and knew he was qualified for the positions. He doubted his competition had a stronger background— shit, the same people that were constantly coming to Jimmy for help with homework were getting jobs. For him though, the offers just weren't coming.

Jimmy had an idea of what was holding him back.

I would be willing to bet that reading this, you are thinking the same, basic thing that I was thinking. They didn't see the resume; they saw the wheelchair. They see his little body, his weak arms, and the look of disability—of incapability.

But Jimmy thinks deeper than that. On one of our weekly date nights, he explained to me that it wasn't his wheelchair that was preventing him from getting a job. On a much more basic level he said it was the fact that he couldn't show how capable he was to perform at the workplace. Jimmy didn't grow up in a bubble. He knows that there is an assumption of inability and dependence when people see him. He also knows that there are all sorts of laws making discrimination illegal. Jimmy realized that those same laws that were supposed to protect him were dicking him over in interviews. He explained to me the gray area where the law confuses discrimination with common sense, and that's what Jimmy was in conflict with.

Because you cannot discriminate against someone based on their disability, by law, the people interviewing him were not legally allowed to ask him the reasonable questions that may be related to his disability. Anyone with a brain and no experience with someone like Jimmy would wonder things like, can he type? How does he operate a computer? Will he need someone to help him during the day?

Jimmy could have let this situation get the best of him, blaming the system and his circumstances and just chalk up rejection after rejection as if it was out of his control. But that's not him. He decided to take matters into his own hands. As uncomfortable as it may have been, he knew he was going to have to bring up his own disability, and address the things he knew, or at least could guess, they were thinking.

While most people only worry about presenting what they can bring to the company, Jimmy had to do that *and* steer the conversation in a way to where he could interject the fact he is able to type the average amount of words per minute, and is fine using a lap top or keyboard as long as it's positioned near the edge of the desk. He would explain that he is even more efficient with his phone, and there is an app that allows to him to control his computer via his mobile device. He would explain that he would have a nurse come every day at lunch time to feed him, and do anything else necessary, but that she would be professional and quiet and it had never been an issue at any of his internships. Those were some of the things Jimmy would sprinkle into the interview, and those were some of the things that made the job offers start popping up.

It was during this time that Jimmy first really saw the misconceptions of those with a disability. He always understood that he was looked at differently, and treated differently, but the experience of having to explain his basic capabilities in an interview really opened his eyes to just how far-off the misconception was.

When finding a job becomes a harder job than the job itself, it would be understandable to jump at the first available offer. But that's not Jimmy. He's too hardheaded to do anything other than what he wants to do. He got an offer on Long Island that he thought was good fit, but he was worried about leaving his city behind. I remember him telling me, "Everything about me is Philadelphia. My friends, my network, what I like to do for fun. It might be a little crazy to leave all these connections I made behind."

He had a lead on a job that was in Philadelphia, for a great company, with a good salary, and it was a position he wanted. With nothing to go on except confidence in himself, he declined the offer in New York and waited to hear from the company in Philly. In less than a week, he was offered the job. He was ready to move into the next step of his life, when he got a call that would change everything.

Someone from the health services company that oversees Jimmy's case called to inform him that if he were to take this job, he would lose the 115 hours of home health care Medicaid provided each week and be forced to pay for his aides out of his own pocket. In order to do that, Jimmy would have to earn over $100k per year just to break even.

Jimmy was confused, heartbroken, and upset. When he told me about it, I was pissed. It didn't make any sense to me. Jimmy had become one of my best friends because I could be real with him. I told him that I know there are all sorts of government programs for those with disabilities. College funding, discounts around every corner, the government covered healthcare . . . hundreds of millions of dollars spent to make sure buildings and sidewalks and public transportation adheres to the ADA . . . all for what? To encourage those with disabilities to sit at home and not work? What killed me most was the college discount—why fund someone's education if they are basically incentivized to not get a job afterwards? Just for show? So we can say as a nation, "Yahoo, whoop-dee-doo, a guy in a wheelchair got a diploma?"

In my humble opinion—fuck that. That's the stupidest shit I ever heard.

Now, I know it's status quo to complain about your job and talk about hitting the lottery, quitting, and doing nothing for the rest of your life, but the truth is, that's a bunch of malarkey. After a couple days of not doing anything, I think most people would go nuts. People need, want, and like purpose. Don't get me wrong, I'm not hating on disability subsidies or unemployment programs—they are necessary, and there's good and bad to them, like most things. But this was a black and white situation to me. Jimmy was qualified for a job he wanted and was capable of doing said job . . . so Jimmy should get to work. It's a win-win-win situation for all parties involved. The only thing holding him back were the very laws that were supposed to protect him. It is almost as though these policies are set up in a way to make sure that we don't tap into the large talent pool of people like Jimmy. Patronizing him does no one any good.

Jimmy didn't know what to do, and neither did anyone in his circle of family and friends—it's not like they teach you how to handle this type of thing in school. The model citizen he is, he turned to his state representative, only to find that they weren't of much help. Though they offered to advocate for him when possible, and shared with him kind words of encouragement and support, they couldn't give him a clear solution to fix the problem.

Undeterred, he turned to the media, hoping that would help expose this issue, and maybe put pressure on the politicians who could actually change it. He was in the paper, and on television, talking about the situation and how disappointing it was.

Sure I was upset about it, as evidenced from my rant above. Sure, it makes me upset as a citizen that we have silly lawmakers who care more about the appearance of a law than the implication of it. When I step back and try to put myself in Jimmy's shoes, however, I can't imagine how frustrating that must have been for him.

He is treated so differently that they need to make a law to protect him, which inadvertently was a huge obstacle in the interview process. Then, once he figured his way around that and got a job, the same laws that provided funding for him to go to college to be trained for the job he wanted, basically tell him, "Well, you can't actually use what you learned in school to have a life where you work and contribute to society—instead we set this up so you can be completely state-dependent forever."

His career's fate was in the balance for a couple of weeks, but an answer finally came. It wasn't from the state representative or homecare agency he was working with—it was someone who had read about Jimmy's situation in the *Philadelphia Inquirer*. And it wasn't a fancy politician with years of experience, or a highfalutin lawyer, or a well-educated government official—it was just a regular person with a disability who had the same experience, and was capable enough to figure out what even those who made the law, couldn't.

Apparently, there was a loophole. All Jimmy had to do was fill out a couple of rarely-used forms, and then just like that, he would be eligible to work *and* receive homecare. This solution was almost too simple, from such an unexpected source, that Jimmy wouldn't believe it until it worked. And, as sure as his chair rolls, it did. It's a good thing, too, because Jimmy was fully intending on showing up to his job regardless of the benefits situation. "Everything is going to work out, somehow, I just know it," Jimmy said, in defense of his bullheaded plan. "I'm not going to miss my first day of work!"

Sometime later, over one of our Thursday night dinners, I explained to Jimmy something* I remembered learning about in one of my classes, which somewhat reminded me of his job search debacle. It was about the "Ban the Box" campaign. There

---

* "Ban the Box, Criminal Records, and Statistical Discrimination: A Field Experiment" by Agan and Starr. Also, "Perceived Criminality, Criminal Background Checks, and the Racial Hiring Practices of Employers" by Holzer, Raphael, and Stoll.

was a big push to outlaw the box on job applications that asked if the applicant has a criminal history. The campaign was started under the idea that the box disadvantaged ex-felons, and disproportionally affected black men. Ironically, it turned out that the removal of the box actually had the most negative effect on black males, especially those who had not committed a crime.*

When applicants didn't have a way to share that they did not have a criminal history, the potential employers fell back on negative stereotypes and preconceived notions. Based on nothing more than the name on the application, they were much more likely to assume certain people had a criminal record.

Jimmy and I talked about how lucky we are to live in the era we do—after things like the Civil Rights Acts of the 1950s and '60s, and the American with Disabilities Act, among other laws geared toward protecting civil rights and giving everyone in this country a fair shake. The world we grew up in and know is very different than the world we read about in history books, despite it being only decades away. What I really took away from our conversation, though, is how obvious it was, through things like the "Ban the Box" study or Jimmy's job search struggles, that a politician signing a piece of paper doesn't create the change that is needed. Though blatant acts of discrimination have been outlawed in this day and age, it is foolish to think the thoughts and feelings that motivated the discrimination disappeared as well. We talked about how the government can change the way people act in public, but laws can't change the hearts and mind of people.

No matter if their ignorance came from a place of innocence, their stereotypes from a place of normalcy, or their hatred from a place of stupidity, Jimmy had just witnessed the amount of misconception involved with disability in his job search—and where the hearts and minds of people lay. He saw firsthand that no law would ever change that, but maybe, just maybe, he could.

He just didn't know how.

---

* Researchers sent out 15,000 applications to companies both before and after the "Ban the Box" laws went into effect. The only difference in the applications is that some had traditionally white names while others had traditionally black names. Before the box was banned, there was a 7% difference in callbacks, more calls going to the "white" sounding names than the "black" sounding names. After the box was banned, that gap rose to 45%.

15

The Two Dreaded Tasks

Now that he had a job in the city, Jimmy's next step was to do something he always wanted to do: move downtown. He knew I was living at home and wanted to get back into the city, so he asked if I wanted to look for a place with him. I didn't hesitate to say yes.

I will never forget the reaction from my friends and family when I told them I would be moving in with Jimmy. People who I believe respected me and my decision-making were now quick to tell me I was naïve and had no idea what I was getting into. Others told me it was going to be an impossible situation—that I would have to be available for Jimmy's want and need around the clock. Some, perhaps most troubling, said it was nice of me—that I was a good person to do that for him. I wanted to scream at them. I wasn't signing a year-lease for thousands of dollars as a fucking charitable act.

Don't get me wrong; I'm no fool. I knew that living with someone with a disability would be different. What I couldn't get past, though, is how so many of these people automatically assumed that this different would be bad. The same people who would comment about how I was a college grad living at home, were now critical of me changing that situation. The same people who were so vocal and enthusiastic about their respect for Jimmy showed that it was just a veneer, and apparently didn't actually believe it was reasonable for him to do things like getting an apartment with a friend. It made me see firsthand the hypocrisy of "tolerant" and "accepting" people. The kind of people who "love" the guy in the wheelchair and rant and rave about how accomplished and inspiring he is, but don't actually see him as a person like anyone else.

As for me, I didn't see it as an issue, and I wanted to get back to Philly. Living with Jimmy's crazy ass was just an added benefit. In retrospect, our apartment search was very limited, as the majority of homes in the residential areas of Philadelphia are not wheelchair accessible. There are people that would throw a big fuss, and act as if it was the end of the world, but Jimmy never made it an issue. If anything, he would prefer an apartment building anyway, as there would more likely be doormen, security, maintenance, or neighbors around if he ever needed anything. He just accepted housing accessibility for what it was, and I guess it forced me to do the same.

The ADA ensured that the bigger apartment complexes were accessible, but what that means is different for every location. One place was only accessible via cargo elevator, and another had a hallway that was too narrow for Jimmy to turn his chair around in. Personally, I kind of liked it, as it forced my indecisive self to eliminate certain options. It didn't take long before we ended up stumbling upon the nicest apartment, at the best price, probably in the entire city . . . if not the world. It was as if everything in the universe was aspiring to come together in our favor.

It was a two-bedroom apartment right near the corner of Broad and Walnut Street, which is about as Center City as Center City can get. Walnut was one of the few accessible stops on the subway line, and the apartment had two bathrooms—one in a bedroom with a stand-up shower, which was perfect for Jimmy, who uses a shower chair. It was spacious, with wide hallways and open living areas, and the second the building manager was out of earshot me and Jimmy talked about how it would be perfect for a party. It wasn't anywhere as expensive as it could have been, but even with that I still needed help in order to afford it.

People tended to assume that Jimmy didn't work, or that he had some bullshit job. Some even assumed I was paying rent for the both of us. I knew this because, in addition to people explicitly telling or asking me about those things, I could see and hear their surprise when they found out where Jimmy worked, or what he did. They would have never guessed that Jimmy was earning almost three times as much as me when I would joke that he was the family breadwinner.

I wouldn't have been able to afford living in the apartment if I didn't get a job as one of Jimmy's direct care workers. All I had to do was spend a couple hours at the home care agency for a training, and then boom, I was officially on the list of Jimmy's aides. From our sleepovers in college and our trip to Penn State, I had an idea of what the task would entail. It did not include staying over in his room at night, or showering him and getting him ready for work in the morning. I would eat with him, or help with little things, on certain, scheduled days, something I usually did anyway when I wasn't "working." I knew I had done almost everything a direct care worker does at some point in our relationship.

There were still two things, though, that I had never helped him do. And neither of us was looking forward to either of them.

The first time I was "working," we both knew one of these dreaded tasks would have to be done. And that task was pooping. I was definitely more uncomfortable than Jimmy was— he has had people help him do it his whole life. But like all uncomfortable things that have to be done, when the time came, I just did it. I guess I realized it was just kind of in my head . . . you make things as awkward or as uncomfortable as you want them to be.

There are people who automatically assume Jimmy is a charity case, and will compliment me, or whoever is around him, just for hanging out with him in a normal social setting. Those idiots aside, there are people who know Jimmy, respect Jimmy, and are friends with Jimmy, that will *still* give me compliments and say that I am a good guy and a nice friend. I am sure it is times like this they are talking about—I mean, I don't take any of my other friends to the bathroom. They stand there and say, "I

could never," or, "I would never," and that it's incredible that I
do.

The thing is, I truly believe in my heart of hearts, the
majority of these people are wrong about themselves. They could
do it, and would do it. On the most basic level, this was the "job"
I had to do in order to afford living at that apartment. The things
people can and would do when they need, or really want,
something is damn near unlimited.

On a deeper level, I think the part that is missed is that I
didn't meet Jimmy doing these things. It wasn't like I was walking
around campus and stumbled upon a handicapped kid who
needed to take a shit, and then decided, "let's be friends!" Sure,
wiping an ass may not be a typical destination in the progression
of a friendship, but it definitely occurred after we became friends.
It was weird to hear people say they would never be able to do
what I was doing, especially since I saw them going above and
beyond for the people close to them. What they were doing—
helping a depressed roommate, being there for a friend battling
addiction, working through a girlfriend or boyfriend cheating—
were all situations I had a hard time imagining myself in. In every
relationship there are things that no one signs up for, but we do
them anyway because . . . well, to put it simply: you do things for
people you care about. It is just the way we are wired.

Ok then . . . let me step off my soapbox and get back to
the scene where I have to help Jimmy shit for the first time.
Under his instruction, I took him out of his chair and laid him on
the bed, and then took his pants off. I carried him to the toilet,
and set him down, not facing forward, but to the side. He told me
lean his head against the wall, so as to help with his balance.
Then, just like every twenty-something guy I know, he wanted his
phone to play with while dropping his logs. He called me when
he was finished, and as I started the cleaning process I was
shocked when I saw the mutant that Jimmy left in the toilet bowl.
I couldn't believe something that size came out of something so
little—I was in disbelief. The moment I started to mention my
amazement, however, he screamed, "EDDIE SHUTUP!!"

It startled me so much I dropped the poop-smeared
toilet paper. It bounced off the back of the toilet seat and onto
the floor in front of Jimmy.

"AHHH, get that the fuck away from me," he snapped,
as he closed his eyes.

I started laughing. "What the hell is wrong with you?"

He didn't open his eyes until I told him the toilet paper was gone. He explained that he has seen his own poop only once or twice. His situation doesn't really lend itself to ever seeing *in* the toilet. As for the times he did see it, he thought it was the grossest, most disgusting thing in the entire world.

Now knowing this repulsion of his, after I washed my hands, I scooped Jimmy up, and, like any great friend would, titled him so his line of sight was directly into the toilet wherein lay the wrath he had just brought upon the world. With his eyes closed, he was doing everything in his power to turn his head, and I refused to put him in his chair until he saw what he had done.

"Eddie, no!"

"Open them!"

"NOOOO!"

"This is a pound for pound the best poop any human has created. Guinness Book type of shit. Literally."

"No, please, no."

"Do it, Jimmy."

He knew I wasn't going to budge. He simultaneously let out a roller coaster yell as he opened his eyes. Then, coming to an objective conclusion after seeing his own poop for one of the first times in his life, he said, "That is the grossest thing I have ever seen!"

Satisfied, I put him in his chair. Now I knew if he was ever pissing me off I could threaten to show him his own poop. Somehow, this increased my comfort with the whole bathroom scenario.

It's not like me taking him to the bathroom would ever become the number one thing on either of our lists, but it got me thinking about the idea that people can and would do anything— it is just a matter of comfort, and that comes with experience. Whether it's wiping a butt, or seeing your own poop, or washing the windows of skyscrapers, or dealing with a classroom of first graders screaming and crying and causing pure chaos . . . people adapt. Now, I don't know if the nurse on the cancer floor is immune to sadness when a patient dies, but I bet she definitely has a better grip in handling a person dying during her workday than someone who works at a post office. All of those people who were hating on my decision to live with Jimmy, well, we all have this tendency to create fears of things, making them bigger or more important or scarier than they actually are. We also have an undeniable and fascinating ability, I was learning, to adapt to almost any situation life hands us.

While Mother Nature forced us to handle the pooping situation the first day, it would take some time before we hit a tipping point in dealing with the other dreaded situation. Believe it or not, the only other thing that stressed me out about being Jimmy's "aide," was helping him get dressed.

Don't get me wrong, I had changed a shirt or two before... but I never helped him get dressed head to toe. See, Jimmy is a full-blown metrosexual. He cares more about the way he looks than most people care about their bank account. He is the type of person to want a different outfit for different dayparts. I had heard him be very direct with his other aides who did not give the proper attention to detail or have the patience that dressing him required. I guess when you are relying on someone else for something as important as the way you look, settling for less than what you want is not an option. I wasn't looking forward to taking on that responsibility, and I know Jimmy wasn't either.

For the people who say our friendship is an unlikely one, they are correct, simply because we could not be more different in this department. I am the type of guy to postpone shaving or a haircut for months just because I don't want to deal with the huuuge hassle of it. Jimmy, on the other hand, stares at the mirror daily, telling himself how good-looking he is, while searching for the smallest hair out of place or slightest imperfection to fix.

That being said, it takes him forever to get ready, and still to this day I can't understand the hassle of trying on multiple outfits per night in order to find the one that works. I understand the concept of matching, even if I am not good at it, but I don't get how the same outfit could look good one night and then not good another. Within the first couple weeks, we had a few little tiffs where Jimmy's indecisiveness intersected with my impatience. Here he is thinking that his fashion choices could potentially make or break a romantic interaction, while I am yelling, "Just pick something! All this shit looks the same!"

I always thought it somewhat of a paradox for Jimmy to care that much about his clothes or his hair. No matter what, I knew the first impression of Jimmy's appearance would come from his wheelchair and a body that looks so very different. Heads turn, and he is remembered because of these things.

One day as we were getting dressed, and he couldn't make up his mind, and I was getting annoyed, I asked him why the hell he cares so much about the way he looks. He explained to me that he has always been very deliberate and intentional in his appearance because he wanted to be the one to decide the way he is perceived. Jimmy wanted to look good because the moment person got past his chair he wanted to meet them with the button-down Polo, fresh haircut, Burberry scarf, 7 for All Mankind jeans, and one of the gems from his vast shoe collection. That reason was well and good . . . but it still didn't make the dressing process easier for either of us.

Our mutual frustration in this department would eventually reach its peak. We had taken full advantage of the "two-dollar Tuesday" beer special the night before, and had each been dealing with the consequences during a long day at work. I was his aide that night, and when we both got back to the apartment our usual dinnertime banter was nonexistent. We must have been in our pajamas before nine o'clock, watching television in his room, waiting for the overnight nurse to come. He was laying in his bed, and I was sitting up in the aide's bed, when I realized I had forgotten to tell Jimmy that a package had come for him in the mail.

"Where is it? Go get it!" he exclaimed. I immediately regretted telling him.

"You sure you don't want to wait 'til tomorrow?" I asked with a smile.

"Eddie, nooo!" Usually Jimmy's enthusiasm is contagious, inspiring me to enjoy each and every moment . . . but not tonight. Tonight, I just desperately wanted the overnight nurse to show up and to get my ass to bed. Though I didn't feel like moving, I grabbed the box from the kitchen and brought it into the bedroom. His wide eyes and repeated demands to "open it" made me start to think it was actually going to be something worth getting up for. When I cut the packaging tape and peered inside, my fashion sense (or lack thereof) left me extremely disappointed.

"What the hell are these?" I said, holding up a pair of kid-sized dress shoes.

"Put them on," he said.

"Gucci!" I said, looking at the label. "Jimmy! How much were these?"

"You don't want to know." I stared at him. He could tell I wasn't budging until I got an answer. "Four-fifty. Now put them—"

"Four hundred and fifty fucking dollars?! Are you shitting me? And I'm the one always buying drinks when we are out? This ain't right, man!"

"Eddie! Put them on!"

"Dude, we are about to go to bed, can't we just—"

"No. I want to try them on tonight."

I never lost sight of the fact that I was his aide, and I had no right to deny the request. There was something about feeling like I didn't have a choice, though, that made an already long day, and night, and getting up from what I thought was the end of it all, that much more frustrating. Up until that point of living there, when I was his aide, I was always just doing my job. But the truth is, whether I was his aide or not, I was going to put those goddamn, overpriced, ridiculous shoes on my friend's feet, albeit begrudgingly. I figured if I was going to make this work, I was going to have to be myself, and not so damned polite.

"Fine, asshole." I said. Jimmy smiled as I ripped the plastic packaging.

It was immediately obvious that it was going to be a tight squeeze getting Jimmy's block feet into these narrow shoes. I loosened the laces and opened the shoe as wide as I could. With Jimmy laying on his back, still in bed, I lifted his foot with one hand as I tried to slide and shimmy the shoe on with my other. It didn't seem like there would be a chance of fitting it on this way. So sliding my forearm under his leg, I used both hands to bend the shoe at the middle, just like I would with some of his tighter sneakers, hoping to slide the toes in and then the heel would follow suit.

"STOP! Eddie, STOP!" Jimmy snapped. I jumped backed as if I had broken a bone. I don't know what I did wrong, but I thought I must have I hurt him.

"Don't bend them!"

"Are you serious right now?"

"Yes! Don't bend them."

"How the hell I am supposed to get them on?"

"Lift up the tongue as far as you can, and just wiggle it on."

"I tried that! It's way too tight, wiggling isn't working."

"Then just shove my foot in as hard as you can. But don't bend the shoe!"

"They are shoes! If you could walk you would bend them with every step you took."

"Well I can't. So don't fuck my shoes up."

I grabbed his foot and shoved it into the stiff Italian leather as hard as I could. Jimmy screamed in pain, and after a struggle, and couple more groans and whimpers, and the process repeated for the other foot, with Jimmy clearly uncomfortable, the shoes were on his feet.

"Happy now?" I asked, holding his legs up so he could see them on his feet.

"Put me in my chair."

"Dude—"

"I want to see!"

We stared at each other for a moment, silently engaging in a contest of stubborn will. It wasn't long before I realized I was fighting a losing battle.

"I hate you, Jimmy," I decided, picking him up and putting him in his chair. As I plopped back onto the nurse's bed, finally able to relax once again, he slid over to his full-length mirror, and indulged himself in the sight before him: a throwaway t-shirt, plaid pajama bottoms, and his brand new, crisp, navy blue Gucci shoes. I looked at him, looking at himself, basking in his own reflection.

"Shoes are meant to bend, you idiot!"

"Not my shoes."

16

The Overnight Nurses

Most orgies that you go to, I have found, most of it is
sad. All that wildness, all those laughs were like the
shining silver and gold paper on packages, but there was
nothing inside.

—Sammy Davis, Jr.

The overnight nurses were important for two reasons: they
had to get Jimmy ready for work, and they had to deal with
Weekend Jimmy. The two overnight nurses during the time I was
living with Jimmy couldn't have been more opposite from one
another, and both were very much needed and appreciated for
their own specific reason.

Loraina was the type of nurse a mother would want her
son to have. She understood Jimmy's desire to look professional
for work, and was meticulous in every aspect of the daily
dressing, grooming, and preparing for the workday. It worked out
perfect, since Loraina was scheduled to work Sunday to
Wednesday, and rarely had to deal with weekend Jimmy. Sure,
there were a couple of Two Dollar Tuesdays that may have
brought Weekend Jimmy out midweek, and sure Loraina may
have worried about whether or not she should take some kind of
action, but most of the time, weeknights out stayed somewhat
reasonable.

Then there was Barbara. She was the kind of nurse a "pull my finger" uncle would want Jimmy to have. Barbara had been with Jimmy through college and understood (through personal experience, it would turn out) his want for a party, and had patience for his drunkenness.

In her sixties, she was big and round, with fire red dyed hair, and a face that said she had seen it all. No one really knew the true extent of what that meant, though, except for Jimmy. Having spent a lot of time with her, he knew the ins and outs of Barbara's private side, and the two interacted more like brother and sister than caregiver and client.

As much as Jimmy loved having a nurse who put up with any and every drunk antic on the weekend, it was a trade-off for the days that she had to get him ready for work. Every Friday morning, along with the random times Barbara was covering Loraina's weekday shift, the two would be ready to kill each other, lacing profanities all through a conversation that I could hear from my bedroom. It typically sounded something like this:

"You're being so lazy! I am going to be late!"

"If it didn't take you an hour to get ready you would be on time!"

"My hair looks like shit!"

"It looks fine, Jimmy! Why do you care so much?"

"Some people care about how they look!"

"Yeah, yeah, yeah."

"You missed a spot shaving!"

"How about I cut you!"

"You're the worst."

At times, it wasn't clear as to who was taking care of who. One night, I was awakened by Jimmy's nightly calls for help. This was odd—usually he would be turned over before his yelling became loud enough for me to hear it. After a couple of minutes he was still screaming, so I went into his room to investigate.

Just as I stepped foot into the dark bedroom, Barbara came bursting out of Jimmy's bathroom yelling, "I'm here! I'm here!" I headed back to bed, and Jimmy never woke up—he had been on autopilot the entire time.

The next day, I found Barbara in her infamous position, sitting with a towel around her waist as her pants were hanging to dry. Jimmy was consoling her, telling her that's its ok, and she has nothing to be embarrassed about. Standing at his bedroom door,

I wanted to help, but Jimmy shook his head, signaling me to let it go. He would tell me later that the reason she was in that position, and the reason she was in the bathroom when I heard Jimmy screaming, was not an issue of the bladder.

In the wee hours of the morning, in the silent and tranquil apartment, Jimmy signaled it was time to be turned over with a piercing shriek of agony. The sudden noise startled Barbara, scaring the shit out of her. Literally. The woman pooped her pants, and her client was trying to make her feel better about it.

Whenever company was over, he would make her stay in the bedroom—whether Jimmy was embarrassed, wanted to protect us, or he just didn't want to share the spotlight, we didn't know. That is, until one time . . .

After the bars closed and we got back to our apartment, we were goofing around, talking, and inhaling Domino's—exactly how any great night should end. As per usual, Jimmy had Barbara strip him down to his birthday suit.* But for some unknown reason, on this night, he allowed her out of the bedroom and invited her to join the after party.

As she fed naked Jimmy forkfuls of pizza, Barbara asked us how the night went—specifically if there were any pretty women we had met. She started going on about how, when she smokes her cigarettes outside, she gets a little excited watching the groups of "sexy ladies" walk past the apartment to the bars. We were surprised at hearing her talk like this. We knew she had been married, so we were half-joking when we asked her if she was into women.

"Honey, I am into anything with legs."

Naturally, the only follow up question for your roommate's overnight nurse at 3 a.m. after hours of drinking is, "Have you ever been with one before?"

"Honey, the better question is how many have I been with . . . at one time." She enjoyed that fact that she raised our eyebrows, and knew she had our attention.

---

* Jimmy had a habit of disappearing from the after party, only to reappear completely naked. Sometimes it was only for a naked lap around the apartment; other times, he reinserted himself into the party as if nothing changed. The first few times this happened, it left the room in stitches. But after awhile, seeing Jimmy with nothing but a seatbelt on at three in the morning almost became an afterthought.

"I was pretty into the '60s, and if there was a drug you could put in your body, I was doing it. I stopped taking acid, though, after a bad trip. We decided to take a ride up to New York, and I swear the Statue of Liberty was on fire and trying to attack me. I never touched that shit again."

That craziness aside, we were stuck on the multiple sex partners. I guess the way people write off Jimmy as an asexual object, it is easy to forget that people above the age of sixty are, or at least once were, sexual beings, and that we all have the capacity for promiscuity. It is especially easy to dismiss that fact when the subject is a chain-smoking, oval-shaped nurse with loose bowels.

Loving the shock she had put onto our faces, and ignoring the embarrassment on Jimmy's, she continued, "You know, it's not like I kept count. But it was about however many people we could fit in the bedroom. It's where I met the true love of my life—Alan." She went on to explain that she loved that man, and the two were soul mates, but that he was gay and that was the reason they never worked out.

"I was willing to marry him and live as life partners, and I would be fine with him doing whatever he wanted," Barbara explained, "but he said he wouldn't do that to me. He was actually the one who encouraged me to marry Hank. I was on the phone with him on my wedding day, hoping he would change his mind. But he didn't."

It was obvious that this was something she has struggled with, but maybe because we grew up in the era we did, we didn't give the shocked reaction she seemed like she was expecting. I am sure that back then, the world treated Alan, and her with Alan, very differently than it would have today. What we couldn't get over, however, was this free-loving '60s hippie nonsense. A friend asked the very fair question, "How is it exactly that an orgy starts?"

"Well, I don't know, you drink some of that white lightening—you know, moonshine—until you don't know what's going on anymore. Then you take your clothes off and go into the bedroom and let the liquor take care of the rest."

My shock may have been mitigated if I could imagine Barbara as a young and sexy partygoer, but unfortunately, the visual that the story unwillingly placed into my brain involved the present day Barbara—all seven decades of this plump, borderline-incontinent woman stripping off her well-worn scrubs in a room full of horny, drunk men and women. My ever pragmatic friend, however, continued his questioning, undeterred. "How exactly do one of those things end?"

"I don't know, I guess you starting coming out of the blackout and you think, 'What the fuck am I doing here?' And you leave."

There is a part of me that wants to find some sort of life lesson in here—something like that it is kind of like Jimmy's chair—before you know it, you're hanging out with a guy in a wheelchair and you just kind of black it out, and forget it's there. And part of me wants to be all cheesy sentimental and say something like, "Fortunately, there is no coming out of that blackout and leaving the friendship with Jimmy." You know, some crap like that.

In reality, though, the biggest part of me is simply thinking, *holy fucking shit* on so many levels. I went to take a drink, hoping it would help alleviate this disturbing revelation, but then remembered alcohol was the catalyst of her story and decided to put the bottle down. God forbid one day I drink too much and wind up in a bed, elbows deep in a Barbara and a couple of dudes looking to do unspeakable things to me. As we sat there in silence, Barbara turned the topic back to Alan and how perfect he was for her. As she droned on and on to a room that was pretending like they weren't thinking about moonshine and orgies, I couldn't get past the fact that the activities this round, older woman took part in blew the minds of four American men in their twenties—literally the most perverted demographic on the planet. To be clear, while blacked out group sex with someone I love who won't marry me because of conflicting sexual preferences may not necessarily be my cup of tea, I am not condemning any of that stuff . . . I am all about if it makes someone happy, and no one else is getting hurt: Go for it. It's just crazy to think of someone a certain way, or assume certain things, and then be confronted with a conflicting reality.

17

The Nurses File

For times when Jimmy was afforded home healthcare but did not require a certified nurse—every weekday from noon to two for lunch and a bathroom break, dinnertime six to eleven, and weekend day noon to four—there were direct care workers. With a CPR cert and about an hour of training, the homecare services company could pull just about anyone off the street and start them at $8.50 an hour, meanwhile billing the government upwards of twenty-five dollars an hour. There have been many bumps in the road Jimmy has had to endure before he could settle into a group of high-quality caregivers he is comfortable with, but even to this day if a nurse calls out for whatever reason, it is a wildcard as to whom they may send. With a background of some pretty freakin' weird people, Jimmy was pumped to have me, a friend, as a caregiver.

Obviously, I wasn't his only direct care worker while we lived together. Aleesha was a very slim, and very attractive girl our age, and she and Jimmy built a relationship that crossed just about every boundary the homecare agency places on their workers—in a good way. The two were extremely similar—loved the same kind of music, fashion, and the shy Aleesha would talk to Jimmy with a comfort she felt with no one else. Jimmy loved having her around, and they would even hang out at times when she wasn't working.

Aleesha, Barbara, and Loraina felt just as much like roommates to me as Jimmy was. As for the others, between my time living with him in the same dorm building, sharing an apartment together, and knowing him afterward, I have witnessed and heard about a lot of crazy shit. Jimmy has no problem getting along with people of all sorts of different personalities and backgrounds, but he has been handed some pretty crazy characters as care givers. The following are the standouts:

The First Aide I Ever Met

The first time I ever met one of Jimmy's nurses really gave me a grasp of just how peculiar that situation may be for him. On an average afternoon in the dorms, Jimmy, Tommy McConnell, Darren, and I went to Jimmy's room to grab something before we headed out. We walk into his room and heard the foulest sounds coming from the computer screen—the audio alone insured this film had an X rating.

"Jimmy!" Latasha said, a large and equally loud woman who was not the least bit startled to see us—she was excited. "You have got to see this one." This woman turned out to be a pornography connoisseur. She ranted and raved and shared the top videos her search that day had produced, told us the kind of porn she liked the most, and told us the kind of porn we should be watching—basing it off of what she gives her son to watch and his responses.

The Full Service Nurses

One day in college, a female friend of Jimmy and I texted me with a question. I knew it was going to be good because she prefaced the actual question text with the "Can I ask you a question?" text.

"I don't know how to say this, but . . . does Jimmy's dick work?"

When I had relayed the info to Jimmy he had the reaction that any young adult male would have when finding out that there is an attractive young woman curious about his penis.

"Eddie." He separated the texts for emphasis. "It's going down . . . tonight."

They never ended up doing the deed, and when not misguided (as so many men can be) by the brain below his belt, he will admit that he understands the misconceptions and the curiosity people may have. Besides the fact that I don't typically spend time thinking about the utility of another man's penis, I can't say that I ever remember thinking about whether or not Jimmy could or couldn't have sex. I guess just spending time with him, talking about the things guys talk about, hearing the comments he made, I simply assumed he was just like anyone else without every really thinking about it.

Over the years, there have been a few jokes made between the two of us concerning this topic. I'll take him to poop, sure. I'll shower him, no big deal. I'll even throw his pants on and adjust the guy downstairs if need be—it comes with the territory. One thing I will not do, nor would Jimmy want me to do, however, is anything related to that monster when it is standing at attention.

Throughout our time together, I would come to learn that there have been certain times Jimmy has opted to stay in his bed, or not get out of his chair, for no apparent reason, and it is because he had a boner and he didn't want to risk any contact during the transfer. One day, however, Jimmy was sleeping in his bed and I had to head out. He had told me to make sure to put him in his chair before I left. I was in a rush, and didn't bother to wake him up before I began lifting him out of the bed and into the chair.

Before Jimmy really came to, I had my hand under his head, swooped my other arm under his legs, and began to lift when I felt something like a hammer hitting my forearm. I had Jimmy about a foot off of the bed before it registered what I was feeling, and I dropped him like he was hot potato back onto the mattress. He cursed at me as he bounced on the mattress, and I started cursing back at him for having that, and then we swore to each other that what just happened, never happened.

Homecare agencies have plenty of rules and regulations, but none of them seem to deal with real life scenarios like what to do when your client has a boner. Meanwhile, these caregivers are coming in and dealing with these odd situations for the first time, and they all handle it differently. Some of them ignore it, some of them make jokes about it, and some of them even make pet names for it.

Some go the extra mile.

The first time Jimmy ever got action below the belt was from a nurse. This girl had expressed to Jimmy that she liked him—like, *liked*, liked him. She was saying he was more than a good client to her. This didn't translate to the nurse finding a note that said "check yes or no if you will go out with me" . . . this translated to the nurse finding an erection the size of the Statue of Liberty when she took Jimmy's pants off to go the bathroom.

She laughed when she saw it, and then she laughed a little more when Jimmy couldn't pee because of it.

With the funny nature of the exchange, Jimmy saw this as an opportunity to take a shot. "Well, I can't go when it's like this..." he said, smiling and laughing.

The girl laughed again, thought for a second . . . and then went to work.

This turned out to be a regular thing—every time she came over, Jimmy wouldn't ever explicitly ask for it, but he made sure he either went to the bathroom or took a shower, and boom, it would happen.

The problem was that this nurse started to believe she was entitled to certain things, treating Jimmy like a sort of sugar daddy. At no point was she stealing from Jimmy behind his back, but she would take a couple of bills out of his wallet and say she was going to buy herself dinner, or something petty like that.

Jimmy faced a conundrum. Like many men, there are two driving forces in his life—money and women. He was finally getting one, at the expense of another. After toiling over this dilemma for a few days he finally came to a decision. He chose to protect his money, and told the homecare agency to never schedule that woman ever again.

Fortunately, he next experienced a strange phenomenon, one that is almost always true when it comes to women. Every man who has ever been in a drought in the female department will attest that when it rains, it pours. Some will say that after one success a man is more confident, but in reality, I think women have this weird sixth sense that can tell when a man has been deemed territory fit for claim, then instinctually want him for themselves. Regardless, after that cherry popped, within days there were others doing the same thing.

Since then, there have been a plethora of aides and nurses who have undertaken this task. What baffles Jimmy is that he never can tell who will undertake the (literal) task at hand. Different ages, religions, stages of life—there was even a married woman who would talk to Jimmy about her husband before and after the act. Jimmy would ask her if she felt guilty, and she would respond, "Oh, don't be silly, this doesn't count."

Like trying to peg anyone for anything, Jimmy will never be able to tell for sure what kind of nurse will be the one to hook him up. But whenever Jimmy was taking his lunch break back at our apartment instead of at the office, sometimes trekking home through torrential downpours or blistering cold weather, I knew that he found one.

Weird Asian* Guy

During the year we lived together, I was working with a Saturday School program and would usually leave in the morning, around the same time the overnight nurse did. One morning, as I was getting ready, I heard Barbara talking very loudly, with the omission of syntax people employ when speaking to foreigners. I found her in the kitchen, repeating herself over and over again as she was trying to instruct a new aide. This guy could barely understand English, let alone speak it. Barbara was trying to inform him as to what he would need to do for Jimmy, and it was obvious that he wasn't picking anything up.

Barbara had stayed well after her shift ended, and at this point, there was nothing else she could have done. She directed him into Jimmy's room and told him to wait there until Jimmy woke up, and then to listen to Jimmy for instruction. She left extremely frustrated, and I was a little worried this guy wouldn't

---

* This note is specifically for you PC folk (not that you typically care about Asians, since they don't really have that mainstream media appeal): I am not implying that all Asians are weird, or that the fact that he was Asian makes him a certain type of person. We refer to him as Weird Asian Guy because of all the weird nurses Jimmy has had, he was the only Asian Guy. It is the most obvious and easiest identifier.

be able to do his job. Then, peering into Jimmy's room, a greater fear came over me.

Weird Asian Guy was not sitting in the chair, or laying on the nurse's bed—no, he was standing over Jimmy, hands folded at his waist, staring at him. It was one of the creepiest scenes I have ever witnessed in my entire life. It looked like he was fixing to eat him.

Hoping not to wake Jimmy, as forcefully as I could whisper, I am pointing and telling Weird Asian Guy to step back and go to the nurse's bed on the other side of the room. He is looking at me and loudly says, "OK YES" without budging, obviously not understanding a damned thing I was saying.

At this, Jimmy wakes up, and sees Weird Asian Guy hovering above his face, staring. He screams, "WHAT THE FUCK?!"

Weird Asian Guy shoots his hands up like he's been caught, and I barge in. I grab Weird Asian Guy by the shoulders and guide him to the bed, and speaking to him like I would my dog (who may have had a better grasp on the English language), I tell him to sit and to stay. I tell Jimmy that I have to head to work, and ask him to text me when he gets up (code for: let me know this psycho doesn't kill you). Luckily, Jimmy hates waking up so much he let the situation go and fell back asleep. Before I left I peeped back in the room, only to see the Weird Asian Guy sitting at attention, like a dog for a bone.

After three of the longest hours ever, I finally got a text from Jimmy. The entire time I was thinking that I had left my friend to get chopped up and made into a soup. Needless to say, Jimmy made sure the homecare company never sent him again.

Kerry

It was not atypical for Jimmy to be out on a weeknight and me to stay in. People always seemed to assume that Jimmy wouldn't go out without me, but that was not the case. Many times, the nurse or aide would come to start their shift and Jimmy would be out at a club, or having a drink with a girl, or what have you, and it would just be me and the caregiver. I didn't mind, they were nice enough—might as well have been another roommate.

So there was this one nurse, we'll call her Kerry. More often than not, it seemed, Kerry felt the need to unload her feelings on me. Despite the fact that her shift started at the end of the day, I was usually the first person she really had a chance to talk to. She was the caregiver for the people she lived with, and her nine cats didn't really qualify for quality conversation. Every now and then, I would be sitting on the couch, minding my own business, enjoying a game or a TV show, the door would swing open, slam against the wall, and in would come Kerry, plodding down the hallway in her very own cloud of despair. She would immediately dive into some story about something she did wrong, why she is a terrible person, and the tears would flow as she claimed life wasn't worth it.

At first, I was scared. I didn't know what to say to my roommate's elderly, female nurse who may have suicidal tendencies. I felt like "it's going to be ok" from someone who couldn't relate to a damned thing she was going through just wouldn't cut it. Like all things, however, I just kind of got used to it. The uncomfortable and awkward situation became familiar to me the more it happened. Eventually the only unpleasant part of these conversations was that it was distracting from the television.

One night, I was tired of hearing the self-disparaging remarks. "C'mon, Kerry," I said. "At the end of the day, you're a good person. I mean, it's not like you killed anyone."

She froze. She looked at me with a face of pure guilt.

"Kerry!?"

She put her head down like she was caught. "They were in pain!"

"They?!"

"It was only twice!"

"Kerry!"

"It didn't hurt, and they asked me to!"

She went on to explain that there were two times where she gave into patients who had begged her, repeatedly, to overmedicate purposefully, to end their misery. She said she only did it because they were terminally ill, in great pain, they really wanted it, and she thought it was the right thing to do.

This shocked me, to say the least. I was sure this would freak Jimmy out a little bit. God forbid one night Jimmy complains about having to get up for work the next day, and

Kerry decides to remedy the problem. But even after knowing him all those years, I still underestimated his carefree approach to life, and the undying faith he has in people. He told me I was overreacting, she was a good person, and it would be fine. Kerry the Killer would continue to work with him throughout our time at the apartment, and continue to interrupt my TV shows with her daily tales of depression and sadness.

Jimmy turned out to be right, I guess. No one, to my knowledge, at least, was killed in our apartment while we lived there.

Vicky

Vicky wasn't a caregiver—she was one of the receptionists at our apartment building. She was more than accommodating to us, mostly because we were one of the few tenants that actually took the time to get to know her. She was one of best parts of that apartment building, bringing an energy and a good-time attitude that always left us with a smile. She would greet us as we walked in, shouting extremely appropriate and professional phrases across the lobby about how last night she was "fucking like a teenager," or "knocking the cobwebs off," and then relaying the newest developments on the three to five men she kept on rotation because the one she really liked wouldn't marry her. She would also brag about what and how much she had to drink, what she liked to drink, and sometimes even forced us to sniff her coffee mug in order to prove she was getting her weekend started a little early.

In no time, when he would get home from work and our apartment was empty, Jimmy would ask her to bring him upstairs and open the apartment door, sometimes even requesting her to set him on the couch, or on the bed, or grab some water for him. Before long, he was even asking her to help him use the bathroom. Desperate times call for desperate measures, and for Jimmy, that particular situation is like asking someone to hold a door. Being the kind and caring person she was, she went above and beyond for Jimmy.

One day after work, as I was walking into the building alone, Vicky starting scolding me the moment she saw me. She was telling me that Jimmy came in drunk the other night, and that it was wrong of me to let that happen, and that I need to stop Jimmy from drinking, and that it was my responsibility to make sure he didn't.

I tried to protest. I tried to tell Vicky that he is an adult and able to make his own decisions. I tried to tell her that his body responds to alcohol just like hers and mine. She didn't want to hear a word I was saying. She kept insisting that "it's different with him," and that he was my responsibility. *Does she think I'm his fucking babysitter or something?*

In the moment, I hated how she looked at my roommate as less than, and put me on a pedestal that I didn't deserve. After some thinking, I remembered what Jimmy's always talking about—how it's ignorance, not maliciousness. Some people are too blind to see what is right in front of their face. Some just don't want to see the truth. I don't know which Vicky was. I do know that she had never seen Jimmy do anything harmful or dangerous due to alcohol, and yet she had stories every Monday morning (albeit entertaining ones) about her own mistakes and regrets under the influence. And I know that to his face, she treated Jimmy like anyone else, but behind his back, she decided he was incapable of making certain decisions on his own because he has atypical limitations. She had put him in a box, and wasn't interested in letting him out.

Terry

After our time living together, Jimmy changed his care plan, and because of that, had to change nurses. Under the new agency, he found a new overnight nurse, Terry. If there was ever a nurse who demonstrated maternal instincts, it was her. She would give her two cents about the women he was dating, scold him when he drank too much, and put up with his complaints. She was one of his favorites, and she was good at her job. The two really got along, and truly enjoyed each other's company.

A problem arose, however, when Jimmy got New Nurse for the days Terry had to call out. It was not as if the other nurse was better at her job—the main difference was that she didn't mind if he slept in. Terry had a second job to get to in the morning, and would have Jimmy up, ready for work, and out the door not a second past 7 a.m. Meanwhile, New Nurse didn't mind letting Jimmy sleep in as late as he wanted. New Nurse was available for, and wanted, Terry's shifts.

Jimmy was dreading a decision for weeks. That extra hour (or more) of sleep each night was truly life changing, but he didn't want to cut Terry—he really liked her. Finally, after practicing on the phone with me, and making every excuse possible to delay it, he broke the news to Terry that he would be using a different nurse. He carefully and kindly explained that he really liked her, she was great nurse—it was just that for Jimmy's lifestyle, scheduling was a lot better with the other nurse. Basically, the "it's me, not you" approach.

He knew she would be upset. Not only did they have a great relationship, but he was a steady, reliable client for her, which was something the homecare agency could not always offer. He wasn't sure, though, as to how upset she would be.

Terry freaked out. She was cursing, ranting, and all fired up. "I treated you like my son!" she yelled. The worst part about it was that Jimmy thought he was doing the right thing by telling her that night, at the start of her shift. He didn't want to mention it in the morning right before they parted ways for good. He wanted to give them time to talk it out, and hopefully end on good terms. It didn't take long for Jimmy to realize that was out of the question.

He didn't count on her taking it that hard, and it meant Jimmy was stuck with her sleeping over, and getting him ready the next morning for work. It was like having a nasty break up with someone and then having a sleepover. He had texted me his goodbyes, final requests, and well wishes, just in case she killed him in his sleep. Fortunately, Jimmy awoke the next day, unharmed . . . but he did pass on shaving that morning out of fear of being cut "accidently."

From an outside perspective, this whole situation was crazy, and it makes sense why the homecare agencies try to have rules and policies to prevent clients and caregivers from becoming too friendly. On one hand, it is business—it is a job for Terry and a need for Jimmy. On the other hand, how could you spend that much time with a single person and not build a connection with them—especially someone as personable as Jimmy.

After seeing how upset Terry was, Jimmy felt bad about it for a little while. I tried to tell him that Terry didn't understand that this was about Jimmy's quality of life. It was not like he was choosing someone else because of something trivial. He was choosing to get a couple more hours of sleep every day. That's a major part of everyday life. Take any sort of relationship, and present the opportunity to either stick together or to sleep an extra hour every single day . . . I'd bet dollars to donuts there's going to be a lot more well-rested people in the world.

18

First Concert with Jimmy

Not long into our time living with each other, Jimmy came home from work one day with an envelope on his seat, under his leg. He told me to open it. Inside were two tickets to the Jay-Z and Kanye West Watch the Throne tour.

"You're going," he said.

Didn't have to twist my arm.

I'd never been to a concert with Jimmy, but back in college Jimmy was notorious for not only going to every show on campus, but also for getting to meet the artist. In the same manner he got onto the floor at the basketball games, Jimmy would use his chair as a VIP pass and simply go where no other regular ticket attendee was supposed to go, leading whatever friends he decided to take with him. "Act like a boss, get treated like a boss," he always said. It got to the point where if Jimmy didn't get to meet the performer, he considered it a letdown.

I knew this concert would be different, being that it was at the Wells Fargo Center and was one of most anticipated shows of the year. I didn't even want to know how much Jimmy dropped on those tickets, and I told him I'd take him to dinner, anywhere he wanted, beforehand as a thank you.

I should have known better. While some would call Jimmy's taste in restaurants cultured and refined, I call it fucking stupid. I worked in restaurants. I know how it goes. A $100 meal isn't ten times tastier than a $10 meal, but they get away with charging that because people like to buy into the way it looks. The way I see it, the leather on the menu, or the linens on the table, or the waiter refolding your napkin when you get up to go the bathroom has absolutely zero effect on the way the food tastes.

Jimmy has heard me rant about this before—but did that matter to him? Absolutely not. I'll be damned if he didn't pick the most expensive steak place in the city, order a steak that weighed about as much as he did, and a $20 drink to go with it. And I'll also be damned if he ate more than a quarter of the thing before saying he wanted to look at the dessert menu. I almost lost my shit when he said he didn't want to take it home.

"You know I'm not the biggest fan of leftovers," he said.

"You're taking it home, and you're eating it for the rest of the week, and you're going to love it." Jackass.

After we dropped off the food at the apartment, we went down into the subway, and the guy working the gate waived me and Jimmy through the handicap accessible entrance for free. It was a small financial victory, but one that I needed to lift me out of gift giver's remorse. To this day, I still think I would have saved money if I simply paid for my own ticket.

We get to the concert and, as always, headed to the customer service desk to get our seats changed to the handicap section. We got to our seats, and Jimmy set up on my right. He is almost always on my right. Walking, sitting, eating, whenever and wherever. Because of the way his muscles formed and degenerated, his head is at a constant tilt towards the left. It works out for me too, because my left ear is more than fifty percent deaf, so I try to make sure everyone is on my right side, especially people who aren't as loud as others.

On my left is a stranger in a wheelchair—not a surprise, being that I am sitting in the handicap section. When a song I liked came on, my inner-dork naturally yelled out, "Oh snap, this is my jam!"

When the guy to my left heard my teenage girl-esque exclamation, he said, "Well shit, man, if this is your jam get up and dance." Motioning to the rest of the section, he continued, "All of us here can't, so you better take advantage!"

I brushed off his suggestion with a laugh. I don't usually put on my dancing shoes in public unless the time and music is right (a couple of drinks in me don't hurt, either), and I was just fine sitting and observing as usual. What struck me about that exchange, however, was that I didn't feel any shame.

I was raised with the guilt-ridden instruction that I better finish my dinner because "there are starving children in Armenia that won't get to eat tonight." And as young kid with that charge levied against me, I would feel embarrassed and unappreciative. The paralyzed guy telling me to "get up and dance" had the same kind of feel to it—but this time, I wasn't ashamed. I don't know why, but I didn't feel like I had to listen to him. I didn't feel bad that I could dance and he couldn't.

I can't say for sure, but if I had a similar exchange before knowing Jimmy so well, I don't think I would have the same level of comfort in disregarding his suggestion. I probably would have felt the same way I did when my mother told me to finish my dinner. I was slowly starting to notice that the more I saw Jimmy as a person—not as a disabled person—the more it was even affecting the way I perceived others. I didn't hear a cripple make me feel bad for not dancing—I heard a man sitting next to me suggesting I do something I didn't want to do.

This reminded me of one day, back around the time I was graduating high school, for the first time ever, I caught my Dad ready to throw away some of his dinner. This was the chance I had waited for. I was ready to return the guilt that my parents had laid into me while growing up.

"You better finish that. There are starving children in Armenia who won't get to eat tonight!"

Without pause, my Dad turned his plate upside down into the trash can. "Whether I eat this or not, those kids are still going to starve."

19

Special Ed

Shortly after we became roommates, I started noticing a strange phenomenon happening with Jimmy, particularly when we were out at the bar. Back in college, everyone seemed to know and love Jimmy. Adding the small-size of campus to his aggressive social life, this only made sense. After college, though, in the heart of Philadelphia, an odd pseudo-celebrity status still followed him wherever he went. Whether he knew people or not, people noticed him. I don't know if it came from sympathy, respect, or just plain human interest.

On one hand, when he would go out, he didn't have to wait in lines, he never had to pay cover, and he was never, ever in want of a drink. And when I could personally reap the benefits of a quick and free entrance, and sometimes even a drink, I didn't mind it at all. But every now and again they would give him the special treatment and leave me out to dry, and I would have to bite my tongue. If I wanted to say what I was thinking, that it was complete bullshit that Jimmy wasn't being treated like everyone else—he might have ended up waiting in line and paying cover like the rest of us shmucks.

When we got into the bar, it seemed like everyone there wanted to meet him and know his story. At the same time, they weren't intimidated to approach him like they would have been with an actual celebrity. Plus, I started to get all sorts of compliments from complete strangers when they would see me out at the bar with him. People I had never even seen before in my entire life were constantly telling me I am a "nice guy" or a "good person." It happened so much that I became critical of their kind words. I realized that compliments are nothing but insults that look pretty. Just because one makes us feel good and the other makes us feel bad doesn't change the fact that they both come from the same place of judgment of another person. And another thing I noticed about these people that were hurling these empty compliments—they would *always* ask me if I was Jimmy's brother.

After a while, it started to get annoying. I started trying to convince the person who complimented me that they don't know me, they shouldn't judge me, and for all they know I could be the biggest scumbag in the entire world.

A friend of mine would always tell me it was the most confusing thing in the world to see, especially when I would be giving this spiel to a female. In a bar full of men doing anything and everything to impress any woman they could, there I was exerting my effort to dissuade a woman who had shown interest in me. It boggled his mind. Until it happened to him. Then he completely understood.

I guarantee if you were to hang out with Jimmy—or almost anybody in a wheelchair—you run the risk of people treating you like some sort of saint. I also guarantee that when that happens, you will understand that empty and annoying feeling an unwarranted compliment gets you. I am hanging out with Jimmy because he is my friend. I am not being nice.

One night out, a random guy—we'll call him Special Ed—approached me with the kind of look on his face that people have when they interject into a conversation that they volunteer at a soup kitchen on Christmas Day. That "I'm trying to be all matter-of-fact and humble but I actually believe in my core that I have moral superiority" kind of look.

"Hi, I'm Special Ed," he said, pointing to Jimmy, over on the dance floor. "Is that your brother?"

Here we go. "No."

"Well, I just wanted to let you know, I teach special-ed, and I just want to say it is just so nice of you to be here for *someone like that.*"

Someone like what? Fun? A good time? Funny? Loyal? And nice to be here for him? We were literally at the newest, hottest club in Philly at the time—it's not like I was stuck inside on a Saturday night eating fast food and watching *Toy Story* for the hundredth time.*

I had enough drinks in me, and this scenario had played out enough times, that I hit my tipping point. When he said "someone like that," it was like he volunteered to be the object of all of the anger and frustration I'd been bottling up from the empty compliments of me and the assumptions of Jimmy.

"'Someone like that?' What is the fuck is that supposed to mean? Who the fuck are you?"

"No man, I get it. I'm a special-ed teacher." *Did he think I didn't hear him the first time? Or is this his way of bragging?* "I know exactly what you're doing here, I do stuff like this all the time."

"Fuck outta here, dude. You have any idea of how fucking disrespectful you are being right now? Why don't you go tell him how nice it is that I hang out with him?" I said, pointing to Jimmy. "How there is no fucking way anyone would actually want to spend time with him. You are a piece of shit, man, get the fuck out of my face."

I stormed away before giving the guy a chance to say anything else. I knew if he said something else I didn't like, I might have completely lost it.

After I had some time to cool down, I started to think about what Jimmy was always trying to tell me: those kinds of people don't mean harm. This guy was just trying to be nice and there was nothing in him to blame except ignorance. I started to

---

* Ok, truth be told, I hate going to clubs—I am more of a dive bar kind of guy. But Special Ed didn't know this, and it was Jimmy's night to pick the spot, and that guy has house music, expensive drinks, and fancy clothes written all over it. So we went to the club. And another thing—leaving a club early by myself to go home and eat fast food while watching *Toy Story* may have happened. And it may have happened multiple times.

feel bad that I took out all the pent up frustrations on some guy with good intentions, no matter how stupid he came across.

So I went back to him and apologized. "Look man, I'm sorry I talked to you like that. Especially because it kind of came out of nowhere. It's just that so many people automatically assume that Jimmy is deadweight. He's a really good friend of mine, and it's annoying constantly having people basically telling me that he's not worth that. You know?" Nothing like alcohol to make an enemy out of a stranger, and then later forge a deep conversation with that same stranger.

I'll never forget his reply. It was as if he didn't hear a word I said. Or maybe he just heard it the way he wanted to hear it. "It's all good man," he said. "I know it can be frustrating. Hanging out with him is probably the last thing you want to do with your Friday night."

I couldn't understand it. Was the wheelchair really that blinding? Did he really miss everything I was trying to say to him? The scariest part is that this guy said he is a special education teacher—it makes me wonder how he actually feels about his own students.

At that point, I was over it, and didn't have the energy to get upset again. I just shook my head and walked away. I was starting to realize there is no getting through to someone like that.

20

Claude Giroux

One day, the pseudo-celebrity that was Jimmy crossed paths with a real celebrity—well, for Philadelphia at least. For being a major city, Philly has a small-town feel and it wasn't uncommon for Sixers, Flyers, and Eagles players to frequent the same bars we did. As expected, when they were there, they would have their asses kissed just like Jimmy, and, in my opinion, more rightfully so. These are people that have worked really hard to become the best at what they do. That being said, I still never understood the way grown-ass men act like little star-gazed children just because someone can put a puck in a net. Don't get me wrong, I'm a sports fan, and think their specific abilities are impressive, but like my grade school football coach would warn us about the bigger, better, opposing players: they put their pants on one leg at a time like everyone else.

One night out, it just so happened that a Philadelphia favorite, Claude Giroux, came into the bar. The NHL All-Star was being drooled over by guys and girls alike. After some time, by coincidence, he happened to make his way over to the section of the bar where we were.

Giroux (who, for the record, I've always heard is a genuinely good guy) went up to Jimmy to shake his hand. I can't say if he thought he was being charitable, or being nice, or maybe felt bad—all I know is that Giroux didn't go out of his way to say hi to anyone in that bar who wasn't in a filled-out shirt and tight jeans other than Jimmy. I am taking a wild guess when I say the wheelchair had some part to play in it.

Jimmy was in the middle of his classic text message conversation he has with romantic prospects. In a loud bar, he foregoes trying to be heard with his voice and instead, types the message he wants to relay into the notes of his iPhone. The girl he was talking to noticed Giroux standing there, and pointed him out to Jimmy. Then Giroux reached out for a handshake.

Jimmy isn't a hockey fan.

Giroux didn't know this as Jimmy starts punching out a new message on his iPhone. It looked like the hockey player was waiting for the dime-a-dozen idolization and praise he is so used to from little kids. What he didn't realize was that there was no little kid sitting in that wheelchair. There was a grown ass man.

Jimmy raises his head, eyes wide, and points at his phone, signaling Giroux to read it. The All-Star hockey player picks it up. It reads:

"Who the FUCK are you???!!!"

Jimmy nodded his head like he was ready to fight. This motherfucker just stumbled into his neck of the woods, and is interrupting his hunt. Giroux was shocked. I don't think he expected to be unrecognized, let alone confronted. He sheepishly put the phone down and walked away.

That night, I would bet Giroux had his choice of women to hop in a fancy car and bring to an upscale home. And that night, Jimmy rolled himself over the cracks and bumps of a Philadelphia sidewalk to go home alone.

But for that moment, in that crowded Philly bar, Jimmy played chicken with a Philadelphia Flyer, and won.

21

Bathroom Beers

Another Friday night, and another trip to the bar, and another call from nature had me following Jimmy to the bathroom. There was a long line that didn't faze either of us. Not only does Jimmy rarely wait in line anyway, but it was the basement bar across the street from our place where we had become well-known. And by we, I mean Jimmy. In fact, after a few months of Jimmy bringing our entire group in through the back, accessible entrance, allowing us all to skip the wait and cover charge to get in, the bouncer started implementing a "new rule from management." People using the accessible entrance could only bring two people in with them. We got a kick out of it because we knew that Jimmy was the sole reason for the creation of this rule, and we also knew that he was the sole person that it was implemented on. We would affectionately refer to this as The Jimmy Rule.

So I followed Jimmy as he bypassed the bathroom line and parked inside the bathroom doorway. The stall isn't big enough for Jimmy to pull his chair into, so he's forced to drop his pants around everyone else in the bathroom, and be carried to the toilet. To be honest, I've always had the suspicion he prefers that, anyway. He wants everyone to know who the big dick in town is.

I did my part, which was oddly becoming like second nature to me. With his chair slightly reclined, I unbuckled his seatbelt, crossed his arms on his chest, and lifted him by the knees so I could pull down his pants. With one hand behind his head and one hand under his knees, I picked him up, and holding him horizontally, carried him into the stall. Angling his body so the monster hanging out was aimed to hit water, I told him to fire away. Jimmy was mid-pee when the stall door swung open. In burst some guy that neither of us had ever met before. He was holding two beers.

"Hey, I wanted to get these beers for you guys. You both are awesome. Seriously, awesome."

Me and Jimmy looked at each other and tried to keep from laughing. As serious and appreciative as I could be, I told the stranger, "Thank you very much, that is super nice of you. I can't really grab them from you right now," nodding to the 63-pound man, half-naked and peeing, who I had in my arms, "and he can't really grab them either, so if you want to set them down on the sink we will grab them in a second."

The guy backed out of the stall. Jimmy and I tried our best to hold in our laughter because cracking up while holding someone over a toilet pissing, who is also cracking up, could be quite a mess.

Moments later, this guy walked right back into our stall, as if it was just another place in the bar. With Jimmy still peeing,* this stranger proceeded to tell us that his brother was in a ski accident and is now a paraplegic, and seeing Jimmy and I hanging out at the bar gave him hope for his relationship with his brother. He went on to talk for a little longer, and was even tearing up a little before he finally left. I couldn't determine if it was a happy cry, or a sad cry—it was probably a little bit of both. But I did know that whatever it was, it was a genuine and kind emotion this total stranger was trying to share with us.

Usually, after the typical run-ins with strangers, either Jimmy or I will make some wisecrack or expletive comment. But

---

* Jimmy has an absurdly trained bladder. He literally went from 1st through 12th grade having never peed at school.

this time, as I put Jimmy back down in the chair, we were silent. Not a word was spoken between us as we exited the bathroom, me now holding two beers. Before we got back to our crew, I tapped the glasses together in an unspoken toast, and gave Jimmy a swig before I took one myself.

Every now and then there comes a sincerity that even my cynicism, or Jimmy's experience, can't ruin.

22

Walk in the Park

"EH-DAY!" I heard coming from the other room, waking me. "EHHH-DAAAYYYY!!!" It came again.

I slid out of bed, and took seven zombie-like steps to Jimmy's adjoining bedroom. Jimmy was lying down, eyes wide as saucers.

"Eddie," Jimmy snapped, letting my name hang in the air. He uses pauses the way others may use hand gestures for dramatic effect.

"What . . ." he said. Another pause, his eyes getting even wider. ". . . happened last night?!"

I plopped down at the foot of his bed, and made myself comfortable. The night before, a bunch of us had gone to Mill Creek Tavern for the karaoke night wings and beer special.

"Eddie! What happened!?" Jimmy repeated, always impatient to get the information he wanted. As it always started, I asked Jimmy what was the last thing he remembers.

"I don't remember leaving," he says.

"First off, you showed up really late with Aleesha." She was most recent aide that he seemed to turn a corner with. The two had moved passed a strictly professional relationship a while ago, and now it was clear that they were way more than very good friends. "You were pretty excited about the extracurricular activity that went down in the bathroom at the happy hour you came from."

"Oh, I definitely remember that."

"Then, you somehow convinced the manager to make you an order of chicken nuggets, even though he was adamant that wings are the only thing available on Mondays."

"Ah, that's right, I did get chicken nuggets. They were good, too."

"I hope they were. The entire kitchen stopped pushing out wings just so you could have your precious nuggets."

"Did Aleesha leave with us?"

"No, you walked her out before the trolleys stopped running."

"I'm such a sweetheart."

"No, you are an asshole. You missed my high quality rendition of 'Bohemian Rhapsody.'"

"How did we get home?"

"By the time we left, the regular buses stopped running, so we had to walk all the way to 42nd and Market for the overnight."

"Yikes. Was I ok?" This was Jimmy's way of asking if he was having a hard time driving his chair.

"Hell no! You were drinking since happy hour, and you didn't stop until we left. Plus, those sidewalks are brutal." This was my way of saying I helped him drive, which is a task that is not as easy as it sounds. Bent over, walking alongside the chair, careful not to let my feet get run over, maneuvering the cracks and holes on a West Philadelphia sidewalk—it's not the easiest thing when you aren't used to the sensitivity of a joystick designed for someone who can barely lift a magazine.

"So we finally get to the stop, and the bus was taking forever."

"It was just us?"

"No. Brooke came with us."

"She did? Is she still here?"

"No, I kicked her out before the sun came up."

"You did?!"

"No. I wish. She didn't stay over."

"You suck again."

"She had work!"

"She had an excuse is what she had."

"Anyway . . . the bus was nowhere in sight, and I started getting a little nervous. It was almost one in the morning on a weeknight." I didn't have to explain to Jimmy that Brooke stood at a massive four-foot-eleven, barely clearing 100 pounds, born and bred in the suburbs and about as street smart as Elmer Fudd. I also didn't have to explain 42nd and Market was not the absolute worst part of the city, but it is definitely not a part of the city you want to be when it's one in the morning . . . especially when the crew backing you up is a tiny woman and a guy in a wheelchair.

"I told Brooke if someone tried to mug the three of us, the plan was to turn your chair off and run."

"Eddie. You should be a comedian. Really. I'm dying."

"So I finally see the bus. It's coming down Market, stops right at the corner in front of us . . . but the driver didn't open the door. She pointed to a sign that said it's not an overnight stop, and screamed "40th street!"

"No. Really?"

"Yup. Blew right past us. We had no other choice but to head to 40th street."

"I'm kind of happy I don't remember all that."

"Well, by that point, you were back to driving yourself. By the time we got to 40th street, we only had to wait a couple more minutes for the next bus." That's how I ended the retelling of our night—though there was one more thing that happened that I decided not to share with Jimmy. I was pretty stressed about it.

"So what do you think is going to happen with me and Aleesha?"

"Geez, Jimmy! How many times are you going to ask me that?"

"Until I get a real answer!" He is the type to fall hard and fast, and like any good friend, I was sick of hearing about it.

"I think it's going to go how it always goes. It's going to be good for a little bit, and then it's going to implode because you are never satisfied with what you have. You always want more."

Jimmy considered this for a second. I was hoping he finally understood what I was always trying to tell him, that life isn't always going to be a walk off grand slam in the bottom of the ninth World Series kind of thing.

"Eddie . . ." *Woah. He seems serious. Did I finally get through to him?* ". . . For real, though. What do you actually think is going to happen?"

"Are you kidding me?!" I put my head in my palms as Jimmy let out a laugh.

"Alright. Get me out of bed. When Barbara gets done smoking we'll head to the park."

I was getting to know Jimmy so well, that I knew "get him out of bed" means put him in the wheelchair. I understood that the night before, he got chicken nuggets, because they are easier for him to eat than wings, and it didn't surprise me to see the owner of the bar make that exception for him. Without asking, I knew that Aleesha was able to go into the bathroom at the happy hour with Jimmy because it was an accessible bathroom and he can't use the facilities on his own, and that riding home with a friend last night or getting a cab wasn't an option because there is no way that large, massive power chair would fit in a car.

What I didn't know, however, is how that part of the story I omitted was going to play out, and now was the time to find out. With him lying on his back, I crossed his arms over his chest. With one hand at the base of his heavy head, my other arm swooped under his two bent legs. I lifted, and the moment I applied the upward pressure to his legs, my fear came true.

"AAAAAAAHHHHHH. WHAT THE FUCK?!" Jimmy screamed.

Jimmy never had a high tolerance for pain, and why would he? He has not dealt with much in his life of sitting in a chair. This pain, however, was real; I could see it in his face and hear it in his voice. I knew exactly what happened.

"What the fuck is wrong with my leg?!"

What I hadn't told Jimmy about the night before was that when the bus pulled up and let down the accessible platform, Jimmy was able to get himself on it. On the bus, however, the driver told Jimmy he had to sit in the designated wheelchair spot, with his chair buckled in. Despite trying to explain that Jimmy's chair wouldn't roll, that the wheels automatically lock when stopped like a car in park, the driver insisted. This meant that Jimmy had to turn his chair 270 degrees on the narrow bus, and then back up into the designated spot. Jimmy was having a hard time trying to swing it, and I just wanted to be home and in bed. I told Jimmy I would do it, and he moved his hand behind his joystick and allowed me to try to make the maneuver. With a bus full of people watching, as I turned the chair, I ran over my own foot, tripped, and slammed the joystick forward, sending Jimmy full speed toward the hard metal seat. What finally knocked my hand off the joystick was when the chair jerked to stop. Unfortunately, it jerked to a stop when the edge of the seat hit smack in the middle of Jimmy's shin. It looked painful when I saw it, but I think Jimmy was having so much fun that night, between his date from earlier, his drinking, and the recent amusement park type ride he just went on, he only groaned a little bit and then let it go. I, however, was afraid I broke his leg.

"Did something happen last night?" he asked.

"I don't know man, that's weird," I said, avoiding eye contact as I set him down in his chair. "Maybe you hit it when you were drinking or something."

"I must have. It kills."

"That's crazy." I ignored my guilt and changed the subject by jumping to *the* question that comes with putting him in his chair: "You good?"

He looked to his right and raised his eyebrows. "That way."

I slid his hips an inch or so, and repeated, "Good?"

He nods. "Eddie. "

The Jimmy Pause. You never know what will come after the Jimmy Pause.

"Happy Birthday, dickhead."

Jimmy made sure he took off work for my birthday, as did I, and after Barbara got him ready to go out, complete with a spat about the way she did it, the two of us were off to the park. On the way there, a bigger, older man wearing a Kangol cap, a bright colored velour track suit, and crisp white sneakers stopped Jimmy to say hello. Jimmy seemed surprised to see him, and after the two talked for a minute, we were on our way. It's not uncommon for Jimmy to come across someone he knows, and I usually don't even bother to find out one of the million ways how, but this guy seemed particularly odd.

"Who the hell was that?"

"Remember how I used to rap?"

"Yeah."

"Well, I used to do these rap battles at bar in West Philly, and he was the bouncer there."

"Wait . . . what? You used to go to rap battles?"

"I didn't just go . . . I was in them."

"Like, live?" I was in disbelief.

"Yeah."

I remember being shocked back in college simply when I learned that he made songs. This was a whole other level.

"When was this?"

"In like, middle school. I haven't seen him in forever. I'm surprised he recognized me. I guess being the only white person in there made me memorable."

"Uh, yea, that . . . or maybe—"

"I know," he cut me off. "It was a joke!"

"How the hell did you get down there?"

"My mom would drive me. And the place wasn't accessible, so that guy would help my mom carry the ramp to the back entrance, and they would lay it down over steps so I could get in."

I was dumbfounded. The thought of middle-school Jimmy battle rapping on stage in a West Philly bar while his angel of a mother stood in the crowd watching left me stunned. That picture was being engrained in my mind as we got to Rittenhouse Square.

The square is to Philly what Central Park is to New York—it's just a lot smaller, doesn't have as many things to do, and is not as nice—so yeah, it is the Philly version of Central Park. All I wanted to do was sit on a bench, hang out and people watch on this beautiful spring day—the same way we would pass time when we first started to hang out at Temple. You can learn a lot people watching.

On a bench, nursing my hangover with a lunch-truck smoothie, I was at peace with the world. I was sitting there with my best friend (who I just found out was a battle rapper in a former life), in my favorite part of the city, with my favorite drink. My comments concerned the look of that girl over there, or the move the yoga freaks were making, or my imagination's take on the band of hobos and their pack of stray dogs. I was thinking about what I wanted for my birthday dinner, and starting conversations with Jimmy on topics like would you rather be able to fly and read minds, or to teleport and be invisible.

When the conversation had died down, Jimmy, out of nowhere, asks, "Eddie . . ." Pause. Dude is so dramatic. "What's your purpose in life?"

He was constantly thinking deeper than most people I knew, and it wasn't surprising for a question like this to come out of his mouth. Knowing that Jimmy is not one to bullshit, no matter how melodramatic it may seem from the outside, this question hit me like a hurricane. I don't know if it was because I was at peace with the world, with absolutely nothing significant on my slate for the day. Maybe it was because it was my birthday, the anniversary of when I came into this world. Or maybe I was still feeling the effects of the night before. I don't know. But for a couple seconds, for the first time in my life, I faced the reality of that question. I didn't think about my possible answers, or what I wanted my answers to be. What I thought about was the question itself.

My purpose? Do I even have a purpose? Does anyone? Is it from birth, or do you get it over time? Do you even get it, or do you earn it? Does anyone really have one?

Frustrated that this question only sparked more questions, I gave up. This was too much. It was too early. I was too hungover, and this was too deep.

"Geez, I don't know. Where does your mind go, man?"

"Answer the question!"

"I told you, I don't know. I don't even know if people actually have one. Think about it, if they did, where does it come from? If it's since birth, that kind of ends the nature vs. nurture argument, right? And if it's developed over time, then doesn't that mean it can keep changing? Or is there a set age where your purpose is fully developed? That seems kind of whack. And depressing. Like, you hit that point, and that's that. Your life is set in stone. And what happens if you miss your purpose? Does that mean you live a wasted life? Or what if you don't like your purpose? Should you spend your life chasing it even though it makes you miserable? How can you even be sure if you know that it's your purpose? It might just be something you incorrectly think you are supposed to do, you know? You know what I am trying to say? Cause, honestly, I'm not sure if I do. This is too much man. Why do you do this to me? I don't know, man. What do you think? Do you think you have one?"

Again a pause. But this wasn't for dramatic effect, or to find to find the answer—Jimmy already knew it. The pause was for him to put it into words, something I don't think he had ever done before.

"My purpose is to change the perception people have about those with disabilities."

For Jimmy, both literally and figuratively, he knew it was going to be no walk in the park.

23

To Open or Not to Open

The best way to lose a friend is to live with them.

—Unknown

It is a rare, if not impossible, feat to find two people who can spend an exorbitant amount of time together and not find themselves in a dispute every now and again. Jimmy and I were no different.

I definitely have the problem of letting things build up over time, and then exploding when I reach a tipping point. One night while we were out, Jimmy wanted to get my attention. He wanted a drink and was trying to be funny about it, and I was in the middle of a conversation when he rammed into the side of my leg. The impact spilled my drink, almost knocked me over, and could have really messed my knee up. Don't be fooled, that wheelchair is powerful, and the metal slab of a footrest is at a perfect height to tear up an ACL, MCL, or any other acronym going on in that joint.

I was especially pissed because when I looked at Jimmy, he was cracking up. This was something I had specifically told him not to do numerous times, but I guess it never stuck. I guess it is like telling a woman it's not funny when a guy gets hit in the balls—Jimmy couldn't relate. He had never been hit in the knees while standing.

I'd had it at this point, and told him off. It wasn't even that I said anything particularly vicious, it was the way I said it. I had never been that mad at him before. A sensitive dude to begin with, the moment my blow up happened Jimmy's mood flipped. He was totally disengaged from that point on. I noticed he wasn't even playing on his phone or looking for someone else to hang with. For the next five minutes, he just kind of looked down into the ground and away into space, and that kind of pissed me off more. How is he going to hit me in the knee, and then be upset with me when I get upset with him? Then, with no further provocation, as we are all hanging around the bar, Jimmy ups and leaves without a word to anyone.

"Screw him, I am not going to go after him," I said to our friends. They were worried about him leaving by himself, but I knew that wasn't an issue. All I could think about was whether or not I owed him an apology. After a couple of minutes of pretending like I didn't care, I decided to track him down in the hopes of getting him to come back out for the night.

I was banking that he was heading home, and if that were true, it meant he would be going down one of two streets. I figured I would look for him on the one that ran parallel to the one we lived on, and then cut over after a couple blocks. After a few minutes of intermittent jogging and walking, with no sight of him ahead, I finally saw him a block down, moving parallel to me, crossing an intersection on the street we lived on.

"Jimmy!" I yelled. "Jimmy, stop!" I knew he could hear me because after I called out to him, he started moving faster. I picked up my pace until I was in front of him, and turned to face him.

"What?" he demanded.

"Look man, I'm sorry. I shouldn't have spoken to you like that, especially in front of other people."

"It's whatever. It's done," he replied, as he tried to go around me.

"Don't act like it's nothing," I said, stepping in his way. "You're obviously pissed."

"Well it was uncalled for."

"Dude, it was uncalled for hitting me in the fucking knee for the millionth time—"

"Get the fuck out of here."

"—and then laughing about it!"

"It's not that serious!"

"It is! You could really hurt me. And I told you this before!"

We started to go back and forth, and in the midst of it, for a split second, I realized the optics of that scene. The people passing by—and believe me, there we plenty—saw me squared up to a guy in a wheel chair, animated and angry, yelling and cursing at him. I was praying that anyone watching would realize Jimmy was yelling and cursing at me just as much. Otherwise, if someone tried to intervene—and there were a few who sure looked like they were considering sticking up for the poor guy in a wheelchair—I might have lost my shit. I just wanted to be able to argue with my roommate on a Center City corner in peace.

Finally, as it goes, we got tired of fighting and both kind of surrendered.

"I just want to go home," Jimmy said.

"Don't be like that, man. Just come back out."

"I'm over it," he said, as he started on his way, passing me. I groaned before I turned and started walking with him.

"I'm fine. Go back out."

"I'll let you in."

"I am fine! Let me go alone."

"Jimmy, there's no one at the front desk right now."

"I don't want your help."

I could have just let him go by himself, and I am sure he eventually would have been fine. But I felt somewhat responsible for him wanting to bail on the night early. I didn't want to make him wait half an hour outside of our building for his nurse—if she was even on time. On the walk back to our apartment there was an uncomfortable silence. We had never been like this before.

When we finally stepped onto the elevator in our building, the confined space seemed to make the silence between us even louder. Tension filled the car, and it seemed to rise with every floor we passed. When the door opened to our floor and we stepped out, Jimmy said, "Fuck you. I don't need you."

I shot my hand back to grab the elevator door just before it closed. I got back on, and said, "Fine, do it yourself, asshole." I left Jimmy in the hallway, knowing he was unable to open the door to our apartment by himself.

I didn't tell our friends what happened, and the next day, as good friends do, we both apologized and put it behind us. To this day, I am unsure about the way I handled it. On one hand, though Jimmy hit me in leg, the way I reacted meant that fight might have been as much my fault as it was Jimmy's. More so, I feel pretty messed up when I think about my knee jerk reaction of leaving Jimmy in the hallway—in exploiting his helplessness in getting into the apartment by himself. On the other hand, I knew his nurse was supposed to be coming soon, and he went for the jugular. He knows more than anyone that I think a direct and sincere "fuck you" is one of the harshest things that can be said to someone you care about. There is something unsettling with what I did, but at the same time, I don't know if it is good to cater to anyone, especially someone you care about, when they are being so disrespectful. That's how resentment is built.

I don't know if there is a right answer, but I do know that Jimmy never hit me in the knee again.

24

Finding Love in a Hopeless Place

There was no "meet cute." There was no eye-locking moment across the room. There were no butterflies, no smooth pickup lines, no clever and playful banter. There wasn't even a memorable moment, and that's not figurative speech, either. At sixty-some odd pounds, Jimmy routinely goes from zero to party as quickly as that frat guy thinks, "Let's take shots with the dude in the wheelchair!" So the next morning, when he received a text that read, "It was so nice meeting you! You are incredible," the only thing that stood out to him was that this chick put her name in his phone, and at that, put it in as "Gloriaaaaaa."

As every single guy would know, a chick named Gloriaaaaaa who texts a compliment before noon after a night out sounds incredibly hot. He had absolutely no recollection of meeting her, or of taking the group photo she sent with her message, but this was not an uncommon occurrence. His affinity for drinking and low tolerance for alcohol was a terrible combination with his celebrity status gained upon entrance to just about anywhere. After seeing this occur so often, I wish I could

think it was something deeper that drew people to Jimmy—
something about seeing a fellow man with an obstacle, something
that had to do with humanity at its finest—but most of the time,
the magnetic pull he had on people seemed totally superficial. I
mean, you see a kid dressed better than everyone, with a head
bigger than everyone, and the body of a first-grader, with four
drinks sitting on his armrest as he leads the train on the dance
floor . . . curiosity has to spike.

We will come to learn that Gloria's version of events is
almost never to be trusted, so we can never know for sure how
the conversation started that night. All we do know is that for
Jimmy, it started at Shenanigans, a Jersey Shore bar known for its
"302" slushy. The drink gets its name from the recipe, which
involves two shots of 151-proof rum. As one can imagine, being
famous for a drink like that, the place can be summed up in one
word: shameless.

As it turns out, a place like that was the perfect spot to
begin the tumultuous roller coaster ride Jimmy was about to jump
on. But who could tell at the time? As someone who had no
choice but to always have his phone on hand, it seemed as
though he had finally met his texting match when he and Gloria
started finger-dating each other constantly.

Thousands of messages and a couple of weeks later, the
two decided to hang out in person again—Jimmy with the hopes
of actually remembering this time. He found out who she was in
the group photo she had sent, and further confirmed that Gloria
was very attractive from head to toe—his wheelchair seemed to
give him a free pass at all times to ask for any sort of picture with
very little risk of coming off as creepy.

In fact, that beautiful chair of his was a free pass for
many things. Aside from never having to pay cover or wait in
lines, he never had a problem starting conversations with girls. It
was a simple play: he would gently nudge—or ram—a girl he
wanted to talk to, and they would turn around annoyed, expecting
to be hit on, or they'd be in pain, ready to yell at whatever just
almost took them out. When they looked down and saw Jimmy,
their attitude flipped like a switch, at which point Jimmy would
start with anything ranging from, "Hi, my name is Jimmy" to,
"That fat ass of yours almost bopped me in the head," depending
on how many vodka-Sprites he's had. No matter what he says, it's
perceived as cute and funny.

Whatever was said to Gloria that first night down the shore, and in the thousands of texts exchanged in the weeks to follow, she was coming over and Jimmy wanted to impress her. He had never really hung out with a girl in this manner before. He had gone on "dates," gotten dinner or lunch or hung out with girls that he had been friends with, but never a "let's get to know each other" kind of date . . . not an uncommon thing for our generation. He thought it would be a good idea to get her a gift of some sort, and knew from their conversations that she absolutely loved chocolate covered pretzels.

The problem was that the store was three blocks away and his chair was very low on battery. His plan was to order in with Gloria, so the battery-life had not been a concern until he had the idea to get the pretzels. In the back of his mind, he knew there was only small chance he could make it there and back—it was much more likely the chair would die. But Jimmy is the type of person who doesn't waste time letting risks and worries stand in his way. He decides to go for the pretzels.

He makes it to the store, as he knew he would, and buys the gift. It was then he knew he had reason to worry. He crosses the first intersection on the way back without interruption, and is moving along pretty quickly. But the next intersection, a red light! Precious seconds go to waste! The light finally changes and there is only one more street before he is back on his own block. The chair starts to beep! Signaling it's about to die! He is only a few yards from the curb cut-out of the final intersection, when he sees the light turn yellow. Visions of having to explain to Gloria where to locate his charger in an apartment she had never been in before, wait for her as she carried that thirty-pound load out to him, then trying to convince a store manager to not only use the store's power but also borrow an extension cord, and then hanging out on the sidewalk until his chair was juiced up, started to flash through his mind. He was determined to avoid that situation at all costs, so Jimmy held his breath and punched his joystick forward, blindly running the fresh red light.

Fortunately, the Philadelphia region did not hear the 6 o'clock news anchor say, "Next up, a hopeful man in a wheelchair misses a first date after being run over by a car." The third and final intersection was cleared without incident and Jimmy zoomed to our building in no time. With Vicky at the desk, he knew he made it.

Back in the apartment, he waited with the pretzels on his lap. When the door opened, he knew the risk he just took was completely worth it. The pictures she had sent, though he liked them, did not do her justice. Blue eyes, long, straight hair, smooth skin, a smile that lit up the room, and, what he liked most, a body that belonged in a music video. And I don't mean some soft pop music video with one of those tall skinny models—I mean one of them hard-ass hood rap videos with the giant booties clapping along to the beat, barely able to fit onto the screen . . . exactly the kind of body Jimmy likes. He was awestruck.

"I got these for you," Jimmy said, pointing at the pretzels.

"Oh my god that's so sweet! You are too cute! Who does something like that?"

"Oh, it was nothing," he said, brushing it off. He didn't know whether she was being serious in her gratitude, or pampering him because he was in a wheelchair. But this girl was beautiful, so frankly, he didn't give a shit.

Over the next couple of hours, Jimmy became convinced he found "the one." She loved to talk, had a flair for the dramatic, and had no qualms about asking any and every question that came to mind, including anything she was wondering about his disability. And Jimmy loved all of that.

That night when I got home, Jimmy told me how well it went. He mentioned all of the dinners out, movies in, and lengthy phone and text conversations with all those other women who, since college, wanted to be a part of Jimmy's life. But with Gloria, it was different. This was the first time *he* felt that way, wanting to be a part of her life—the first time he found himself wanting to build something real.

"She is coming back over tomorrow night. I may lie and say my nurse cancelled to try to get her to stay over."

"What about her boyfriend?" I asked

"She told him about me. He's fine with it."

I shook my head. "He's cool with her hanging out with a guy she met at 2 a.m., hammered, in the scummiest bar in the scummiest city in New Jersey?"

"People are so dumb!" Jimmy laughed.

25

The First Date

Jimmy and Gloria were hanging out yet again, but this time it was different. This time, he was taking her on a date.

After two more weeks of non-stop texting, and hanging out, Jimmy wanted to keep the relationship moving forward. Despite having a boyfriend, Gloria was excited when Jimmy said he was going to take her on a real date. He wanted to keep it a surprise and had found a wine tasting event at his favorite restaurant on Rittenhouse Square that he thought would be perfect. Her reaction when they got there told him he made a solid choice. With good food, good conversation, and good wine, Jimmy knew that if he played his cards right there was no telling where this night could lead.

Like every other time these two were together, everything was going great. Then, Jimmy's phone lit up. It was a text from me. I was out of town and hadn't seen Jimmy in a couple of days, but he made the mistake of telling me he was going on a date with Gloria. I saw it as the perfect opportunity. I blame Jimmy for opening the text. He should have known better.

Regardless, he swiped open the text on his phone, sitting in his lap. After seeing what I sent him, he tried his best to keep a straight face. Unfortunately, it didn't matter.

"WHAT. THE. FUCK?!" Gloria shrieked. To her regret, she snuck a peak when Jimmy opened the text. In my defense, I wasn't counting on Gloria snooping. What she saw was an up close and personal, well lit, crystal clear picture of my penis.

"So, you know how Eddie is my "aide" sometimes . . ." Jimmy started to explain. "Well, I guess at some point, because he was always handling my junk, he started flashing me when I wasn't ready for it . . . like as a joke." I recognize that this must sound super weird to any normal person reading this. I never in a million years thought I would say this, but hey . . . you touch a dude's dick enough, the event loses any and all shock value.

"Go on." Gloria was getting to know Jimmy so well, she wasn't that surprised.

"So, at some point, I had to get him back."

I will never forget where I was when the battle began—in the office of the radio station I was working at, in front of a computer, with a very attractive female coworker at the computer right next to me. I saw a text from Jimmy, and like getting any text from a good friend, I get a little excited when I saw the notification. I open the message to reveal, in between two skinny legs in a birthing position, that giant monster of his. I threw my phone onto the desk like it was on fire, as the girl next to me asked what was wrong.

"Uh, nothing," I stammered as I felt my face turn red. I had never seen a dick pic before. Don't get me wrong, it's not like I have never seen another man's dick, or even a dick in a picture in some secondary or academic capacity—but this was my first official "dick pic" . . . where the dick is the center and sole focus of the image. I have to say, it was the weirdest fucking thing I ever seen. I can't imagine the kind of crazy a guy has to be to think sending an unsolicited picture of that odd looking appendage would actually improve his chances with a female. Regardless, the pic Jimmy sent, that he had an aide take of him during his lunch break, started a picture battle that, in all our maturity, lasted much longer than I would like to admit.[*]

---

[*] At least until the time of this writing, and most likely until present day.

As weird and misunderstood as that aspect of our relationship may be, believe it or not, a good thing came of it. Back at the apartment, Jimmy appealed to Gloria to help him get me back.

Little did I know that the obnoxious picture I sent to Jimmy because I was trying to mess with him would lead to these two things: for the first (and unfortunately not last) time, Jimmy sent me a picture of the monster . . . *fully erect*. Gloria's hand was gripping it like she would never let it go. This instantly became the new lead candidate for the weirdest fucking thing I'd ever seen. I swear that thing was thicker than his thighs, looking like a lethal weapon. And after Gloria prepped, snapped, and delivered that picture, she wasn't finished. As I was trying to erase that traumatizing image from my brain, for the first time with Gloria, Jimmy was getting some action below the belt.

Still to this day, Jimmy and I are in amazement at how something so good could come from something so fucking weird.

26

Moving Out

Jimmy was my roommate and one of my best friends, so when I would relay stories to others about my weekend or going out, he was usually in them . . . but it's not like I referred to him as my friend or roommate *in a wheelchair*. Unless the story called for it, I never felt there was a reason for the qualifier. So when people came over for the first time, especially during the beginning of our time living together, I would sometimes feel the need to preface it—like I needed to let them know that they will be meeting someone in a wheelchair. As the year went on, though, that feeling subsided. I guess the more comfortable I became with my living situation, the more I forgot about what others might think of it.

I always thought it was kind of cool to see the different and raw reactions people had when meeting Jimmy. Some people took it in stride, as if there was nothing weird about the situation. Other people were obviously uncomfortable, acting in a way I'd never seen them act before. Sometimes people would raise their voices, as if Jimmy was deaf. Other times, they would laugh hysterically at anything he said.

My favorite reaction, however, was from my cousin. I think he knew I was living with a guy in a wheelchair, he may have even met Jimmy once before . . . I'm not really sure. Regardless, one night he came over with plans to head out in the city. As we pre-gamed at the apartment, Jimmy and his very attractive dinnertime aide kicked it with us. They even joined us for a couple rounds of shots even though they weren't coming out. And as if on cue, minutes after eleven o'clock, Barbara came barreling through the door in a huff, complaining that it took so long to find a parking spot, and that she had to pee so bad, that when she finally found one, she took a squat right there in the parking garage.

"Barbara!" Jimmy cried. "Get in the bedroom!"

When my cousin and I left the apartment for the bar, his only comment was, "You have a pretty interesting living situation."

I never really thought of it so simply. I guess I knew that a lot of people thought it was bad, or weird, and I guess in defense of that I tried to focus only on the normalcy of it. I was so worried about how it might have looked to other people— good or bad, weird or normal—I didn't fully appreciate the incredibly unique situation I got to be a part of.

One day, towards the end of our time living together, Jimmy showed me a piece of paper his mom had recently found cleaning out the attic. It was one of those middle school projects where you had to write a handful of goals for your life as an adult. In his very familiar chicken scratch, which ironically does not look too different from my own handwriting, among other goals, it read, "Get an apartment in Center City with my best friend."

Jimmy was proud of that, and it was pretty cool to be part of his realized goal. What I can't say is if that was the dream of an average middle-schooler who wanted to live in the city, or if even at that young age Jimmy knew the adversity laying ahead in making such simple goal. I don't know if this was merely something he wanted to do, or if there came along with it an element of proving people wrong. Knowing Jimmy, it was probably both. All I could think, though, is that if I was looked at funny for wanting to live with Jimmy . . . I can't imagine the kind of patronizing and humored conversations Jimmy may have encountered when sharing this plan—something so readily attainable must have been treated as if he was asking for the moon and the stars.

Thinking about all those people who treated Jimmy like that, or who told me what I should have known—all of those who were *sure* they knew better—I can only help but laugh because moving to Center City Philadelphia, "working" as a caregiver, having nurses coming in and out around the clock, and living with such a great friend, was definitely one of the most interesting, and best, living situations of my life.

After living the life of luxury, according to Jimmy's standards, in Center City for a little over a year, it was time for me to find a more affordable place. Jimmy was getting another roommate—another very close friend of his—and would stay in that same apartment for another year. With a legendary year under our belts, having turned that apartment into the designated spot to start and end the night among our group of friends, we were able to walk away from our time together in apartment 808 with our heads held high.

It just so happened that our mutual friend Poker Josh had a must-see event in Las Vegas the very weekend I was set to move out. It would only be right to punctuate our time as roommates with a trip to Vegas.

"Honestly, Eddie," Jimmy told me after we booked our flights, "if there was a way for me to go out . . . this would be it. There's a very good chance I don't make it back."

I politely laughed, but he and I both knew that he wasn't joking.

27

Victim of Chance

My mother always told me this story growing up:

There was once a peasant man in a village who had nothing but one son, and one horse. One day, the horse ran away, and all the villagers were very sad for him, saying, "Oh what bad luck you have," to which the peasant man replied, "How can you be sure it is bad?"

A week later, the horse returned, and with it were two wild stallions! The villagers were ecstatic for him, exclaiming, "What great luck you have!" To which the peasant man replied, "How can you be sure it is good?"

A few days later, as the peasant's son was trying to break in the wild horses, he was trampled and left paralyzed. The villagers visited the injured young man and shared with the father, "Oh, what bad luck you have. He is your only son, who is to care for you, and now you must care for him." Again, the peasant man replied, "How can you be sure it is bad luck?"

The next week, word came that the nation would be going to war, and the army recruiters came to take all of the able young men of the village. All of the young men of the village fought and died in a terrible, horrific battle—all except the peasant man's son, who was passed over by the recruiters due to his inability to walk.

By total chance, Josh McDowell and I were assigned to be roommates freshman year of college. We ended up sticking together all four years at Temple. Ok, it wasn't total chance—our lack of attention to detail put us in a smaller pool of students that were planning to live on campus but were not assigned to a room. Josh, because he forgot to pay his bill on time, and me, because I misspelled my name on my college application.*

The first day I met Poker Josh was move in day, and within minutes of exchanging greetings his mother told me that he would be helping me with my math homework. Even if I wasn't good at math, I thought that was kind of a frank statement to make, but being that I felt pretty confident with the subject, and competitive with just about anything I do, it didn't sit well with me.

That is until the day Poker Josh challenged me to a contest in mental math—I guess it's something math nerds like him do for fun. I accepted the challenge, and Stephanie acted as the moderator, coming up with any random multiplication problem or what have you.

It was unreal. It didn't matter how many digits a number had before or after a decimal, Poker Josh was going to figure it out. And fast. I am talking Rain Man kind of shit. He was studying to be an actuary—someone who uses probabilities and statistics to assess risks. He absolutely hates the following reference, which he's heard numerous times, so being the good friend I am, I will be sure to relay it here: "Have you ever seen *Along Came Polly*? Ben Stiller's Character . . . who is super conservative and assesses the risk of every life scenario . . . well, he's an actuary." After college, Josh was planning on working at an insurance company, but what he discovered during sophomore year would set him on a path that no teacher or university could prepare him for. That year, his brother introduced him to poker.

For hours and hours at a time he would play this game. He would wake up sometime around 11 a.m., take two steps from his bed and plop down at his computer desk. He would bring up sixteen poker tables, and play until two or three in the morning. The only breaks he took were to use the bathroom or meet the Dominos delivery guy downstairs.

The summer after graduation, before starting at an insurance company, he lived in Sin City with fellow online poker friends (that's a common thing to do in the poker community) and played in some live tournaments. He earned a decent penny,

---

*I typed my middle initial twice. Edward P. PDoyle had to explain to every professor on the first day of each semester that, no the P isn't silent. I still haven't opened my diploma to this day out of fear it was never corrected.

especially with a couple of top ten tournament finishes, raking in around $100k. The poker lifestyle is full of ups and downs, however, and even with those winnings, it wasn't enough for him to forego the steady and stable lifestyle of the nine to five.

In July of each year, thousands of people pay $10,000 to play in the World Series of Poker Main Event. For about a week straight, they play cards all day until there are only nine players left. Those nine then finish the tournament a couple months later in October, in a big event broadcasted on ESPN. It is the Super Bowl of the card-playing world. Even while working his full-time job, Poker Josh played in these tournaments every summer, and the third time around was his charm. Out of nearly seven thousand entrants, he made the final table of the Main Event of the World Series of Poker.

If there was ever a reason to go to Vegas, it was to see a friend take home, at minimum, more than half a million dollars if he finished ninth place and nearly nine million if he placed first— all on national television. It was not a question of whether we should go, but how long should we go for? We were going to roll into Vegas squad deep—The Kid, Red, Calvin, Big Perm, and many others.

I had never traveled like this with Jimmy before, so I wasn't really sure how it would go. Jimmy never had any hint of trepidation about the trip, though, so I guess that kind of caused everyone else to not worry. As far as traveling with a disability, there really wasn't anything different Jimmy had to do. All hotels have elevators, so that wasn't an issue, and the only thing about the plane was that Jimmy had to check his power chair like luggage. He would then have someone push him to the plane in one of the manual, airport chairs, and would sit in the airplane seat like anyone else.

It must have been a little confusing for the other passengers to see a group of ten young men pointing out the window at the wheelchair being loaded on the plane, and yelling at our friend in the airport wheelchair that we hope they lose it. They were probably even more confused when Jimmy returned the smack talk when he got to pre-board the plane because of his disability.

If anyone was made for Vegas, it was Jimmy. Upon landing around noon, Jimmy was up and at it for thirty-six hours straight. He started by immediately going to one of the infamous hotel pool parties, and that would only serve as his pregame. An all-night stay at XS was his main event, and that was followed by a nightcap at the famous strip club, The Spearmint Rhino. The excursion was completed with a picture of him and the four guys in the crew who managed to keep up, taken as the sun came up over Las Vegas just as they were leaving the strip club.

And all this was before we even watched the Main Event Final Table.

When it was time for the card game, Poker Josh's fan crew walked in with matching t-shirts like we owned the place. Josh had t-shirts designed with spaghetti splattered on the front and read, "One shot, one opportunity" — a reference to the Eminem song "Lose Yourself" and its opening lines: "If you had one shot, one opportunity, to seize everything you ever wanted, in one moment, would you capture it, or let it slip?" It wasn't only about the money for Josh—the guy has a true passion for poker.

There was a section on the second level of the arena reserved for us, but we noticed a handful of open rows in the very front, next to the stage. Being the passionate Philly sports fans that we are, we wanted to move down. The staff at the Rio was fine with it—for everyone except Jimmy.

They said his wheelchair was a fire hazard if he parked it in the aisle, and there was no handicap seating anywhere in the front. Instead, he would have to sit in the way back, apart from everyone else. I had tickets to sit on the stage, and Jimmy, probably because he was still tired and hung over, didn't protest. As he went to the accessible seating, Red went to sit with him— the two of them in the back by themselves, the rest of the group up front near the stage.

They didn't mind—the two of them loaded up a drink tray and settled in for the show, but I couldn't have it. Over the years, one thing I have found to be very frustrating is when certain situations force separation. It wasn't that the place was not accessible—Jimmy could have very well gone down to be with the group. Instead, he was prevented from doing so either because of silly rules or a staff member who didn't know any better, or both. What's more, the handicap section was on a flat level behind the last row, meaning that if anyone stood up, Jimmy wouldn't be able to see.

I was fixing to have one of the best days of my life. I didn't want our group to be separated, and I didn't want Jimmy to be unable to see. I spoke with the Rio staff, and explained to them the situation. At first they were adamant that it was a fire hazard. Now, I understand that there are rules and regulations that have to be in place so that when something does happen, people can cover their ass from lawsuits and such. I really appreciated the staff at the Rio that night, however, because they saw the big picture. When I explained that a close friend of ours was playing, and that we all wanted to be together to watch it, and that he wouldn't be able to see in the back, and that if there was a fire he would be picked up and carried out of his chair anyway . . . they let him come down. Because of that, our group was able to stick together as we gave a boring game of cards the Philly fan treatment. The ESPN cameras were loving it. We weren't there to golf clap and sip our drinks. We yelled. We screamed. We started the wave and got loaded on the bar tab Poker Josh opened up for us. A couple members of our crew were even given warnings for taunting the players. Apparently, personal attacks are frowned upon.

Poker Josh did not win first, but he placed high enough to rake in over two and a half million dollars that day. What I will never forget, however, is how disappointed he was. He didn't even want to celebrate that night, retiring to his room in a sullen mood. I understand that he is a competitive person, but at the end of the day, when playing a game with so much luck involved, how upset can you really be? To this day, I still don't know if he was upset because of how he played, or because he missed out on the first-place payout. It was probably both. What I couldn't understand, though, was that he was disappointed for months after. Literally, months. I would text him almost weekly, asking him, "You proud of yourself yet?" He would constantly, consistently, and simply respond, "No."

Poker is a game of luck. Don't get me wrong, there is a ton of skill involved, but there is too much luck for me to consider it a game of skill (I can feel Josh rolling his eyes as I write this). I consider my poker skills comparable to my basketball skills, relatively speaking—I am good enough to not be considered bad. Thing is, if I were to go against the professional player Poker Josh 100 times, head to head in poker, he would beat me anywhere from 60 to 80 times, every time, almost guaranteed. On the other hand, if I were to play the 12th man on any NBA team 100 times, I would lose 101 times, every time, guaranteed.

The chances of Josh getting to the final table in the Main Event of World Series of Poker are slim. He won millions of dollars and a deal with a poker company that allowed him to quit his desk job and travel the world playing cards. Meanwhile, you would have thought that he had just been diagnosed with Lou Gehrig's Disease. Jimmy, on the other hand, who had an astronomically low chance of being born with SMA, was tackling that trip as if he was luckiest man in the world, happy as anyone could be.

One night while we were out—years after our Vegas trip—some Random Jackass attempted to spark a conversation when he saw Jimmy. Tapping a stranger, and out of Jimmy's earshot, he nodded towards the wheelchair and said, "Holy shit, talk about unlucky." Unfortunately for Random Jackass, the stranger he chose to share his comment with was Jimmy's brother, The Kid. We called him The Kid because Jimmy had been bringing him around for years before we found out he was a lot younger than the rest of us. Anyway, as you can imagine, The Kid didn't take this comment too kindly. In a swift motion, fit for a football field, Random Jackass was jacked up against the wall. Apologies immediately started spouting out of his mouth. I jumped to pull The Kid off of Random Jackass, as Random Jackass' friends rushed to defend him. As I am trying to tell The Kid to let him go, one of the friends shoves The Kid off of Jackass. Now me and The Kid have a group of four guys looking to fight us, as I am still trying to keep The Kid from getting to Random Jackass, as Random Jackass is between us and them. He is still apologizing to The Kid as he trying to convince his friends to back off, to no avail. He knew what he said was wrong.

In the midst of The Kid wanting to kill Random Jackass, Random Jackass' friends wanting to kill The Kid and me, and Random Jackass arguing with his friends that they should let it go, who broke it up? Jimmy, who couldn't throw a punch if his life depended on it. He rolled his chair right in the middle of the hostile circle. All he could do was shake his head no, as it was too loud in the bar for everyone to hear him. His presence alone was enough to quell the situation, quicker than the bouncers could make it over to kick people out. By the time they got there, they couldn't even tell who was at fault and they let everyone be.

Even after that comment from Random Jackass, Jimmy was able to go on with his night and have a grand old time, just like eventually, Poker Josh was somehow able to come to terms with winning only a couple million dollars. I know Poker Josh would cite studies* that claim Olympians who get Silver are more upset than those who get bronze, as the Bronze finisher is happy they got to the podium, while the Silver finisher is only thinking how they were so close to Gold. I always wonder what it would feel like to hit the five white balls but miss the red ball while playing the Powerball—I would have just won a million dollars, but would have been only one number away from winning hundreds of millions of dollars. Would I be happy with what I got, or disappointed that I was so close to so much more?

It seems like no matter what luck is thrown your way, whether good or bad, millions of dollars or a rare genetic disease—the only determining factor of any importance is attitude.

---

* When less is more: Counterfactual thinking and satisfaction among Olympic medalists. Medvec, Victoria Husted; Madey, Scott F.; Gilovich, Thomas. Journal of Personality and Social Psychology, Vol 69(4), Oct 1995, 603-610

28

The Subway Cop

Technically, Jimmy's disability entitles him to a discounted subway and bus fare of a dollar, but no SEPTA cashier or bus driver ever charges him. In fact, most of the time they allow me to ride for free as well. There isn't even a place to put a token at the handicap accessible entrance, and I would usually just get waved through as I held the door open for Jimmy. I would always have a token out, ready to pay—but hey, if they were going to invite me to slide through, I wasn't going to protest.

This happened quite often, as we took the Subway down to Pattison Avenue for many Sixers games, events, or to watch games at the giant sports bar venue nearby. When the games ended, we would head back to the subway, and it would be packed with a crowd of people trying to file through the turnstiles to get into the station. There was a separate handicap entrance that was idiotically placed right in the middle of all the turnstiles and surrounding chaos. It was a bear to maneuver our way through the crowd, especially because everyone walking toward the station naturally had their back to us. I would usually tap people on the shoulder, and kindly ask them to make a path, but sometimes the masses were too much for a couple of "excuse me"s to handle. Times like these, I would tell Jimmy to forge ahead, and stand behind him yelling, "Heads up! Coming through!" We felt bad for the innocent legs and feet that fell victim, but in that situation, it was our best option. Otherwise we would have had to wait for the entire stadium to empty into the subway. Plus, anyone who did get hit by the wheelchair, as Jimmy plowed through, would turn around in anger, only to quickly change their expression and immediately apologize to Jimmy. This always baffled me.

The police were always present at the stadium subway station when the games ended due to the large crowd. They were usually squad deep, too, sometimes with full-on riot gear. And those damn police dogs. I swear there is nothing more intimidating to me than a full-grown German Shepard with a vest on. I know the cops are there for crowd control and couldn't care less about the subway fare, but I was always afraid that I would rub one of them the wrong way. Even though there was nowhere to put the token in the accessible entrance, I would make it clear that I had one out and was willing to use it, just in case one of them thought I was trying to sneak in with Jimmy. One time I even tried to hand a token to one of the officers because I thought he was eyeing me funny. He told me not to worry about it, and helped clear a path to the elevator Jimmy and I take down to the subway platform underground.

One night, we were barely into the fourth quarter of a Sixers game when Jimmy convinced me to leave. He always wanted to leave early when we were down by a lot, and since it felt like the millionth time the Sixers were down by a lot, I finally gave in. We beat the crowd and arrived at a near-dead subway station. We were in mid-conversation as I mindlessly opened the handicap gate and walked through it with him towards the elevator. I was with Jimmy, and without the SWAT team present, I didn't even think to put on the charade of trying to pay. We are steps away from the elevator when I hear a voice yelling from outside of the station, and it sounds like it is getting closer.

"Oh no! You are not getting away with this!" A police officer is in a dead sprint towards us, and hurdles the turnstile as if he was in action movie. "I see you pull this shit all the time up at Walnut Street! Get the fuck out of here, you aren't riding this subway!"

I was in shock. Not just because of his anger, but also because he recognized me from Walnut Street. I felt kind of important. "Relax, man, it's a token. I got it right here," reaching into my pocket.

"No, don't give me a fucking token. You pull this shit all the time. You aren't riding my subway."

By no means am I anti-cop (to be honest, I hate the fact that I feel the need to clarify that) but I whole-heartedly despise people in any profession who use their position to abuse power. "It's not *your* subway," I said. "I got a token right here. I am riding the train." I pushed the elevator button to call the cart to our floor.

Jimmy started to yell at me to calm down—he could tell I was getting pissed, and didn't want me to escalate the situation. The only thing worse than a cop on a power trip is an angry cop on a power trip.

"Son, you aren't riding the subway."

I held up the token as I walked over and slammed it into the fare slot. "Bullshit I'm not." Pointing to Jimmy, "You going to make him ride it on his own?"* I was thinking this idiot cop assumed Jimmy was incapable of doing this, and thought it would be the dagger to the conversation.

Subway Cop didn't like that option, but he wasn't giving up that easily. "I should write you a fuckin' citation for trying to sneak on the subway."

That sent me over the edge. "Why the hell are you giving me so much shit? What's your problem? It's a fuckin' token! A silly token that means absolutely nothing to you!" As I heard Jimmy trying his best to shut me up, it gave me a thought. "Why aren't you making him pay?"

"Don't give me that shit," the cop replied.

"No, seriously, that's discrimination. You are letting him on for free just because he is in a chair. That's total bullshit. You

---

*For the record, this is something Jimmy can and does do all the time—it's just a pain in the ass because he has to rely on finding strangers to push the elevator button. This is particularly a pain at the Walnut station due to the fact that it takes two separate elevators to get to street level, and one of them is well off the beaten path in a station that can be kind of sketchy late at night.

don't care about the city, or what's fair, you're just giving me shit cause you feel like it."

At this point the argument is reduced to him telling me to "shut the fuck up," and me repeating to the African-American officer that he needs to "stop discriminating," as Jimmy is telling me to chill out as he shepherds me into the elevator.

We get onto the elevator, with the officer still fuming about five yards away from us. As the elevator doors are closing there is that complete silence that typically comes about at some point in every argument, where each side takes a breath and either sees it as over, or questions why they were arguing in the first place. Sometimes, however, this is the moment when one party decides to claim the last word. In all my wisdom and maturity, as the elevator doors slowly started to close, I felt it necessary to mutter, "This is fuckin' bullshit."

The words had barely left my lips when the officer took off in a full sprint towards me. I didn't know what set him off—we had both been slewing profanities around the entire argument—but he looked like he was ready to end me. Standing still, cornered in the elevator, I tried to appear as calm as possible. Inside, though, I was hoping to God and all the heavens that the doors would shut before he reached us.

Thankfully, they did. Through the glass doors, we watched him jam the button numerous times in hopes of opening it back up, and breathed a sigh of relief as he punched the wall and the elevator started moving down. The relief didn't last long, however, as just before we went underground, we saw the officer turn and sprint towards the steps, presumably running to meet us.

"Look what you did now." Jimmy was disappointed and mad at me.

"He was being an asshole,"

"You're going to get arrested."

"For a token?" I was trying to play it cool, but I was scared. I let my youth and hubris get the best of me. I felt so stupid for getting into it like that with someone who had a gun. That's the thing about police—in the moment, who cares who is right, and who is wrong—you got to listen to the person that the government gave a gun and its blessing to use it. Simple as that.

That firearm on his hip was on my mind as we went down to the lower level. I knew the elevator brought us to a spot that was out of sight from anyone else riding the subway, and even though I was almost certain this guy wouldn't shoot me because he was angry, it was pretty scary seeing how hostile he was. I had no idea what it was that made him flip, and was afraid of what he might do with no one else around.

When the elevator got to the ground floor, I saw the officer sprinting from around the corner of the staircase and heading straight for us. Images of being thrown onto the train tracks flashed through my mind as we waited for the elevator doors to open. I was snapped back to reality, and slightly comforted, when I saw another officer peek around the corner, curious as to what got his coworker so fired up. If this guy was going to try to turn me into rat food, at least Jimmy and another officer were there to witness it.

My heart was pounding as the elevator doors opened. Jimmy had moved his chair so that he could get off first, letting me know, without using words, that he was going to try his best to stay in between me and the officer. As calmly as I could, I stepped out of the elevator, directly behind Jimmy. The officer screamed as he approached, arms flailing and in a rage, "DID YOU CALL ME A NIGGER?!"

That was a game changer for me. Sure, there was no denying that I had lost my cool upstairs. This officer had pushed me to a place that I don't go to often. I would be lying if I said I would not have socked this guy in the face if I thought I could get away with it. But as much as I could not stand this person, and believe that it is people with power like him that make the world a worse place, upon hearing that accusation, my mood immediately changed.

"Whoa, whoa, whoa," I put my hands up as if to show innocence. "I would never, EVER, call someone that."

I know there are some people reading this who use words like privilege and genocide out of context who may not believe me, that might think in my anger the inherent racism that's at the core of every white man may have slipped out, but with the upmost sincerity, they can go fuck themselves. I usually try to refrain from defending myself in such a simple and inconsiderate manner, but I have really strong opinions about race and race relations, and especially this word. The way I see it, that word is doing just as much damage now as a "term of endearment" as it was when it was strictly hostile. Never have I ever even considered dropping the N-bomb like that. Shit, I usually skip over that word when singing along to my favorite songs—I don't want it to become anywhere close to a comfortable part of my vernacular.

My mood changed so much with this accusation that the officer immediately believed me. He could see in my face, despite our mutual feelings of disgust in each other, that I was being honest. He just stood there, frozen and silent, knowing he misheard. I kept repeating to him that there was no chance in hell I would ever say that, as Jimmy and I walked passed him towards the subway car.

On the ride back, I reflected over that whole situation. I was mad at myself for my short temper, and I was mad at the world because there were people who care more about power than what is important. Most of all, I was in shock about that accusation.

As I sat in the subway car, I noticed, as I always do, the inevitable glances at Jimmy from the strangers on the train. It was always easy for me to catch people stealing peeks, or even staring, as I was basically invisible next to the wheelchair, and the guy in it, that they were curious about.

Wrestling with my own thoughts, as the people in the subway car stole glances at Jimmy, I wondered what kinds of thoughts were sparked in their heads when they looked at him. Then it clicked—people see what they want to see. I could never say what their thoughts are exactly, but if I remember back to the days before I knew Jimmy, I know that I had a lot of ill-informed ideas—assumptions really—about what it meant for him to be in a wheelchair . . . for him to look the way he does.

For whatever reasons, from whatever he may have experienced in his life, that officer approached the situation assuming that because I was white, and angry with him, I was probably a racist. In his mind, I was treating him a certain way because he was black and I was white. In reality, I couldn't have cared less about his skin color—I was treating him that way because he was being an asshole.

29

A Normal Relationship

He must have gotten over a hundred texts from her over the last three days, and had yet to answer a single one. He knew her frustration was building, but when he swiped to see the most recent text from "Gloriaaaaaa," he wasn't prepared for what he was about to read. Under a picture of a hand full of different color pills:

> *If you don't answer me, I am going to take these pills and drive to the emergency room.*

Jimmy had promised himself that he wasn't going to text her anymore—he was tired of the bullshit. He was tired of the lies, the games, the constant worry and insecurity she brought into his life. He told her—begged her even—to leave him alone, but she needed his attention. This threat of her harming herself finally broke through to Jimmy, even though in his heart of hearts he knew she was being more manipulative than serious. He answered her, setting their merry-go-round in motion again for another make up and break up.

For all intents and purposes, Jimmy and Gloria had been dating exclusively for three months. She had been staying at his place at least three times a week, and even introduced Jimmy to her parents, as well as some extended family. When they weren't together, they were talking on the phone—anything from serious talks to the kind of nothing conversations that involve asking if the fries were eaten before, after, or with the cheeseburger. When they weren't talking on the phone, they were texting each other. And when they weren't texting each other, they were sending unanswered texts that read, "Where are you?" or "What are you doing?" or "WTF answer me!"

If Gloria got a ride to the gym with a guy, Jimmy would be on guard. If one of the thousands of girls that follow Jimmy on social media reached out to him, Gloria would get an attitude. When they were together, any sort of phone activity would cause suspicion, as if the two believed their cell phones were devices only meant to use for each other.

At the time she met Jimmy, Gloria had just moved in with one of her exes in an attempt to mend the relationship. That didn't matter though, because at first, even Gerald, who Gloria described as an extremely jealous person, did not care that Gloria was hanging out with Jimmy. I guess one never thinks that a handicapped little guy is going to steal your girlfriend.

The relationship progressed, as Jimmy's willingness to listen was a perfect match for Gloria's need to share. Jimmy started going into work earlier so he could be done the same time as Gloria, who worked at a school and got off around 2:30. She would rush to Jimmy's, where the two of them would lie in bed until the latest possible moment that would still allow Gloria to beat Gerald, who worked late, home. She even began intercepting the phone bill so he wouldn't see the amount of texts she was sending Jimmy's way. At its peak, adjusted for waking hours (note: not work hours), Jimmy and I did the math and figured out the two averaged about thirty texts per hour, every hour for one month.

As Gloria and Jimmy's relationship moved onward, the physical aspect did as well. In retrospect, who knows the kind of guy Gerald actually was—he could have been an All-American, class act for all we know—but at the time, Gloria made him out to be a demon. Who wouldn't root for their friend to win the girl he wants? So when Jimmy told me, with a shit-eating grin, that Gloria had stopped kissing Gerald because she felt too guilty after where her mouth had been on Jimmy, I couldn't help but laugh. I mean, Jimmy literally couldn't hurt a fly, but here he was tearing a relationship apart, and loving every second of it.

One day after work, I walked into his room to say what's up.

"Eddie." Pause, as always. "I need to figure out how to have sex."

The act was coming soon, he could feel it. But he didn't know how it would work. He can't stand, thrust, kneel, hold, or do any of the many other unspoken requirements of the Kama Sutra. It required some brainstorming and troubleshooting, but we finally figured it out.

Because Jimmy doesn't have much muscle, he doesn't move most of his joints. Because his joints do not move, the ligaments and tendons in and around them harden, almost like concrete not being stirred. When he was younger, he would go to physical therapy every week, where a therapist would bend his legs and arms and wrists and ankles for him, to prevent them from hardening. After an inattentive physical therapist broke his kneecap by stretching his leg out too far, Jimmy decided he was done. He was tired of spending all that time there, especially because there would never be an end. He quit going, and because of that, lost flexibility in his knees and elbows. When Jimmy is being carried, his arms hang at an "L," and his knees stay bent even when lying on his back. If someone were to forcibly straighten them, it would be extremely painful and tear every ligament in the joint.

With all that sexiness in mind, Jimmy was afraid that being on the bottom would not work because of his knees sticking up. I reminded him that he has crazy flexible hips—the result of having little muscle in his legs and always crossing and turning his legs while he sleeps. He could spread his legs wide like a woman giving birth, and then Gloria could get in a position where they could do the deed. I'm not usually one for that bullshit frat-boy conquest kind of grandstanding, but hey, if the wingman of the year award doesn't go to the guy that helped his friend realize how he could have sex, then I quit.

After they knocked boots, Jimmy was expecting the ball to start rolling even quicker. She never said she would leave Gerald, but her complaining about him, and her dependency on Jimmy, was skyrocketing. Jimmy knew he was the one who made her happy and was holding out hope that she would eventually realize that. As the fights between Gloria and Gerald were becoming more frequent and cutting deeper than ever before, Gloria would call or text Jimmy for hours after, and he would be there for her no matter what. He would stay up until the wee hours of the morning, consoling Gloria, who would even reach out via text as she lay next to Gerald. With every fight, Jimmy was feeling more and more optimistic about their future together.

That is, until Gloria sent him a two-word text on Christmas Eve:

He proposed.

It took some probing, but she finally admitted to Jimmy that her answer had been "yes." She played it off like she said it out of obligation, but couldn't honestly tell him that she wasn't going to marry him. Jimmy didn't answer her for two days, which felt like a decade to the both of them. Eventually, Jimmy gave in to the constant calls and texts from Gloriaaaaa, hoping against hope that if he was in her life, she would realize that he was the one who made her happy. But then time passed, and wedding plans were made, and Jimmy started to grow skeptical.

The emotional relationship between Jimmy and her was still in full force, as Gloria always had some tragedy that made her turn to Jimmy for advice and comfort—but the physicality subsided and then disappeared. Gloria said she couldn't do it with a ring on her finger, but that she still loved Jimmy more than anything or anyone else. This is when he first started to give up on her. He didn't want to be treated as a backup—just a shoulder to cry on when things got tough. Jimmy no longer felt like an exception. He didn't think he was special—that he was reason Gloria would lie and cheat on her boyfriend. Instead, he started to think that was simply who she was, and now he was the one being cheated and lied to.

Without Jimmy at her beck and call, Gloria started having a hard time. She realized how much she missed him, and would tell Jimmy often, usually after a fight with her now-fiancé. Eventually, a blow-up would officially end their engagement, and I'll never forget how excited Jimmy was to tell me the news.

"She was texting me as they were fighting, giving me the play by play," Jimmy said. "At one point, he was so frustrated that she was texting during their fight, he said, 'What do I have to do for you to pay attention to me? Fall out of a window and be in a wheelchair?'" Jimmy was cracking up as he told me.

Jimmy thought he had finally won. Without missing a beat, Gloria was back in the picture full time. She was basically living at the apartment, and the two were unhappy only when they weren't together. Jimmy even went to Gloria's family beach house for an overnight stay. He was as excited as a teenager when he got back from that trip, telling me that Gloria took him into the bedroom "to go the bathroom" during the afternoon, with the entire family on the other side of the wall.

In our apartment, the two would lock themselves in Jimmy's room and I would hear Gloria go on and on about God knows what, and Jimmy would console her. She was there every day after work, and he even rearranged his nursing schedule so that she could get paid to be a caregiver. I knew how happy he was when I walked in on him one day and caught him looking through her profile pictures while belting Frank Ocean's "Thinking About You" out loud. Believe me, if he wasn't about to shed tears of happiness singing to himself, thinking about her—I did everything I could to make him cry over the fact I would never, ever let him live that down.

I don't know if I have ever seen such a dependent relationship, and I am not talking about the needs that came with Jimmy's disability, either. The caregiver aspect of their relationship was easily replaceable, but Gloria only had one Jimmy, and Jimmy only had one Gloria. As unhealthy as that may have been, it was everything he wanted—except commitment. Gloria would not say they were dating, and never introduced him as her boyfriend. The routine and cliché excuses were used: "I just got out of a relationship," and "I am not ready for a new one," but Jimmy knew it was something more. His entire life people have been indirect and delicate with him, and he could sniff out the bullshit from a mile away. He wanted the truth.

Eventually, she told him what was holding her back. She told him her friends thought she was being irresponsible by hanging out with Jimmy so much. She told him that her family didn't approve—her aunt said that the fun with that handicapped little friend needed to stop, and her dad said she needed to stop spending so much time with "that retard."

When Jimmy relayed this to me, I was surprised . . . not so much by what those people said, but that Jimmy seemed fine with it. He was telling me this story, laughing, as if they were characters in a movie—something entertaining and not real.

I try my best to not care what others think, but Jimmy takes this to a whole other level. I have asked him a million times, in a million different ways, how he feels when he hears these kinds of things, or why he isn't bothered when people on the street give him money for no reason, or what goes on in his head when people turn around and are audibly startled by him in his wheelchair, or the multitude of other ways he is presented with the ignorance and misunderstanding of so many people. It is so common, he says, that he is used to it, and can brush it off as if it is nothing. He knows that people with disabilities are often seen as less-than, and that he can't control what others think. All he can do is control what he thinks, and he chooses not to let it bother him. What does bother him, though, is when that stuff affects his life—when it intrudes on the things, and the people, he cares about.

"What they think doesn't matter," Jimmy said to Gloria, after she told him all of those things that were holding her back. "What do *you* think?"

All of the problems and worries and fears she was talking about were not things that have happened—they were opinions and thoughts and feelings of others. She couldn't give Jimmy a straight answer to his question, but he knew that had to be one of two things. She was either putting too much value on what others said, or she actually felt those things herself.

This was the root of the fight that led to Gloria threatening to take the pills. She told Jimmy that she couldn't be with him—not because she was unhappy—in fact, she said he made her happier than she could have ever imagined. She couldn't be with him because of all the drawbacks that come with his chair. She talked about things that didn't make any sense to Jimmy—things like not being able to vacation at the beach, even though that is where they met, or how it was uncomfortable having an aide around, even though privacy never seemed to be an issue.

What did make sense to Jimmy was that she couldn't be with him because of how he was born—not because of something he did, not because of the way they were together, and most certainly not because of the way he made her feel. It was because of who he was, something he could never change.

I will never forget Jimmy telling me that night that no one had ever made him feel more like a man than Gloria had . . . and no one had ever made him feel more handicapped, either.

30

The Creation of [dis]ABLE

"I had always wanted to change the perception of those with a disability, but was never sure exactly how. Every day, I tried to do that with the way I presented myself, and the way I interacted with people, but I always wanted to do more—to really leave my impact on society.

When I started looking for a job after college—despite an immaculate background, transcript, and experience—I realized I was being seen for my wheelchair and not my resume. After securing a job as a market analyst at a major insurance company in Philadelphia, I started the brand as a project on the side, coupling my passion for fashion with my mission to change the connotations of the word "disable." Messing around on a notepad one day, I came up with the logo, put it on a shirt and then social media, and the response was overwhelming."

At least, that is the story Jimmy tells the people he meets at events, and the people interviewing him for the paper, and the anchors talking to him on television. It's what he puts on advertisements and in the "about" sections of social media. It's not a falsehood by any means—that story is entirely true. The part that is left out, however, it the tipping point that drove Jimmy to actually create his brand.

Though he always wanted to change the perception of those with a disability, and he always loved fashion and wanted his own clothing line, it took a major event for Jimmy to actually move forward with it. I know this may seem cliché, but the reason Jimmy created [dis]ABLE was because of a broken heart.

After Gloria laid out the reasons she was unsure of their relationship—all of them pertaining to Jimmy's disability—it broke Jimmy's heart. He knew he was what Gloria wanted, and saw how he made her happier than she ever was before. But he was being rejected for who he was physically, something he could never change. The worst part was that he knew in his heart of hearts the fears she was having were unfounded—it is far from impossible to be happy with someone who has a disability. Anything she had brought up was a problem or situation that existed only in her head, or was voiced by other people—none were things that had actually happened to them.

After they had broken up, he had been scribbling on a notepad one day, and finally put on paper an image that had been dancing around his head for a while. He'd written 'disABLE,' emphasizing the ABLE. Then he bracketed the 'dis' and crossed it out, "Because," as he told me, ". . .fuck it."

He put the graphic on the computer and then onto a t-shirt, and was going to wear it loud and proud, not only as a testament to who he is, but also (as the tagline read) "for all those who said I couldn't." Especially her.

I found out about it one night when I walked into his apartment before we headed to a 76ers game.

"What the hell is that?" I asked, pointing to a giant framed poster with the [dis]ABLE logo on it.

"It's my brand," Jimmy said. He loved to downplay major events.

"Your what?

"My brand."

"Do people do that? I didn't know that was a thing."

"Shut up. Look." He pointed to a little flyer he made. As I started to read it to myself, Jimmy yelled, "Eddie!"

"You vain bastard." I should have known better—Jimmy loves nothing more than to hear his own writing read aloud.

"DISABLE is defined as 'to deprive of capability or effectiveness,' however, having lived with a physical difference, Spinal Muscular Atrophy (SMA) type 2 (a form of Muscular Dystrophy) for my entire life, I know this to be grossly inaccurate; hence why I created this brand. Everyone has limitations. So if you believe those who are 'disabled' are just people who need to achieve personal greatness differently, you can support the brand by purchasing some of its fashionable apparel. Place your order at www.disablethebrand.com. A portion of the proceeds will go to the Muscular Dystrophy Association."

I looked at his couch, covered in [dis]ABLE t-shirts, towels, and even a onesie made for his baby nephew.

"Grab one," he said. "You get the first."

The thing about Jimmy is that he the embodiment of that Nike slogan, "Just do it." The guy puts himself out there, and doesn't care. This was something he wanted to do, and he did it. That attitude is special, and I felt lucky to be around someone like that. And since he was such a good friend, I most certainly couldn't tell him that. "Great," I said, grabbing a shirt. "And here I thought my wardrobe couldn't get any worse."

As always, Jimmy demanded a picture, and I suggested that since we were heading to the subway for the game anyway, we take one on our way there. When we got to Broad Street, we asked a group of girls if one of them would take our picture with City Hall in the background. The one who said yes shared with us that it was her 18th birthday, and I told her she is lucky because on the day she became a legal person she gets to meet the founder and creator of [dis]ABLE the Brand. I told her the brand was going to be a big deal, and someday she would find Jimmy and tell him she was the one who took that first picture. (In my defense of such an extraordinary claim—my thinking was that it's not every day you turn 18 and take a picture of two guys wearing matching shirts in the middle of Broad Street during rush hour, one of them in a wheelchair).

On the subway ride down to the game, with his chair fixed and set in place, Jimmy dreamed about the day my prediction would come true. At the game, he fantasized aloud about which NBA players he will have wearing his gear. On the way back from the subway he said he would know he made it for real when a giant, customized disABLE shirt adorns the statue of William Penn atop City Hall.

That night, I slept over Jimmy's, and when I left for work the next day, I couldn't find the shirt he gave me. I was running late, and told him I would grab it the next time I saw him.

He claims that he never found it, and suggested I must have taken it with me—but I know better. In the next year, the wall around the [dis]ABLE poster in his room would slowly be surrounded with pictures of family, and then friends, and then strangers wearing the brand that he created. In that first year, he sold over a thousand shirts, and he even managed to get his brand onto the backs of some NBA and NFL players, as he predicted, as well as other celebrities.

The City of Philadelphia has yet to order a XXXXXXXXXXXXXXXXL sized t-shirt for Billy Penn, and Jimmy is still waiting for that girl to find him and tell him that she is the one that took the picture in the middle of Broad Street. Whether those things will ever come to fruition, I don't know. What I do know, however, are these two things: first, with every t-shirt, or Facebook post, or Instagram tag, or simple conversation where "disable" is used in reference to a clothing line—to represent the initiative and dream and confidence of a young man—the connotation of "less-than" slowly fades. No matter how microscopic those events may be, they mean Jimmy is inching and progressing closer and closer to his goal.

The second thing I am sure of: that asshole stole back my damn t-shirt.

31

Superbad Courtside Seats

When Jimmy was given courtside seats to a 76ers game for the first time, he was so wrapped up in his clothing brand, [dis]ABLE, he saw it as a business opportunity more so than an incredible fan experience.

After our college days, Jimmy and I decided to graduate from attending Temple basketball games to the 76ers', even though there were times where it felt like the latter could have competed only at a collegiate level. We went with a ten-game plan and took the cheapest seats available, knowing that we could work the system in our favor.

The arena the Sixers played in was not the most accessible venue, and there were limited options for handicap seating. Plus, the available seating could prove to be quite a hassle. There were a handful of accessible areas on the lower level, but half of them weren't elevated—they were just the cement space directly behind the back row of the first level. That meant that when people stood to catch a t-shirt, do a dance with hopes of getting on the Jumbotron, or the big moments at the end of the game when the announcer tells those watching at home, "Everyone in the building is on their feet," Jimmy is left out.

To be clear, I am not making an asinine complaint that people in wheelchairs don't get a fair chance to get on the Jumbotron or to catch a t-shirt (especially because anyone who does catch a t-shirt usually tries to give it to Jimmy), and I am most definitely not implying that there is anything at all offensive about the announcer saying, "Everyone on their feet." I think it is kind of silly that political correctness is so prevalent that I feel the need to explain that.

What I am saying is during those times when everyone rises to their feet, the people sitting in the wheelchairs behind the crowd can't see the fun halftime show or the game-winning basket. Instead, they get a row full of asses in their face. You would think someone might have considered that when designing a section for people who can't stand.

If all of the first level handicap sections were full, they would move us to a club box in between the first and second level. This was always a pain in the ass.

Now I know what you're thinking—complaining about getting assigned to the club box? What is this entitled asshole's problem? The thing is, in the club box, there is no space for a wheelchair, and Jimmy is told to sit *behind* the back row of the box, encountering the same problem of 100% butt-vision whenever the crowd stands. As for me (or whoever else goes with him), I am told to sit *in* the back row of the box. When that happens, I have to explain to the ushers that I came to the game to sit and watch it *with* my friend, not in front of him. Every time, they insist that there is no other way, and I get frustrated. And every time, I tell them, "Frankly, I think it is a little disrespectful to suggest we sit separately," and then challenge them with the idea that the next time they go to an event with a friend, they should buy seats in two different rows, since, as they would claim, it's no big deal.

If they still don't know what to do, I explain to them that every time we are faced with this situation, they get on their little walkie-talkies and someone brings a fold-up chair to the box, so I can sit next to Jimmy in the back row. Then, after all that, we can finally accomplish our unreasonable and unthinkable goal of watching a game together at the stadium.

When I first started going to 76ers games with Jimmy, I thought I would be forced have the unfortunate experience of actually having to sit in the seat I paid for. With designated wheelchair sections, Jimmy wouldn't be able to partake in the longstanding tradition for fans of terrible sports teams to buy cheap tickets and sneak down to an empty section in the lower level. Tragic, I know. I was pleasantly surprised, though, when Jimmy figured out a way to beat the system.

He realized that customer service relocated people from regular seating to accessible seating on a first come, first served basis, filling up the lower level first before sending anyone to a club box. Technically, if both of those levels were filled, there was accessible seating on the upper level, but we are talking about the time when the Sixers were historically bad. They couldn't give those tickets away for free. So instead of paying a premium for lower level seats, or going with the cheap accessible seating on the upper level, we would simply buy the cheapest tickets available. We knew that we could trust the process of seat relocation, and our friends at customer service would hook us up with the lower level.

Being that we had been working the system in our favor for years with our $10 lower level seats, we had no idea the kind of hassle we would encounter when we had legitimate courtside tickets. Jimmy serves on the board for a company that provides resources to those with disabilities, and to his delight he found out they had two courtside seats and would pass them around to the board members when they weren't being used.

It was pretty awesome taking the usually dreaded walk to the elevator and, instead of saying "upper level," delightfully telling the usher we were going courtside. As we walked out from the bowels of the stadium and into the arena, we were greeted by an attendant with an unpleasant attitude who snapped, "Who let you down here?"

All my life I have snuck down to sections I didn't belong in—it's the Philadelphia way—so I thought once I showed that I had legitimate tickets, it would be a non-issue and we would be on our way. He must have taken us as newbies when he tried to come off as smooth and helpful and advised us that we could head back upstairs to guest services and get accessible seating. This wasn't our first rodeo.

I told him that there was no shot that we were going to guest services to get relocated to a section that was higher up. We had courtside seats, and we were fully intending to sit in them. This prompted him to call his supervisor, Frank.

Frank was quite the unpleasant character. He interrupted everything I said by calling, "Timeout," while making a "T" with his hands. He kept repeating that Jimmy could not sit on court level because of logistics, but he wasn't offering any explanation as to why the suggestions I was making wouldn't work. All I got was a perfect "T" in my face and, "Timeout."

It is a sad truth of this life that sometimes, the more you fight, and the more you argue and the more you are a pain in the ass, the more likely the other side will just give up and you'll get what you want. I wasn't letting this go—we can pretend it was for some noble cause of fairness or equality or sticking up for my friend . . . but the truth is, I really wanted to sit courtside myself. Finally, when I asked for the umpteenth time why I couldn't leave the chair under the bleachers, out of everyone's way, and carry Jimmy to his courtside seat, Frank finally gave an answer. "He is a fire hazard on this level, he would take too long to exit in case of an emergency." This wasn't the first time I heard this.

"With that logic, there should be no wheelchairs on the upper level, or club box level. But there are. Also, there shouldn't be any slow-moving seniors or really anyone who moves slow sitting down here either. They would take too long to leave, also. I'll tell you what, Frank. I'll let this go if you kick out every person who looks like they would take too long to leave."

I like to think I stumped him, but it is more likely I had just become too annoying to deal with. With one final motion of a timeout, he told me that there was nothing they could do, and that I needed to go to guest services, and "the chair has got to go, immediately."

One of the more annoying things that happen when hanging out with Jimmy is when people only address me. I get it—people may be uncomfortable, or unsure, or even afraid of how to approach Jimmy, but I can't stand when waiters look to me and say, "What does he want" or when people ask me, in front of Jimmy, "What is your friend's name," like he is a fucking pet. Above all else, I hate when Jimmy is addressed as an object—reduced to a chair, especially "a chair that has got to go."

With a long argument preceding this statement, and courtside seats to a game I was missing, I was over it.

"What are you telling me that for? Tell him."

Frank looked at me dumbfounded.

"He's got ears, and a mouth, and it's a power chair—he is the one that would have to move it anyway. So you tell him to move it. I am done with this situation."

I turned to watch the game where I was standing. He told me to hold on; he was going to call his boss.

Enter Mark James, who introduced himself as the vice president of something—at that point I was too pissed to pay full attention. I didn't even need to say a word to him. He immediately informed me that they would bring a ramp down, and would make space on the first level of the bleacher seats, located three rows behind the court. We would be able to stay on court level. He gave me his card too, and said if there is anything I needed, to give him a call.

It was the closest I had ever been to the court at and NBA game, and I was too tired of arguing to argue anymore. As we sat down in our new seats, I was satisfied with the fact that we didn't get sent back upstairs.

Jimmy, however, didn't want to settle for being a little back. He wanted to sit on the court, like the tickets he had entitled him to. We must have been in the makeshift seats for two possessions when Jimmy told me he wanted to go courtside. He hadn't worn the Gucci shoes for nothing.

Sitting there at halftime, letting the ridiculousness of the first half sink in, I said, "Fuck it, let's do it. What's the plan?"

"Alright. Grab my phone and wallet. Unbuckle my seatbelt. Then get ready to lift me on my signal." I do as I'm told. Sliding my one hand under his knees, I leaned over to him as if he was talking into my ear.

"I'm in position, sir!" Jimmy kept his eyes peeled for the right moment, and when all the ushers were preoccupied Jimmy said, "NOW!"

I scooped him up and carried him right to the seats we had tickets for: two big leather chairs right in the middle of the baseline.

"Eddie, the glasses!" Jimmy said after I set him down.

"How'd we forget?!" I ran back to his chair, and grabbed the two cases he had in his [dis]ABLE duffel bag. He brought them to the game, one for him and one for me, because as he said, "It wouldn't be legit unless we're wearing Versace shades."

Just then, the Sixers came out to warm up from the halftime break, and we called out to Lavoy Allen—a former Temple player and good friend of Jimmy's. The ushers had finally spotted us and were making their way over—but backed off when they saw Lavoy coming towards us to say what's up.

Waiters started swarming from everywhere, handing us drinks, and food, and programs. Here we are, two guys sitting courtside, calling out to our friend, an NBA player, outmaneuvering the staff—all while rocking the stunna shades.

We made it.

When the game started back up, Jimmy's mind immediately turned to what he came for. He wanted a celebrity in a shirt. Finally, he thought he spotted someone.

"Oh shit, is that Mark Wahlberg?"

"I don't know, watch the game."

"Is it him? Look!"

Unfortunately for me, a kind woman overheard Jimmy, and told him, "No that's not Mark Wahlberg . . . but Michael Cera is sitting a couple rows behind you. Curious, I turned around, and sure enough, in tight khaki's, a t-shirt, and one of those beanies with the fluffy pom-pom ball on top, there he was.

"Which one is Michael Cera?"

"The skinny guy from *Superbad.*"

"Oh shit! Eddie, get him a shirt!"

"Watch the game!"

For the next twenty minutes, Jimmy was persistent. He knows I am not one to go gaga over a celebrity, and I don't like to bother people when they are just out and trying to enjoy their night. However, Jimmy also knows that I got his back. For me, that means if Jimmy would do something himself, but for whatever reason he can't, I'll try my best to take care of it for him. The point is, I knew Jimmy wasn't trying to use me to do something he was afraid to do himself.

His asking turned to pleading, which turned to, "Stop being a bitch and just do it." Eventually, he broke me. It was probably at the worst time, too. There was less than two minutes left, it was a close game, and the crowd was hype. Furthermore, it was the part of every Sixers game when they show this morbidly obese superfan who takes his shirt off and does a dance to rile up the crowd (it's a lot cooler than it sounds—he's a well-known fan favorite).

I expressed to Jimmy my current feelings toward him with a common two-word phrase, went back to his chair to grab a shirt and a flyer, and then headed for Michael Cera. When I got to him, I kneeled down next to his chair. "Hey man. Look, I hate bothering you like this, but, uh . . . well, see that head of brown hair sticking out above the seat?" I pointed to Jimmy's chair, and the back of his giant head. "Well, he started this brand, and he's a big fan, and wanted you to have a shirt, and I feel bad for bothering you like this but, um, he's a fan and wanted to give this to you." When he didn't take the shirt I was holding out for him, I more or less shoved it in his hands, and he held it like he didn't know what to do with it. "Again, thanks, and sorry to bother you like this, but, oh yeah, uh . . . if you wanted to take a picture holding it up that would be cool."

"Wow, that's really nice," he replied, looking at the Jumbotron, with the close score and now a giant belly of truffle doing a shuffle across the enormous screen. "There's a lot going on right now, it's a lot to process, but I really appreciate it."

When I heard him answer me, I was kind of surprised. He sounded and talked and acted exactly the way he did on screen. Later, I realized how silly it was of me to be surprised by this. I guess I just expected him to be different—a different voice or speech or mannerisms or something. Even though he is so relatable on screen, I kind of assumed his celebrity would make him not relatable in real life. I think it's a lot like what happens to Jimmy—except the opposite. While celebs are assumed to be on a pedestal until an interaction with them makes them human, with a disability, Jimmy is assumed to be "less than" until his actions change that perception.

Michael Cera did not take the picture, and people later asked me if I thought he was a dick for that. I barged in on this dude during a game and talked to him for less than a minute, and I'm supposed to make a judgment on what he's like as a person? If anything, I was the asshole for interrupting his night out. I hate when people say this or that actor is a jerk because he didn't tip well the one time they came into a restaurant, or a musician is a dick because they once refused to take a picture. Maybe they were just being normal people, having a bad day, or in a rush, or whatever. Again, I think it mirrors what happens to Jimmy. When celebrities show that they are in fact human, they risk being ridiculed for the most mundane things. Meanwhile, when Jimmy's actions show that he is not all that different, he is put on a pedestal for simple things like going to a bar or eating at a restaurant.

What I am trying to say is that when other people don't live up to your expectations, it reflects more about you than them—especially because these expectations are usually unfounded, based on stereotypes or assumptions. At least that's what I took away from interacting with ~~a movie star~~ some skinny guy with a soft voice and goofy hat at a Sixers game.

Despite that interesting perspective I gained from that encounter, at the time, I was pissed at Jimmy for making me do that. I hate that kind of shit. Michael Cera was cool about it, however, and I went back to my seat feeling like I did my friend a solid after delivering the shirt. But with no picture to show for it, Jimmy was begging me to go back and get one.

He could go fuck himself.

32

Jimmy Almost Dies

"Do you have Harry's number?" The text read. I saw it when I woke up one Thursday morning. It was from Jimmy's nurse, Aleesha. I noticed the text was sent at 3:30 a.m., and like the rest of the normal world, I had been sleeping. I brushed it off thinking it was just Jimmy being Jimmy, going out too hard and too long on a weeknight.

I texted him later that day, asking him if he got into anything good, and shared with him the odd text I had received from his nurse.

"Eddie! I almost died!" he responded.

I assumed correctly that he did go out on a Wednesday night, and as expected, he went extra hard. He went out with Harry, who bounced after Jimmy gave him the signal—he had an in with this girl that was coming on to him hard. Hugging, kissing, sitting on his lap . . . the whole nine yards. They headed back to his apartment as the bars were closing, a little before 2 a.m., and all signs are pointing to this girl wanting to Marvin Gaye and get it on. They had just stepped onto the elevator when then this chick has a come-to-Jesus moment, and confesses, "I can't do this." She stopped the elevator door as it was closing. "I have a boyfriend."

The button was already pushed for his floor when the girl stepped off. As if this girl couldn't get any worse, with the door closing, she melodramatically blows him a kiss as he sits there, alone and confused.

The greatest tragedies occur nearest the goal, and Jimmy literally had opportunity at his door when it felt apart. I imagine Jimmy riding up the elevator by himself, just full of disappointment and trying to figure out what he did wrong, feeling alone and dreading the early wake-up for work the next day, thinking that it doesn't get worse than this.

Then it does.

When Jimmy gets out of the elevator, CRICK, CRACK, WHOOOOOOOOSSSSSHHHH—the back of his chair gave out. In his new, reclined position, his joystick was out of reach. His phone was also out of reach, so blindly pushing buttons in hopes of getting lucky and calling someone was also out of the question.

He tried to yell and scream. Nothing. Jimmy was stuck there for fifteen minutes. Then thirty. Then an hour. His back started to ache. Two hours. He was getting so fatigued in that awkward position, with his head tilted straight back, that breathing was becoming difficult. Three hours. Dehydrated, in pain, and barely breathing, Jimmy thought that this could very well be it.

Just before 5:30 a.m., a neighbor was leaving for work. She found Jimmy, almost three and half hours after the chair back gave out, stuck in the hallway in the same position the entire time. She lifted the chair back, and Jimmy was finally able to take the deep breath he had been yearning for. On the ground, there was a single screw that must have somehow come loose.

Jimmy was able to get a couple hours of sleep before his alarm went off. He went into the office that day, on time, as if nothing happened.

Now, for anyone to show up to work after an ordeal like that, is incredible. Couple that with what I know about the way people look at Jimmy and the assumptions they make about him—the shock and awe that comes when he shares he has a corporate job—I couldn't help but think about the huge disconnect in people's perception. That very day, I would bet dollars to donuts that somewhere, at some point in his trek from home to the office, someone thought or mentioned to a peer how incredible it is simply that he goes to work. Little did they know that he was powering through a slight hangover, barely any sleep, and the aftershock of a near death experience, as if nothing happened.

"That's messed up that girl would do that," I responded to Jimmy's story, thinking that she should have walked Jimmy back to his room and this all would have been avoided.

"I know," Jimmy replied in agreement, though on a slightly different page. "Like, if you're not going to cheat on your boyfriend, why lead me on all night?"

33

Renting a Beach House

Remember when you told me that renting a beach house is something I could never do?

Jimmy texted Gloria, sending that message first before delivering the blow.

I just put a deposit in for a full summer.

Jimmy is too kind, too non-confrontational—but I personally thought *so fuck you* was warranted at the end of that second text. By the time Jimmy got in on the beach house, it had been months since the two had talked. Their split was solidified with the familiar salt on the "I'm not ready for a relationship yet" wound when, not long after feeding Jimmy that line, Gloria started dating Boyfriend No. 2. In fact, Jimmy had such little faith in Gloria, he was convinced there was some overlap in the relationships. Regardless, despite being out of his life, she was still on his mind. He wanted her to know how stupid she was being.

Sea Isle City is a small piece of paradise about half an hour south of Atlantic City. Every summer, hordes of young adults from Philadelphia and the surrounding area rent houses from Memorial Day to Labor Day, not as a season long vacation, but as a weekend getaway. The weekend ritual was almost a rite of passage for a young professional in the Philadelphia area: after work on Friday, sit in terrible traffic along with everybody else heading down to the Jersey Shore.* Upon arrival, enter into a drunken fantasyland where calories don't count, twenty dollar bills are fun tickets, and dignity, respect, and responsibility become four letter words. The most seasoned weekend warriors would stay for Sunday Jam, drinking an alcoholic lemonade until the day was done. They would get a couple hours of sleep, and then partake in the age-old tradition of "The Drive at Five"—departing fantasyland at 5 a.m. Monday morning, heading back to the city in time for work.

Up until that summer, Jimmy and his brother routinely rented a room at this hotel that was so old-fashioned it looked like a retirement home—simply as a place to crash. They rented from there because it was wheelchair accessible, one of the few options they had in the type of old beach town that doesn't have chain hotels. They frequently got complaints for the loud music they played, or about the guests they would bring back. They would get a warning call from the front desk, and when they wouldn't listen, there would be a knock at the door. The manager would threaten to kick them out . . . until he saw Jimmy. Then, his attitude would change and he would let it slide.

As for me, I would usually stay with friends, crashing wherever there was space, but I was getting tired of sleeping on floors and wanted to be able to head down whenever I wanted. So that year I decided to put together a house myself. Little did I know how frustrating trying to find a place would be. Every house that was wheelchair accessible was either too expensive or too small. I figured there would be six to eight people in our group, and there was nothing I could find that would accommodate our needs . . . and a wheelchair.

Finally, I homed in on a place: a three bedroom, one floor apartment in a complex within walking distance to everything we needed—the bars, the beach, the stores, the

---

* Pronounced "headin downa shore."

basketball courts, mini golf, and Wawa.* Perfect location, perfect size, perfect price. Unfortunately, it wasn't wheelchair accessible.

Jimmy had known I was looking, and I remember explaining to a friend how much I was dreading having to tell him that the place I got wasn't accessible—that he wasn't going to be able to join in the fun.

"I got a place," I told him over the phone.

"Nice . . . what street?" Jimmy replied, automatically assuming he was in. That made me feel even worse.

"Dude, the thing is . . . I couldn't find one that was accessible." I felt terrible.

"It's alright, we'll figure it out." You would think after hanging out with Jimmy for the past five years, I would have learned that for him, there is no such thing as "can't."

"Jimmy, it's not accessible, how would you operate?" I didn't know how to explicitly tell him he couldn't get in on the house with us.

"It's only a place to sleep, I can just be carried in."

"I don't know man, we will be in there a lot."

"I know what we can do . . . I have an old wheelchair at home. We could carry that into the house in the beginning of the summer, and just leave it there. I can use that one when we are inside, and leave my other one for when we go out."

"Dude, you don't get it. It's not accessible. Like, on the third floor kind of not accessible." I thought this was the kicker. There was no way. Three flights of stairs? That would be absurd just to carry Jimmy up—let alone a 250-pound wheelchair.

"So? What's your point?"

"Third floor is my point, Jimmy!"

"And . . ."

"You think that would actually work?!"

"Why wouldn't it?" That was easy for him to say—he wouldn't have to do all the carrying.

Sure enough, when the summer came, four of the guys in the house took about twenty minutes to lug the 250-pound wheelchair up three flights of stairs. Every time we went to the beach, or to the bar, or to get food, one of us carried Jimmy

---

*I know the name looks weird to an outsider, but those who know the area know it is a staple of life in the Philadelphia area. I very well could have just said it was a convenience store, but that would be a disservice to the truth—it's so much more than that.

down the steps, to the wheelchair he left parked under the staircase, or in the storage space if it was raining. And every time—actually, only some of the times—when we came back to the condo, one of us would carry Jimmy back up the steps.

A lot of times, for no other reason than to mess with Jimmy, we would make a house pact to not carry him up. He would be left to garner the kindness of a stranger to give him a lift back upstairs. He didn't mind—he would just make sure that the girls he struck up a conversation with looked like they were up for the task. It was usually a well-endowed female, and on the way up the steps he would encourage her to hold him tight to her chest "so as not to drop him."

At the end of first night, at 3 a.m., when Jimmy completed the challenge and was carried up by an unknown and attractive female, we thought it was the most hilarious thing in the world—especially when he asked her to take him to bed. She did, and was in his room for a bit too, until she made an exit, hastily, to the door. I can only imagine what Jimmy may have said to get her to leave like that. Alone in his room, Jimmy started to call out for us to put him back in his chair, as he didn't want to miss the post-bar party.

As the summer went on, though, Jimmy being carried in by a stranger became less of a spectacle and more of a forgettable routine. We would be gathered around the kitchen table burying our faces in pizza, or glued to an intense game of Mario Kart, when, at 3:30 am, yet another big-breasted female would enter, carrying our roommate Jimmy. We wouldn't even turn our heads. We'd just point to the back room where Jimmy slept. And when the stranger would leave, and Jimmy would call out, incessantly, to either be put into his chair, or for one of the female roommates to accompany him ("Hollaaaaayyyyy . . . come cuddle!"), we would silently laugh to ourselves for a minute or two, pretending like we didn't hear him.

Sometimes, he would simply scream himself to sleep. Other times, his yelling would continue until we couldn't ignore him anymore. We were forced to let the animal back out of his cage, and he would force us to continue the party until the sun peaked out over the ocean.

34

The Samantha Hoopes' Story

Getting back from breakfast one day, I walked into the middle of what seemed like a pretty intense argument. The Kid had invited some of his college friends down the shore for the weekend, and they were all in the living room going at it. Jimmy was on the couch, silent.

"Dude, I think that was her."

"There is no way."

"Her Instagram has her pinned in South Jersey."

"She wouldn't go to the freakin' Ocean Drive."

"She's from the area!"

I was standing there listening, very confused. I had gone out with the other members of the house to a different bar the night before. The Kid filled me in on what they were talking about.

"So last night, there were these two smokes at the bar. Like I mean, they walked in and EVERYONE stopped and stared. Like not just good looking, but like a different breed of woman. Like it was almost uncomfortable how good looking they were. Literally, every guy in the bar was staring at them. Anyway, somehow, they latched on to Jimmy. Both of them started talking to him." He tossed me his phone, showing a picture of both of them giving him a kiss. "And then the one went away, and Jimmy hung out with the other one for pretty much the rest of the night. Next thing I know, I look over, and they are full on making out. In the middle of the back patio, at the OD."

"Who was she?"

"That's the thing. We are pretty sure it was Samantha Hoopes."

He could tell from my reaction, or lack thereof, that I had no idea who that was.

"She's a model."

"A *Sports Illustrated* swimsuit model!" One of his friends added.

I laughed. "For real?"

"There is no freakin' way it was actually her!" Another friend re-started the argument.

"Dude, look, she has posted from the OD in the past! She's definitely been there before."

Still to this day, it is unknown if the person Jimmy made out with was actually a *Sports Illustrated* swimsuit model, or if she was just some run of the mill tall, skinny, blonde, big-breasted chick he met at a shore bar.

When I asked Jimmy whether it was her or not, what she was like, what they talked about, and how he even got to talking with her, he was a little hesitant and kept brushing off the questions—very unlike him.

"Honestly," Jimmy finally came clean, "I was pretty drunk. I barely remember meeting her."

35

A Weighty Conversation

As much as the beach-for-the-weekend lifestyle was touted and celebrated, people usually partake in it for only a few summers. I have always noticed the same people who claim that it is the best time of their lives and party harder than anyone else, are usually the ones who say they need to take a weekend or two off, as if it was an arduous task to go down the shore. These are usually the same people who are loud and proud about being single for the summer, and usually end up in a relationship—or at least the 21st century resemblance of it—halfway through. There is a reason that every year, as Labor Day approaches, people start to say, "I'm ready for this to be done."

The thing is, it's not a sustainable lifestyle. As fun as it looks to escape the real world and enter into that drunken fantasyland, at the end of the day, that is all it is: a fantasyland. Beneath it all, there is a sadness and emptiness that manifests itself in the dreaded booze blues, Sunday scaries, or the Monday morning demons.

Despite his almost unshakeable confidence, Jimmy is no different. Every now and then, he succumbed to valleys that came with the peaks of a Jersey Shore summer. Though it is the number one party drug, at the end of the day, alcohol is a depressant. Mix that with the passionate and sensitive Jimmy, and then throw him in the mix of the very beach town where he met Gloria, doing the things she said he couldn't when she broke up with him—it was bound to happen.

One day on our walk home from happy hour, Jimmy told me he wanted to call Gloria. I told him it was a bad idea, but he did it anyway. When she didn't answer, it set him off. He wanted to be with her, not just in that moment, but for good. Even more so, he wanted to understand why she didn't want to be with him.

"I'm not meant for this world, Eddie," I remember him saying. This was so out of Jimmy's character, I kind of chalked it up to the alcohol. I know they say drunken words are sober thoughts, but that doesn't mean those thoughts are valid. Though I wasn't really worried about what he said or how he was doing in his drunken and exaggerated pain—I knew he would sleep it off—I did know it was genuine pain from a place of confusion. I mean, that was the only night that summer that Jimmy decided to stay in after happy hour. If that doesn't speak to how upset he was, I don't know what does.

The next day, he asked me why there was a call to Gloria on his phone, and if they had talked. I told him he wanted to call, I advised against it, and he did it anyway, and got really upset when she didn't pick up. I stopped there—I didn't think it was good to get into just how upset he really was. We had another day at the beach to enjoy.

Back in Philly, during the week, when it was just the two of us grabbing dinner, I told him how down he got.

"I said that?" Jimmy laughed, as if it I had just told him a funny joke. "I don't believe it."

"I know man, I couldn't believe it either." I thought for a second, before I finally decided to ask him something that had me confused for quite some time. "Why do you like her so much?"

"Eddie, you know this!"

"No, I know, you think she's hot—"

"What else is there?" Jimmy interrupted me, laughing.

I shook my head before I continued. "I know she's hot, and you guys get along, but there's other hot girls, and you get along with just about anyone you spend time with. I guess what am I saying is, is she worth all this trouble? Like what makes her worth all of this bullshit you keep putting yourself through?"

"So, I usually weigh, like, 63 pounds or whatever . . ." Jimmy started. That girl seemed to be the only thing on Jimmy's mind lately—I wasn't surprised he had an anecdote on deck. "The doctor's always said my weight is really important. I should weigh at least 67 pounds, but I started losing weight as my jaw got weaker. It got harder for me to eat. I think at one point I was even down to 60. Well, when Gloria found all this out, she started buying me Ensure and Pedialyte. You know, that stuff old people drink," he laughed. "And when she found out I skip breakfast, she wouldn't only make sure I drank a full one every morning before she left, but she would put me on the scale. I gained like 5 pounds because of her."

I was silent. It wasn't often that Jimmy talks about anything this specific to his condition. I had no idea he had been underweight, and though I didn't know exactly what that meant, it seemed like it wasn't good.

"The point is," Jimmy continued, "other than my family . . . I never felt someone else care about me that much."

That sounded sweet and all, but I didn't buy it. He and I both knew that her "caring" comes and goes as is convenient for her. But I also knew you can't talk someone out of loving someone, and you most certainly can't talk Jimmy out of something when he's made up his mind. I was going to be in his corner regardless. What was more of a concern to me, at this point, was his weight.

"You never mentioned anything about your weight before." I said, trying to conceal my concern with curiosity.

"Yeah, it's not that big of a deal."

"It sounds like it is."

Jimmy rolled his eyes, obviously not worried about it.

"Dude, how can you just brush something like that off? I don't know much, but it sounds pretty important. I would be freaking out."

"I like my lifestyle. And I don't want to give that up. They wanted to give me a feeding tube, and I wasn't about that. I'd rather lose a little weight, and deal with whatever that brings when it comes, than to change what I am doing. I never weigh myself and I never want to know—since I know I don't want to adjust the way I am living, there's really no reason why I need that information. But it was important to her, and that meant something."

His attitude baffled me. I don't know if I have, or ever will, meet someone else who is so determined to live the life he imagined for himself. As I continued to cut up his food, I decided that I was going to force-feed the rest of this cheesesteak down his throat, whether he liked it or not. If he was going to lose weight on his own time, that was fine, but damn it, it wasn't happening on mine.

We moved the conversation on to other subjects, but I could tell Jimmy's mind was still on Gloria, and the question I asked. He knew I didn't buy his answer, and if he was being honest with himself, he didn't either. When there was a break in the conversation, he brought it back up.

"I think the reason I can't . . . I don't want to let her go," he started, "is because I need so many things in my life from other people. I depend on so many people for so much. For the first time, I felt like I was needed by someone else. Not just wanted, but she *needed* me. I was a crutch that she couldn't do without. And that felt good."

That honesty gave me pause.

"Well," I started, after I had a second to think, "that sounds like a super healthy relationship," I said smiling, as I loaded up another forkful.

"I know, right?" he laughed as he chomped down on another bite.

36

Plan B

I don't know if it was because Jimmy proved he could rent a beach house, or if it was just the part of the merry-go-round where Gloria was due to interject herself back into the picture, but she started blowing him up again—texting, calling, wanting to hang out.

Jimmy knew she was still in a relationship, and knew that it was a bad idea to start talking to her again, but those things have never stopped anyone from trying to get back with their ex. He loved her. And he knew that she loved him back. He was desperate to show her that they could work, and wasn't going to turn down a chance to make that a reality. He had nothing but hope that one day, she would be his. He was ready and willing to do anything—and I mean anything.

One Wednesday night back in Philly, sandwiched between those beach weekends, Jimmy called me. I could hear his smile through the phone. "Guess what I'm doing?"

"I don't know, dinner at Rittenhouse?" I knew he had plans to hang out with Gloria that night but I didn't know what his exact plans were.

"No. Plan B," he said, excitedly.

"Plan B?" I didn't know what that meant. I figured Gloria bailed, and I started naming a couple other girls I knew he had been talking to, but I was still confused. I never heard him refer to anyone as a Plan B.

"No, Eddie. Plan B! I'm at the pharmacy . . . you know, getting Plan B."

"That bastard was supposed to tell me when to stop!" Gloria yelled in the background, never one to shy away from even the weirdest type of attention, no matter the setting.

As the two bickered about what brand to buy, I couldn't help but think about the optics of that scene: A beautiful woman going into a pharmacy with an abnormal looking man in a wheelchair on a Wednesday night. I am sure that most people would peg Gloria for an aide or a family member, and may assume Jimmy is going to the pharmacy for a medicine his condition required—or at the very least, something like toothpaste or deodorant. I don't think anyone in the world would have guessed what was actually happening.

"Eddie, could you imagine?" Jimmy chuckled into the phone, "Not only would I get to be a dad, but she would be stuck with me for eighteen years!"

"Not funny, Jimmy!" I heard Gloria say in the background.

37

The Fault in Ourselves

As another weekend down the shore started, Jimmy let it slip that he would be breaking the normal routine and would be heading back to Philly a day early. At first, he wouldn't say why. Finally, after some coaxing, he revealed that he was heading back for a Sunday date with Gloria.

"That's it? What's the big deal?" I didn't understand why he wanted to keep that a secret. Jimmy was silent.

I would find out later that the date was to see a movie, based off of a book, called *The Fault in Our Stars*. He had confided with the girls in the house all of the details, and after Jimmy left, the girls ratted him out. They explained what the movie was about—something about two teenagers who meet in a cancer support group and fall in love, one of them in remission and the other not doing so well. It made total sense why Jimmy wouldn't fess up to that kind of romantic nonsense. It sounded like exactly the kind of movie every guy has to pretend he is too cool for but secretly cries while watching. Apparently, Gloria made Jimmy read the book and wanted to see the film with him, because it "defined their relationship."

The very next weekend, Gloria was invited down to the beach house. The two did what they always do. Had fun, had fights, made up, rinsed and repeated. It was a cycle that seemed to continue indefinitely, a circus ride that would not stop. But what I will always remember from that weekend was sitting on the beach with everyone, in a circle of beach chairs and sprawled out towels, with Jimmy and Gloria in a lengthy debate. Gloria was adamant that life is all luck, while Jimmy asserted that one chooses their own fate. He asked me what I thought, and though I hated to do it, I sided with Gloria . . . and luck. I told him that so many things in life are either available or not, simply because of circumstance.

It wasn't lost to me that, by any normal standard, I have had any and every opportunity in life handed to me. And I pointed that out to Jimmy—so many things in his life were set in stone from the start just because both of his parents, by total chance, carry a gene that only 3% of people have. By having SMA, so much was already determined—he would never walk, or play with toys, or play sports, or hold a job that involved any sort of physical work, among so many other things.

"No, Eddie. Those are things that happen. That doesn't matter. What matters is how you feel about them—your attitude."

Still to this day, I can't get over the fact that I was being told by a man who, since birth, through no choice or design of his own, had so many limitations placed on him, who had so many avenues that would never be open, that life is what you make of it; that you decide how you will interact with the world.

I don't know what it is. I don't know if it is luck, or choice, or both. But I did know that Gloria and Jimmy seemed to do better together than apart, and the option to be together was there for Gloria to take. I just didn't know if it would take some good luck for her to realize that, or if she already knew it was a choice that was hers to make.

38

Talk about Time

"Eddie . . ." Jimmy greeted me, as serious as he was excited.

During the routine dramatic pause, I braced myself for yet another tale of conquest. Despite Boyfriend No. 2 still being in the picture, Gloria and Jimmy were as serious as ever. During this second go-round, Jimmy seemed to have a personal quest in, shall we say, making special memories in public places. The wheelchair lent itself to that—managers didn't think twice about giving him keys to the accessible and spacious family bathroom, and always allowed him to bring along a female companion. He had planted his flag at the most popular bars and clubs, five-star restaurants, and his proudest achievement: The Diamond Club— an exclusive seating area behind home plate—during a Phillies game.

"We had the *realest* talk you can imagine."

"I am sure you did, Jimmy." *Ok good, it wouldn't be another sex tale. Now, bring on the philosophical gibberish.* Between the two of them, there was always a melodrama brewing. They would talk and talk and talk until they came to some sort of conclusion or truth, which they would share with the same kind of overdone reverence that people have when they tell others the meaning of their Chinese symbol tattoo. That shit was exhausting—I don't know how they constantly did it.

"Eddie . . . we talked about time."

Whoa. What did he say? I looked away, too afraid to meet his eyes.

"You know . . . *time.*"

Was this really happening? Was this it? In all our years hanging out—in perhaps the most intimate friendship I have ever had—this was the one topic that we had never breached.

"What did you talk about?" I mustered up the courage to ask, my mind racing as to where this conversation would go, and how the hell I was supposed to handle it.

"We talked about how time is limited. And we talked about how I don't want to waste it. I want to make it count."

The first time this subject was brought to my attention was back in college, within the first couple months of hanging out with Jimmy. Stephanie had called me one day, and said she needed to talk—it was urgent.

She was knocking on my dorm room door in no time, and I opened it to the face of a ghost. She was so scared, and though she wasn't someone I would usually take seriously, her mood had me a little worried.

She was quiet for a while, and I had to beg her to get it out. Finally:

"Ok, so I looked up what Jimmy has, and I saw online that he is expected to die in his twenties."

"Say what?" This was probably the last thing I would have thought she wanted to talk about. In fact, my 19-year-old male brain could only imagine one scenario where she would be that scared, and it could not have been more opposite. I thought she was pregnant.

"I know, right. What do we do?"

I was never one to have an immediate reaction. Whenever there is a possibility of emotion taking over, I tend to throw up a wall. It's a super healthy thing to do, I know.

"I don't think there is anything we can do." Not to sound insensitive, but I definitely laughed a little at the suggestion that we had any sort of say in the matter.

"Well, do we tell him?"

"NO! No, Stephanie, no." A suggestion like this is why I usually had a hard time taking her seriously. "He probably already knows, and if he doesn't, how would it help?"

Over the years, there have only been three other times where this subject was brought to my attention. What I found interesting about my reaction in each exchange was that it only reiterated what Jimmy has always talked about—intent. The way I felt about these situations had more to do with my perceived intent of the people in them, than with what was actually said or done.

Once, while playing cards, someone was asking about Jimmy's condition—not an unusual occurrence. What was unusual, though, was that they weren't asking me about it, and I was more than content to not partake in this conversation for the millionth time. Focused on the card game, I was half listening to the questions that are always asked about his health. My ears perked up when I heard one that, at that point, I had never before heard asked.

"So, like, does it affect how long he can live?" I checked my cards, but the only thing I was interested in was in the way this guy, a mutual friend of Jimmy and me, was going to respond.

"It does," he said, rather bluntly. "Honestly, at this point, he is on borrowed time."

There was silence for a moment, as everyone acknowledged the implication of that answer. When conversation picked back up, it drowned into background noise. All I could think about was how I felt like that response should have upset me . . . but it didn't. He didn't mean to be disrespectful—he was just trying to answer the question the best he knew how. And it seemed like the information was received with the respect it deserved. As I thought about what he said with an open mind, my inner dialogue to hearing Jimmy being on *borrowed time* was, "Aren't we all?"

The second time I encountered this same exact question of life expectancy was one of the most absurd conversations I have ever been part of. Sitting around a dinner table, somebody was talking about Jimmy in a way that would let the world know that they were friends with a guy in a wheelchair.

"We will be out, and people will be looking at us, but I don't care." *You care enough to bring it up now, asshole.* "And I'll tell Jimmy, who cares what other people think. Let them look." *Yeah, like Jimmy needs to be told that. I doubt that happened. Funny how you're not sharing how often I've heard you unloading your problems on Jimmy, looking to him for comfort, guidance, and encouragement.* "I like to keep it light with him . . . I always tell him if he gets out of hand I am going to pop those tires of his!" I don't know what pissed me off more, the way this person was talking, or the fact that the table laughed at what is probably the most unoriginal wheelchair joke in the entire world. And it doesn't even make sense. *His tires are Styrofoam, dumbass.*

"Really though, it is amazing, all the things he does, despite everything." *Here we go . . . now that you created an intimate and personal relationship with the guy in the wheelchair, here is the part where you get all sentimental and heartfelt, all while making sure you and your loud humility never leave the spotlight.* "I mean, I think of his struggles, and his physical health, it's really so inspirational. Even when I am helping him, I feel like he is helping me . . . "

Classic.

"Does it affect his life expectancy?" someone at the table asked. *Great. Happy for you to have chimed in.*

"I am sure it does, but I don't know exactly." *Everyone needs to shut the fuck up.* "I mean, I know it's not normal . . . like, it's a lot less than normal. But I don't know the exact number." *Stop fucking talking about him like this.* "Eddie probably knows better than me."

Are you fucking kidding me? Are you that fucking stupid that you don't see me sitting here staring at my plate, not speaking? Don't you think that means something?

"Well, what is it?" someone asked.

"I'd rather not talk about this."

"Oh, come on, just say it."

"Yeah, come on."

"What is it?"

"Is it less than 30? More than—"

"Look," I interjected into the peppered demands. "If you care that much, you should ask him." There was an awkward silence, until someone changed the conversation to a totally different subject. I continued to stare at my plate, trying to calm myself down. *Did that really just happen? They were acting like I was holding out on how many pieces of candy were in a fucking jar.*

The third time this subject was brought to my attention, though, was the one that really got me thinking. Jimmy had started writing what he intended to be an autobiography, but instead morphed into the blog he currently runs today. In the early stages, however, he loved nothing more than to show his work to others. One day a friend had stopped by to see Jimmy and fell victim to his demand to read it (out loud, of course). In what seemed to be a completely objective and honest assessment, the friend told me later that he really enjoyed it, but in order for Jimmy's writing to be taken seriously he would have to address what everyone was thinking: life expectancy.

His comment surprised me as much as Stephanie had in my dorm room five years prior. I get how people can look at Jimmy and think dependency, or weakness, or even sadness and struggle. But I had no idea the subject of death was even on the radar when people looked at him, and I wondered why I missed something that apparently was so obvious to others.

I grew up with a grandmother who was once stranded in the ocean atop a piece of wreckage, clinging on to a railing for her life, helpless as she watched her father and brother drowned in a boating accident. She then had to be the one to inform her mother (my great-grandmother) that her husband and only son were gone. I never got to meet her, but I know that was the second time in her life my great-grandmother lost two members of her immediate family in a single day. The first was when she came home from school to discover her own mother and brother were gone, disappearing in the throes of the Armenian Genocide, never to be seen or heard from again. At the ripe age of nine, she had no other choice but to check herself into an orphanage. I would often ask if my great-grandmother was bitter, revisiting the question because I had hard time believing what I was told. Time and time again the answer would come back that she was anything but, and would always say, "You can't get upset at people today for things that happened in the past." I once asked my grandmother what it was like in the aftermath of the shipwreck, and how she handled it. "I gave myself one day to cry," she said, "and then moved on. Life wasn't going to stop, so I had to keep going."

I was raised by a mother who was in that same boating accident, and from a young age, instilled in me that life is a precious and fragile gift that can be taken away at the most unexpected time. Mixed with that, I have an unfaltering optimist for a father—the kind of guy who once got a flat tire on the highway and immediately smiled to my brother riding with him, saying, "Thankfully it's on the right side," because that allowed him to change the tire on the shoulder, shielded from traffic.

Granted, it was probably not the healthiest thing to assume that every time my mother was late picking me up from basketball practice could only and most definitely mean she was in a terrible and horrific car accident. And, granted, there are times when I am convinced my dad's optimism borderlines delusion, particularly when it comes to rooting for Philadelphia sports teams. Regardless, I believe that these things played a major role in shaping my attitude towards death.

I have an uncanny ability to compartmentalize things, as every woman in my life has made it a point to tell me. Like Jimmy, I am good at ignoring the things I know I can't change. Some people seem to think it is a major character flaw—that I shouldn't always believe things are going to work out and I should worry more, but I don't understand why. Maybe because he is such a good friend of mine, I always avoided making Jimmy's death an issue. Then again, maybe because it was never an issue to me, we could become such good friends. I can't say for sure either way.

I had never told Jimmy any of these things, and I didn't tell him on that day he told me about his conversation with Gloria, either. I just asked him questions and let him talk. I didn't think I could add any value to the conversation by opening my mouth. He told me that Gloria got really upset talking about the subject, and admitted to thinking about it a lot.

"She even cried when she thought about not having me around," Jimmy told me. "I said she shouldn't think about that kind of stuff. It does no good. And I told her what I always tell her . . . all you should focus on is what you can control.

"It doesn't make sense to me, Eddie. I don't get how people can get so upset over things that didn't even happen yet."

39

The Pathetic Part of Sympathetic

At that age, it feels as good to feel bad as it does to feel good.

—John Hughes

My maternal grandmother can put on a "sweet little ol' lady" act when she needs her groceries carried to her car, but don't be fooled: she is four feet eleven inches of hellfire. She is one of those people who seem to be at their happiest when they are angry, yelling about the township or the weather or the news anchor's outfit. Raised in the depression-era Bronx by immigrant parents, she went through a lot in her life, but never complained or expected anything from anyone. I am talking about an eighty-something-year-old lady who uses a walker but still rakes her own front lawn. I learned a lot from that woman, but perhaps the most valuable lesson was the difference between sympathy and empathy.

When I would walk into her house with that recognizable *the world is against me* attitude teenagers have, she would hop up from her table and put something on the stove, as all old, round, grandmothers do. She would ask about things, and sometimes gave advice, but usually only if I asked for it. One thing she wouldn't do, though, was give me any sort of sympathy. No matter how upset, or angry, or down I was, I never got that sense that she felt sorry for me.

There is something to be said about the comfort and feeling of safety that comes from being coddled, no matter how temporary that feeling is. But this feeling of respect my grandmother had for me was something different. It was something that wouldn't allow me to believe that whatever it was that had me down was bigger than me. And because I knew that she wasn't ever going to feel sorry for me, there was no sense in feeling sorry for myself . . . especially when I was around her. It was something that made me believe I was going to get through whatever it was I was going through. It wasn't empty or fleeting. It was real.

One day she told me a story from her past about a family friend who always seemed to be having a hard time. She was constantly asking for help—or "handouts," as my grandmother called it. My grandmother was never happy when other friends and family readily sent her the money or the things she was asking for. After a while, my grandmother was insistent on "not giving her anything as much as a slice of bread." She reminded her friend that she was a grown woman, and she could go get herself a job and stop pretending the world was so hard on her.

Sometime later, that woman attempted suicide.

"We are not seeing her," my grandmother said to her husband. She was firm.

Not long after that, the friend attempted suicide again.

Again, my grandmother was adamant about not going to the hospital.

The third time this woman attempted suicide she was refusing all visitors, specifically requesting that no one be allowed in to visit—except for my grandmother.

When she heard of this special request, my grandmother went. She told her friend, as she was lying in a hospital bed fresh off an attempt at her own life, that this was no way to be acting. She told her she had a good life, and she was capable of getting a good job and to "knock the bullshit off." And that is exactly what that woman did.

I am not naïve enough to think that this is the answer for depression or the be-all and end-all way to treat people facing hardships. For every story where tough love succeeds, you can find one where it is misunderstood, or where sympathy is helpful.

What I find extremely interesting about this story, though, is that of all the people in the world, that lady who was struggling only wanted to see the one person who hadn't given her handouts.

The way I see it, she wanted to see the one person who respected her enough not to give her something—the person who believed in her enough to leave her to her own abilities. Sympathy can be a drug worse than alcohol or any pill prescribed when it gives the recipient a sense of entitlement, weakness, and dependence. At first it feels great, but in its aftermath it ostracizes and weakens, leaving the one who gave sympathy feeling elevated and different, and the one who received it only wanting more, since their situation has not changed.

*　　*　　*

From the moment [dis]ABLE started getting a little traction on social media, people assumed I was involved. I am sure some of it had to do with Jimmy and I being such good friends, but I am also sure that most of it had to do with people thinking Jimmy couldn't do it on his own. It would bother Jimmy, and understandably so, when I relayed to him stories of people who thought I was involved with the brand, and he would wonder aloud, "Why the hell would they think you are part of this?"

Almost a year after launching [dis]ABLE, Jimmy had sold over a thousand shirts. In addition to hand-to-hand sales, he had created a website, started a blog, and even made sure to attend celebrity events with the intent of getting someone famous in a shirt. As he was expanding, he was looking to bring someone else on board, and he called me.

I was really good friends with Jimmy, and he knew of my capabilities and work ethic. He could trust me and he also knew that I was 100% behind the brand's mission, believing in it fully. Of all the people who wanted to be a part of what he was doing, however, he wanted me for one reason more than any other: I was the only one, he explained, who ever gave him negative feedback.

When he started selling the shirts, I would hear in passing conversations little details, like the logo faded quickly, or the shirts shrank and no longer fit. Instead of returning these shirts, people would usually keep it to themselves, or sometimes just buy a new one without any mention of the problem they encountered. It wasn't until I told Jimmy about these complaints that he was able to adjust and remedy those problems.

Jimmy told me that he would be excited to have me on board because he was wise enough to know that most people didn't give him the necessary and helpful feedback a non-disabled person may have gotten—the kind of feedback they would share with me but not Jimmy. It's not like I was excited to tell him where he had to improve, I just wanted to make sure he had a fair shot in making his brand the best it could be.

Now, Jimmy will admit that he is terrible at receiving any sort of criticism, being that so few people actually say anything bad to him. On the other hand, when I see something for the first time, my thoughts immediately go to, *What is wrong with this and how could it be better?* I will admit that I am not always the best at relaying that in the most sensitive manner. People often seemed surprised to find out that we get in arguments, and it still surprises me when they are surprised. Just because Jimmy is in a wheelchair doesn't mean that he doesn't have strong opinions, and it doesn't mean that I am going to hold back from telling him when I disagree with those opinions, and vice versa.

When he had approached me about becoming part of what he was doing, it was not a request for some extra help or volunteer time, or even to offer part time work. He approached me with an investment opportunity, because he knew that he had something really good building and believed in his company.

I also believed in the brand's mission, and was excited for the chance to join in a business venture with a friend, but I did have trepidations. First, I had little knowledge about the apparel industry, and absolutely no sense of fashion to go with it. When picking out an outfit for a night out, I have a strict rule of thumb: if I think it looks good, don't wear it. If I think it looks bad, wear it. Believe you me, I get more compliments on the outfits I think look ridiculous than those I think look good.

I got past that pretty quickly, knowing that my contribution to the company wouldn't depend on my middle-school sense of style—that was Jimmy's department. What I was really worried about is how the brand might be received, particularly from those who saw it as a sympathetic and charitable cause.

I had been to a few events where Jimmy was selling shirts. There were people who saw the design and immediately latched on to it. There were others who had their interests sparked with the design, and after hearing Jimmy's story, and what the brand was all about, wanted to be a part of it, even if it was to just take a flyer and follow the blog.

Then there were the people who felt bad for Jimmy. The people who would hear Jimmy say, "I have a clothing brand," and reach for their wallets or purses before they even saw the clothing. The people who would come to the table and hand Jimmy money, sometimes without a single word, other times, announcing to everyone within earshot that they want to make a donation. It was a weird thing, seeing Jimmy tell someone, "That is extremely kind and the gesture is appreciated, but this is a for-profit company and I don't accept donations." Sometimes, they would insist, and against his wishes leave the money on the table.

I get it, and so does Jimmy. After all, it is a brand named "disable." The thing of it is that these are exactly the kind of people that Jimmy wants to reach, to show "disability" isn't synonymous with "charity." I was worried about how hard that task would be, or if it was even possible. Was it actually realistic to think that if someone bought a shirt under that premise, the brand mission would ever get across?

I was also worried because I knew that all of those people making that purchase out of sympathy were doing more to hurt the brand than to help. Still to this day, I wonder if certain people we meet are actually *that* excited about the brand, or if they are just trying to be nice and charitable. It kills us. It would be better to know what customers don't like about the product, so that we could adjust and make it better. It's like, imagine you want to become a great chef, so you decide to cook dinner for your family and friends every week. But the only feedback you ever receive is that the food was "absolutely incredible." Eventually, you would start to wonder if your diners actually liked the meal, or if they were just being polite—all the while remaining clueless as to where and how to improve your craft.

Jimmy and I had quite a few talks about this, and finally I decided to go forward with it. We began "negotiations," and after some conversation, we agreed on a price, and I wrote Jimmy a check for a chunk of my savings that might give my grandmother a heart attack.

I didn't tell her how much it cost me to become a minority-owner of [dis]ABLE. But when I told her I invested, I was reminded of how nice it is when sympathy is there to sugarcoat opinions.

"A t-shirt that says 'disable?' That's the STUPIDEST thing I ever heard! Why would anyone ever wear that? I don't need to advertise that I'm disabled! I have a walker. Everybody already knows!"

40

Notes from a Communications Major

If you will kindly indulge me for just a moment, I must share an observation— sure for the sake of the story, and the theme, and blah, blah, blah . . . in reality I just want to talk about this topic so I don't think that I wasted fifty grand for a piece of paper that says I studied Communications.

Before he took me on as a partner, Jimmy had been making most sales personally, carrying a duffel bag full of t-shirts on the back of his chair wherever he went, telling people about the brand whenever he had the chance. Some additional sales came from the blog he ran, and some via word of mouth. He wanted to expand the brand even further, and we thought Kickstarter would be a good way to help us do that.

We put together somewhat of an event tour to coincide with the Kickstarter campaign. Some of the events were local, but we were particularly excited for a couple that were quite a distance away. The two months in which we ran the campaign were the most hectic, and best, that the brand had experienced up until that point.

One of the most common pieces of advice to running a successful Kickstarter is to get media exposure. Neither one of us had ever written a press release before, but that didn't deter us. We both have the mindset that if someone else in the world figured out how to do it, we could too. Granted, I learned that lesson from my dad, who drilled it into me every time I wanted to quit something, like fixing a car or putting together furniture from IKEA. He'd say that it was just some guy somewhere who built the thing first and I could figure it out. Meanwhile, Jimmy garnered it by thinking things like "if someone else who can't use all four limbs can live by himself at college, so can I." Slightly different journeys to get to the same conclusion, but the point is, you put two people together with that mindset and the idea of not being able to do something gets further and further away.

"This whole thing reeks of irony," I laughed as we looked at our press release. It was titled "MAN with SMA launches a Kickstarter campaign to expand his start-up business."

"How so?"

"The whole point of the brand is that people with disabilities are no different than anyone else, right? But you and I both know we got a pretty good shot at getting some attention because of your disability. Able-bodied people start apparel brands every day and you don't see that in the news."

"Don't you think that speaks to how important and unknown my message is?"

"Oh, I definitely see that. I'm just saying, we are a brand with a message that says disabled people are no different, and are basically titling this press release, 'Disabled person achieving something.'"

"Yeah, well, the media eats that shit up."

"Just another disgusting example of wheelchair privilege."

Within a week, someone from my home-county newspaper reached out to do a story. Jimmy and I both took half days off from work and met the reporter at a coffee shop. She was very friendly, and I followed Jimmy's lead, as he seemed like a duck in water talking to her about his life, and his disability, and what he hopes to accomplish. We both left there in high spirits, happy with how it went and excited that we managed to garner some press.

Jimmy passed that article along to the person at the *Philadelphia Inquirer* who had covered his employment benefits debacle, and within a week, Jimmy was on the phone with me, reveling in how well the interview went with the *Inquirer* reporter.

"He really seemed to get me," Jimmy told me on the phone, explaining how their meeting went way longer than originally planned, but neither of them cared. "And, oh yeah," he added before hanging up. "He asked for your number, he will probably call you tonight to or tomorrow."

"Cool," I tried to play it off like it was nothing, but I was immediately nervous. Not only would this be over the phone, but it would be for a newspaper article, too. Without Jimmy on the call, it would be just me talking to this guy I never met. On top of that, I was familiar with the guy's work in the *Inquirer,* and I thought he was a really good reporter. What that translated to in my mind is that he was going to spend every second of that interview judging whatever I said, in order to form a perception that he could then try to put on a page.

Sure enough, when the call came, I blabbered on and on, tripping over words and running out of breath as I paced up and down in the alleyway next to my building. Afterwards, I called Jimmy, telling him how terrible it went, and he tried to console me to no avail. Fortunately, when the article came out on the front page of the local section in the Sunday edition of the paper, there was nothing of me in it more than a mention of being a college friend and a business partner. It was nice to be reminded that I was just a sideshow to this whole thing, and could totally suck as much as I wanted in these newspaper interviews.

The Tuesday after, Jimmy called me, acting funny.

"Eddie, is today a good day?"

"What?"

"Is today a good day?"

"Of course it is."

"Is Thursday a good day?"

"What are you talking about?"

"Is Thursday a good day to go on *Good Day Philadelphia*?"

"Seriously?" I like to go into things like writing the press release confident it will work out, but that doesn't mean I don't get super surprised when it actually does. Jimmy explained that someone he knew from college saw him in the paper, passed the article along to her producer, and they wanted us to come on the morning show. That meant in just two weeks, we were able to get coverage from the local paper, city paper, and television in a top five media market.

Jimmy didn't know if they were going to have him, or both him and me on, but I figured I would check out the studio, regardless. I planned on meeting the ever-confident Jimmy the morning of our first TV appearance in front of the Fox Philadelphia building—but I had never before met the Jimmy who showed up. He was as nervous as a snowman in a sauna. He couldn't stay still, wanting to sit in the backstage lounge, then go outside, then go back into the lounge—even offered to buy the assistant producers coffee for an excuse to go back out. I was only half-joking when I told him he should have taken a couple of shots before he left his apartment, and he said that it probably would have been a good idea, had he not had to go to work right after the show.

As they were putting his mic on, I tried to talk that "I'm about to see a ghost" look off of Jimmy's face, when another production assistant came up and started wiring a mic onto me.

"Well, I guess I am going on with you, Jimmy." Aside from the fact that Jimmy was nervous enough for the two of us, finding out I was going to be interviewed on live television in just a few minutes did not really faze me. I had been on my high school morning news show, where I learned that if I forgot about the camera and just talked to the people on the set, all the hoopla of being broadcasted would go away. Plus, facing potential rejection and ridicule from an entire student body of vicious teenagers who know you personally is a lot more daunting than a city of strangers that will forget about what they saw within a week, if not that same day. On top of all that, I had done plenty of on-camera exercises in college, and worked at and been in multiple television studies. As trivial as those experiences may sound, I believe it played a pretty huge part in me not having the same nervousness that most people might have in or around a television studio. I figured all I had to do was be friendly, smile, and not say anything racist, sexist, or homophobic. Not a difficult task.

In front of the cameras, waiting for the show to come back from commercial, I was snapping selfies while Jimmy looked like a deer in headlights. Before I knew it, I heard our Kickstarter video playing throughout the studio. I looked at the monitor to see the video being broadcasted across all of the Delaware Valley. I had spent forever editing that damned thing, using nothing but iMovie to try to make the video we shot on an iPhone somewhat presentable, and the fact that *Good Day Philadelphia* deemed it worthy to broadcast had me feeling like the next Scorsese. In that moment, I couldn't have cared less about [dis]ABLE—I was ready to jump on the next plane to Hollywood and take a crack at show biz. As I heard the video come to a close, I had to bring myself back to reality. *Ok Ed, stop daydreaming and focus. You are about to be on TV.*

The interview went exactly how I thought it would go, except for the part where the host—who I had seen earlier in the men's room, wiping his eyes and holding his head, telling me "Sure was one hell of a night last night"—introduced me as Greg Doyle. They talked about the celebrities in the video, the brand and its message, and asked Jimmy what he hoped to accomplish with the brand and the Kickstarter. I did find it funny when I saw a banner across the monitor that read, "JIMMY CURRAN HAS BEEN IN A WHEELCHAIR SINCE HE WAS 2-YEARS-OLD." Not saying that isn't a point of interest, it's just that on the screen it looked like it was breaking news.

Once off air, Jimmy's short answers to anything I said let me know how disappointed he was in how it went. "I was so nervous," and "I don't think I got my point across" were the only explanations he actually offered up as to why he was upset. In my personal opinion—and I would be the first person to tell him if he sucked—I thought he did a good job. But he didn't want to hear it.

As we walked out of the station and to the bus stop so we could head back to work, I noticed a sad-looking man sitting on a chair in front of a bank. There was a bullhorn at his feet, and he sat in between two large signs that read, "Why does TD Bank discriminate against & take advantage of the disabled & sick?" And "TD Bank. America's most convenient Bank?? I don't think so!! Not if you get sick! And certainly not if you become hospitalized!"

"You better be careful looking all down and out like that, Jimmy. People may think you are here for the protest." Jimmy looked up to see what I was talking about.

"Eddie!" Jimmy finally cracked a smile. "This is the bank where I have the business account!"

"This is too good. We have to get a picture."

"Dude, the signs are literally hanging from the railing of the accessible ramps!"

I try to be as fair and open minded as possible, and I fully realize that I don't know the whole story. I don't know what happened to this man, or the events and circumstances that brought him to stand in front of a business and accuse it of practicing a terrible, terrible thing. And just because he could walk, and hold a sign, I am not implying that severity of disability matters. It is great that this man was exercising his right to free speech, but part of the greatness of free speech that I think a lot of people forget is that it allows others to form an opinion, too.

So there I am, someone who is not disabled, looking at these two people, knowing one of them very well, and not knowing the other from anything more than what I see, and I couldn't help think about the stark contrast. On one hand is a man who brought a chair, a bullhorn, and two signs, in order to spend his time and energy to sit there and blame a bank for his problems, while offering no reason as to why, and right there next to him is another man with a disability who was mad at himself because he thought he could have done much better on the television show he was just featured on, for the business he started, which has an account at that exact bank that allegedly discriminates against people like him.

"Couldn't make this shit up, Jimmy." With my phone out for the picture, I thought to check the Kickstarter account. The inbox was flooded with notifications—we had sold around one hundred shirts in about thirty minutes.

"Told you it wasn't that bad," I said, as I put the phone in his lap for him to see. It definitely lightened his mood, but still to this day, he refuses to watch the clip.

It was interesting to see the effect media exposure had on the brand's reception—especially television. After the publicity, the people who rolled their eyes when told about the brand were now on board, and those who had supported it from the start seemed to think it was now a Fortune 500 company. Literally nothing was different about it from before, but everyone's perception of it seemed to have either flipped or become magnified. Even my grandmother warmed up to it slightly.

More interesting to me was the polar reactions that Jimmy and I had to the two different mediums. I was comfortable being on a live television talk show because I knew there was no filter, no editing, no reporter potentially making me into something I am not—it's just me being me and the audience gets what they see on the screen. It is so much different than talking to a newspaper reporter, where the constant worry of how I may be coming off to him with anything I say or do, overwhelms me.

Jimmy, on the other hand, loves that. He finally gets a chance to be perceived as a regular guy in the paper. He knows that the more anyone gets to know him, the further away that chair gets. The journalist has the time to learn about Jimmy the person, and translate that perception into a story about him—not necessarily the disability. On television, however, the audience has a visual that brings with it so many ideas and connotations— the very misconceptions he is trying to erase—and he only has a short and limited time slot to clearly articulate his message. Perhaps it is that thought that overwhelms him; the nervousness of us each coming from the very common fear of how we will be perceived.

Our second, and last, television appearance for our Kickstarter campaign was at a television station in a smaller city located north of Philadelphia. Though Allentown is the third largest city in the state, the studio was located in the middle of nowhere, and compared to the hustle and bustle of downtown Philadelphia, the perception of low viewership made Jimmy a little less nervous.

Regardless, I am kind of anal when it comes to preparing for any sort of presentation. Shoot, I'll even give a to-go order a practice run if it's a big one. As we drove through the farmlands to get to the station, Jimmy and I were reviewing the list of questions the reporter had sent to us, when we got to one that set me off.

What is it about the word "disability" that bothers you most?

"I'll be honest, man, I don't know if we would have become such good friends if you were the politically correct type. I'd be so nervous and uncomfortable. I never understood that shit—people are so damn sensitive I could very well be offending people by using the word 'sensitive.' Instead, maybe I should say 'emotionally quick to respond.' I'm not advocating insults here, I'm just saying, at what point did it become cool for adults to get offended by words other adults say? I always wonder where the hell those people grew up . . . did they skip grade school? I'm assuming they didn't, so come on. Channel your inner 5th grader and get over it. Especially if they're around our age. I mean, we grew up in the heyday of sexist and homophobic slurs. Shit, most of my childhood—I didn't even know 'gay' meant *gay*. I just thought it was a word the cool kids used to describe half the things I said, did, or wore. If I could deal with it then, I would expect an adult to be able to deal with it now."

I paused for a second, in case Jimmy wanted to tell me how insightful my diatribe was. He said nothing, so naturally I seized the opportunity to keep spouting off. "And who the hell even decides which terms are the offensive ones? You know how people are always bitching about the name of the Washington Redskins? You know that every time they survey . . . uh . . . can I say American Indians? Even though that name comes from Columbus thinking he landed in India? Or do I call them Native Americans? Even though technically, anyone born in the Americas are native to it. How about this . . . whenever they survey actual Redskins, asking them how they feel about the name, it always comes back that they don't give a shit.

"You done yet?" Jimmy asked. This wasn't the first time he has heard me go off on a rant like this.

"No. When the hell are we going to be done with 'African-American?' First off all, most of the time, I could do without the qualifier. Sorry Aunt Gertrude, the fact that it was an African-American who carried your groceries to your car doesn't thicken the plot for me. Second of all, if the qualifier is necessary, can't you just say 'black?' It's not a bad word. God forbid we consider him a normal American. Nope. He is an African-American. Half the time I hear that term I think, *white guilt*, because they sure as hell aren't using 'European Americans' as if 'white' was a curse word." I finally took a breath. "Ok, now I'm done."

"Feel better now?"

"Honestly . . ." I couldn't help but laugh when I realized the answer. "No."

"Do you know where the word 'handicap' comes from?"

"I do not."

"Most people don't. All of these people throw it around, thinking they are being politically correct . . . handicap parking, handicap seating. The term handicap comes from the fact that way back when, I mean before power chairs or accessible anything, disabled people really had no other option in life but to beg, asking for money on the street with their 'cap in hand.' Hence the term: handicap. People don't realize that their P.C. term is rooted in something pretty insulting."

Jimmy continued by asking me if I remembered an encounter we had with a guy who worked for a public relations firm. He was a little older, and he was someone who just didn't get the brand—didn't get the mission, didn't get the idea, and didn't get Jimmy.

He had asked if Jimmy's employer knew that if he had started the brand on the side of his full-time job, and if they were supportive of it. They did, and they were.

"If I can be totally honest, no offense," the PR guy prepped his statement. "From a press standpoint it looks really good for your employer that they hired you, and they are letting you do this brand."

We were almost at the TV station when I told Jimmy that I did indeed remember that encounter, and that specific statement stood out to me as well.

"There was nothing at all wrong about what he said . . . it was a true statement, and it wasn't something that I didn't know. But what I didn't like is that he felt the need to preface it . . . that he was afraid he would be offensive." Jimmy thought for a moment, before he continued.

"I guess that is how I would answer the question . . . what bothers me most about 'disability' is that it bothers other people."

41

The Make-a-Wish Story

At one event, our table was positioned across from the Make-A-Wish Foundation. The rep was super cool, and we carried a solid conversation throughout the event during any down time. At one point, when the rep stepped away to grab lunch, Jimmy had a story for me.

"Remember that audio equipment in my dorm room?"

Back when he started rapping, he told me, he really wanted to get the equipment necessary to make his own music. Unfortunately, that stuff is expensive for the average adult, let alone a middle-schooler. In classic Jimmy fashion, however, he wasn't going to let a little thing like money stand in the way of getting what he wanted. The pre-teen Jimmy did some research, and found a solution. He applied to the Make-A-Wish Foundation. "They ended up getting me a top-notch audio set worth, like, ten grand."

If you are anything like me, you only see those Make-A-Wish specials on ESPN or the nightly news and store them away in your head as a nice little story . . . almost like a fairy tale. What

I tend to lose in that process is that the recipients are just ordinary people in extraordinary circumstances.

"You don't use it anymore, do you?" I asked.

"Nah, I stopped rapping when my mouth got a little weaker," Jimmy smiled. "Lucky for every rapper out there, too." SMA is a progressive disease—he no longer had the necessary strength in his jaw to articulate his Grammy-worthy raps.

"Where's the equipment? Your mom's?"

"Nah, I sold it."

"You what?"

"I sold it. I used to charge others to record on it in college, but since I stopped doing that, I didn't need it anymore."

I kind of found that hilarious. Don't get me wrong; I think the Make-A-Wish Foundation is one of the best around. But if it wasn't for Jimmy, I probably would continue to think of the recipients as unlucky charity cases, instead of just regular people. In essence, Jimmy used Make-A-Wish to get something very expensive that he wanted, and then sold it when he didn't want it anymore. I am not saying there is a flaw in system; in fact, he used the system exactly in the way it was intended. All I'm saying is that in my mind, what usually follows a Make-A-Wish story isn't a sale for profit; it's a beer commercial with talking animals.

All that being said; we didn't bother to relay that story to our new friend at the Make-A-Wish table when she came back from her lunch break.

42

The First Expo

There is a traveling convention known as the Abilities Expo, geared toward people with disabilities. There are companies and organizations promoting all sorts of services and products there, including accessible vehicles, wheelchairs, home care, as well as companies that are not exclusively for those with disabilities, such as financial services, or insurance companies.

We scheduled a handful of events to attend while we ran our Kickstarter campaign. The "event tour" started in Edison, New Jersey, right outside of the Big Apple. It was considered the New York City leg of the Expo, and we were told it was always the show with the biggest turnout.

We were excited and nervous. Not only had we never done an expo like this before, but we considered it our first real test. This would be the first time we would be presenting the limited clothing line we had outside the Philadelphia region, to complete strangers.

Aside from the fact that there would be no friends or family, or even those who knew or heard about us through friends or family, we were especially excited because it was going to be a convention of people with, or familiar with, disabilities. We hoped that meant we would be less likely to encounter some of the things we did at other events, like the assumptions of charity, or the pity purchases, or the conversations that took a turn when I pointed to Jimmy and mentioned that he created the brand. All of a sudden, the person's voice would raise and their excitement blew up, as if they were talking to a puppy that barked at the door to go outside instead of shitting on the rug.

We were starting to realize how difficult it is to grow when people only meet you with positivity. We understand that everyone who comes to our table isn't going to buy a shirt, even if they do like the idea or design. But when 9 out of the 10 people who don't buy a shirt are enthusiastic and in awe and over the top about "what an incredible idea this is," telling Jimmy he is amazing and inspiring, it makes you wonder. I can't tell you how many times someone who didn't make a purchase told us we should be on Shark Tank. I bite my tongue, but on the inside, I'm thinking, *If you aren't making a purchase, what makes you think the people on Shark Tank would? Or can you admit that what you're really saying is a guy in a wheelchair who started a business, no matter what it is, plays well on TV?* We thought it would be much less likely for someone at the Abilities Expo to make a "pity purchase," or worse, to patronize Jimmy, than it would be anywhere else. After all, people don't have sympathy for what is commonplace in their own life.

The first couple hours of the show were a little slow, but then again, we didn't know what to expect. Finally, we found our groove, made some adjustments, and throughout the weekend, continued to make adjustments and figure out what would work best for us. In fact, there was a guy at the booth next to us who had no qualms telling us that there were parts of our setup that were far from ideal. He was with an insurance company, but had worked in retail for many years before and made suggestions that helped us improve our setup. He was probably the best thing that happened to the brand that weekend and he didn't even buy a shirt.

There are often times at events when our table gets swarmed with people, and Jimmy is backlogged, trying to ring up the customers on his iPhone while I am scrambling around to find a requested size or style. The first time this happened, however, at that first expo, is something I will never forget. It was a rush, standing in a booth as part of a business that was new and appealing, being part of a brand that was causing so many people walking by to be interested and excited about it. We had never dealt with anything like that before, and in the midst of all the unfamiliar chaos Jimmy and I paused for a moment, catching each other's eye with a look that said, *"Hot damn! Is this really happening?"*

After the first day of the expo, we talked about how cool it was to see the effect the brand had on so many people there. Jimmy said he was hoping that it would be something new for those with disabilities—something that could represent how they felt about themselves—how Jimmy felt about himself. "This doesn't say 'please accept me because I am different,'" he said as he reflected on the day's success over drinks. "Not that there is anything wrong with that message. It's just not my message. This says 'I accept me,' you know? Yeah, I have limitations, but so what. Don't we all?"

Regardless of the way people feel about the brand, it is undeniable that it takes guts to make something new and try to make a business out of it. It requires doing something most people try so desperately to avoid: making yourself vulnerable to rejection and failure. It is something I feel every time I talk about [dis]ABLE . . . and I didn't even create it.

I always tell Jimmy that having him around is the reason I can go through all the twists and turns of starting something up. It's a funny thing—when I was working at the city's number one radio station, or one of the world's most prestigious universities, I had no problem telling people what I did for a living, even though I either disliked my job or I wasn't happy with my pay. The judgment that came with doing something different, however, was a whole different animal. I've told Jimmy that if it wasn't for his lead, I don't think I would have the guts to wet my feet in the entrepreneurial waters. He never discussed it—the guy has a confidence that could stare down a skyscraper—but I just kind of assumed his fear of rejection must have been a million times greater than mine. It had to have been. This was his baby. It was either that, or he simply didn't have that thought process in his DNA.

There was a family who approached our table at that first expo—a mother, a father, and their young son who was in a wheelchair. Mom and child were looking through the clothing as Jimmy and the father had a conversation to the side for quite some time. The man was interested in Jimmy's story, and Jimmy told him about the path that led him to create the brand and what he hopes to achieve.

I knew how much Jimmy hated being praised for doing regular things, and seeing it happen firsthand so many times, I understood how ridiculous it could get. On the drive home from the expo, basking in our excitement, Jimmy relayed to me the father he had been talking to had told him he was an inspiration. But instead of warranting an eye roll or frustration, however, Jimmy told me this interaction was different—the father was impressed with Jimmy's business.

"It was pretty cool," Jimmy said, "to be praised for something I did—something that I am very proud of."

43

Dana

At this point, Gloria was all but out of the picture—for the time being, at least. This was the part of the endless cycle where she had another boyfriend, but wasn't cheating on him with Jimmy . . . yet. On the way to an event out of state, he told me how annoying she was becoming. He had specifically told her that he wasn't interested unless she was ready to commit, but she wouldn't stop randomly trying to connect.

He was having an easier time dealing with it this time around though, in part because there was a new flame involved. Her name was Dana.

Dana reached out to Jimmy online after reading his blog. The reason she was interested in his blog, she explained, was because she had met someone playing an online virtual reality game who happened to have SMA as well, and the two took an interest in each other. Dana explained to Jimmy that she was too shy and embarrassed to ask the guy she met about certain things she was wondering. She was hoping it would be okay to talk to Jimmy about them.

Jimmy loved it—this was exactly the type of thing he hoped his blog would accomplish, and wanted to help any way possible. She had questions about lifestyle, accessibility, sex—anything and everything, which Jimmy was more than happy to talk about. As time went on, their texts evolved from questions and answers about disability to a more personal conversation between the two.

"Get this," Jimmy said, "she lives only an hour from our event. And she wants to meet."

"I don't know whether to be proud of you for getting a girl to fall for you over text or ashamed that you are stealing that poor guy's internet connection."

"Here's a pic," Jimmy said, pulling her up on his phone.

"Oh shit, she's hot."

"Come on, Eddie. You know if I am going to move on from Gloria, I'm going to move up from Gloria." I just shook my head. She definitely did not seem to fit the mold of a girl who picks up guys on Internet video games. Then again, I guess I don't know how that kind of girl is supposed to look.

"Oh yeah," he continued. "Then there is this . . ." He swiped his phone through the numerous pictures she had sent him until he found the one he was looking for.

It was a picture of a doctor's office. Dana was sitting on the table, waiting. Jimmy said she was vague about why she was there—only that she had to receive another round of medication. She wouldn't say why, or what for . . . but would answer Jimmy's questions if they ever met in person.

"What do you think it is?" I asked.

"I don't know," Jimmy said. "I just hope I don't catch it if we end up having sex."

When our event ended, Jimmy was especially quick in telling me to stack the boxes so he could push them with his chair across the floor to the door. After four trips and moving everything he could, he sheepishly asked me, "Uhhh . . . well . . . since I can't really help pack up anymore . . . do you mind if I go meet Dana? She's already at the hotel bar."

I knew that bastard seemed oddly enthusiastic about moving those damn boxes. His chair had been at full speed the entire time. But I was in no rush. After the event, my only plans were to grab dinner and watch the game, so I wished him well and told him to call me when their date was over.

A couple hours later, I got a call from a number I didn't recognize.

"Hi, this is Dana. Jimmy's phone is dead. He's ready to get picked up now." I called the number back when I arrived, and the two of them came out. Dana gave Jimmy a long kiss goodbye, and went on her way.

"Well, I guess that went well," I said to the awestruck Jimmy.

"Another bathroom in the books. This one was classy, too," he said. "And just after it happened the other guy texted her. I feel kind of bad about it."

"Bullshit you do."

"I'm serious!"

"Well, think if the roles were reversed . . . if some girl you were trying to hook up with went and got with another guy in a wheelchair."

"Yeah . . . what's your point?"

"I would bet a million bucks you wouldn't be the slightest bit upset. You would be happy because you would have proof she hooks up with people in wheelchairs."

"This is true. This is very true."

As we drove to where we were planning on going out that night, Jimmy wasn't talking—he seemed deep in thought.

"Eddie," he finally spoke. "She explained the doctor's picture. You will never fucking believe what she told me."

He went on to explain that she had Leukemia. She was diagnosed a while ago, and amidst the stress and demand of her first round of treatment, her marriage fell apart. She finished treatment before she turned twenty-five, left with the cancer in remission and two kids to take care of.

"This is where it gets fucked up," he warned me.

She recently found out the cancer was back. Whatever the exact situation was, a successful treatment was not likely — the doctors estimated something like less than twenty percent. She already knew the toll going through treatment takes on not only her, but also everyone else involved. She didn't want her children to watch her suffer, especially for what she thought would be a futile attempt to get better. From what the doctors told her, she had anywhere from six months to a year left. She hadn't told anyone—she couldn't even bear to think about how to tell her kids.

"I can't understand it," Jimmy said to me in the car. "I just don't get it. Why wouldn't she just try?"

That night, over drinks, Jimmy talked about how much he cared about Dana and her situation. He talked about how he loved getting to know her over the past couple of months. He felt a connection with her, especially after they met in person.

While we were out, Jimmy tried his best to be involved with the crowd, but couldn't do it. He kept sneaking away—texting her, calling her, thinking about her. At one point, he was gone for a while. I finally found him, hiding outside and around the corner, overcome with a sadness that had brought him to tears. In that moment, on the lively city sidewalk, I wondered if the people passing by who saw his red eyes and wet cheeks assumed it had something to do with his own condition—the assumption of depression that comes with the chair.

I can't say what it was exactly that brought Jimmy to tears, but I know for sure it wasn't that. I don't know, nor will I speculate, the extent of heartbreak Jimmy felt that night over his relationship with Dana. His sadness could have been completely related to her, and the fling he had with her, no matter how brief. I would not be surprised, however, if was rooted in something more—something not contained in a single person or a single relationship. Perhaps his pain came from the unknown—not only the mystery of what happens next, and the looming inevitably of it, but the unexplainable actions that are dictated by worry and fear. Jimmy could never understand how so many people spend their whole lives trying to hedge the pain of anticipated disaster and disappointment. The only certainty about the future is that it will become the past. Jimmy couldn't fathom letting life slip by without seeing the incredible beauty of each and every day. He couldn't imagine not wanting to squeeze every last drop out of what was given to him.

"The roles are reversed," he said, looking up at me with glossy eyes. "This time, she's the one with the disability. She's the one with the time limit."

[dis]ABLE Does Chicago

The Kickstarter campaign was well underway, and Jimmy and I were days from our week-long trip to Chicago and Kansas City when he sent me a book of a text.

He explained to me that he was on a panel for a discussion on independent living for people with disabilities, taking place at a center that helped those with disabilities. He was beyond shocked at what he saw.

He started by telling me how lucky he felt to have the parents and family that he did. He knew that their support and encouragement and belief in him was a huge reason why he could be in the position he was today. After going on and on, spilling his heart out about how much they mean to him, he started to describe the condition of everyone at that disability center. To be blunt, he thought most people there looked terrible. Old, dirty clothes, hanging heads, slouched bodies. What was even worse was the sense of depression and hopelessness that overwhelmed the room.

He wasn't appalled by their physical condition. Let's be honest, Jimmy ranks up there in the disability world for being in bad physical condition. In fact, there was a paraplegic man we met at an event who told us how he loved the brand because "I am tired of all this 'accept me' and 'love me' bullshit I hear all the time because I look messed up . . . Jimmy, you know what I am talking about, you're even more fucked up than I am!"

Jimmy was upset about what he saw at the center. He told me that he couldn't understand how people could present themselves like that—how they could let themselves go as if their lives were meaningless. He wanted to help them, to reach out, to make them see hope, and was excited that maybe he could help serve that purpose. As he went on and on about how bad he felt for those people, it struck me that Jimmy was looking at others with a disability the same way so many people looked at him.

Up until that point, I had never once given him any sort of credit or spent any time acknowledging how he deals with his disability. He never expected, or wanted it. After that text, however, I explained to him that his attitude was a rare quality, and I believed that was a big part of the reason he is so well-liked. From the first day I met Jimmy, he never once portrayed himself as disabled. He was just someone who wanted to be treated like anyone else, and happened to have a disability.

After Jimmy and I attended more than a few disability-related events, it became apparent that there was a split in the community. There were some people, like Jimmy, who wanted to be treated like anyone else, and didn't give themselves the handicap that the rest of the world did. On the other hand, we were very surprised to find, there was a group of people who seemed to identify with their dependence, feeding into and relying on the sympathy of others. It was almost as if they preferred to be seen as victims.

And this split was not exclusive to those who would be labeled as "disabled." It was obvious even with the people who work with them on a consistent basis—teachers, care givers, nurses, etc. Some of these people would view the disabled individuals they worked with as individuals who had the ability to get better or worse at something—capable of having successes and failures. Others, however, were putting on a veneer of respect, but it was clear they didn't see their students or clients or patients with a disability the way they would someone without.

There was even a lady, confined to a wheelchair, who came up to our table at an event only to tell Jimmy that she didn't believe it was possible to be happy with a disability. Briefly thumbing through a couple of T-shirts, she was adamant that she just didn't buy into "all this bullshit" before rolling away. I wish I could have bottled the irony of that moment.

Another encounter will always stand out to me. Late in the day at the Chicago Abilities Expo, we were approached by a man in a wheelchair who said he was a photographer, and had been at the event all day promoting his photography venture. He was a younger guy, maybe in his early twenties, but he had business cards and even a portfolio full of pictures he had taken. Some were strictly landscapes, while others had people in them. They didn't look half bad to me. Now I don't know shit about photography—I couldn't tell you anything about apertures, shutter speeds, or white balancing (I had to look up the photography Wikipedia page just to get those terms to throw in here)—but I knew that, at the time, one of the most popular social media sites and *the* most popular picture sharing app was Instagram. I even personally know a handful of people that have turned their Instagram accounts into successful photographic enterprises, scoring positions in art galleries and paid photo shoots.

We asked this dude what his Instagram handle was, and he looked at us confused. "I think I heard of that before . . . what is it?"

We were astounded. It would be one thing if he had some hallowed reason for boycotting social media, or said something pretentious like he refuses to degrade his art to a common commercial space. But he offered up nothing of the sort. This guy was a photographer and he didn't know about Instagram!

This isn't about him not knowing an app—this is about the implication of him not knowing *this* app. Even if you make the extremely unlikely assumption that no one in his family, and no one who posed in his pictures (whether they were friends or paid models), *and* no one in his inner circle knew about the app, you can't get past the fact that he was at a giant expo handing out business cards to tons of strangers. Am I to believe that Jimmy and I were the first people to think to mention Instagram in a conversation with an aspiring photographer? Get the fuck out of here. That would be like a teenager telling people he wants to play in the NFL and no one asking what position he plays on his high school team.

Jimmy and I couldn't believe it. The young man was in a wheelchair . . . so what? He can still take a fucking picture. Had no one around him taken his career seriously? In my opinion, that dude faces so many more obstacles because he is being handled with kid gloves. He has to take the time to figure out the simple things that any other person would be hit over the head with. Take away the wheelchair, and tell someone you are a photographer who never heard of Instagram, and you would be told to get with the damn program.

And that's exactly what I told him to do. I thought it would have been disrespectful not to. This poor fuckin' guy is pushing himself all around this huge conference center with business cards and a portfolio—he's past the point of being shielded from rejection and deserves a fair shot.

Talking about encounters like these consumed hours of our drives to and from events, as we hypothesized as to why things like that happen. Do people really believe that those with disabilities do not have the capability to improve or succeed at a particular venture, or are people just overly sensitive as to potentially offending someone in a wheelchair? Oftentimes, our conversation turns to the unanswerable question of nature vs. nurture. Are people molded to feel as though they are not good enough, just like Jimmy believed his parents nurtured him into being so confident and capable? Or is it a natural inclination to make excuses as to why you can't live the life you've imagined, to not take the leap that puts you at risk of failure and rejection and success and approval? After all, it is human nature to take the path of least resistance.

I know we can never answer that question, but I know this: for the rest of the three-day event, that non-Instagram-knowing photographer seemed to find his way over to our table, just to kick it with us, every chance he got.

45

Bozo the Bartender

It was our last day in Chicago and we had every intention of leaving the Windy City with a bang. We had been staying out in the suburbs, near the convention center, but that night we were going to crash at our friend's place in the city. We met up with Red in the late afternoon, and kicked it in the park across the street from his house. As we were catching up, relaying stories from our trip and debating who would win the NBA finals, an elementary school-aged kid playing in the park came up to us.

"Is he sick?" He asked me, pointing to Jimmy.

"Nope, but you can ask him about it, it's ok."

"What's wrong with you then?" he asked, turning to Jimmy.

"Well, when I was born, my muscles didn't grow like yours do."

"Oh. Ok."

The boy took it in stride. Jimmy might as well have been telling him that the grass is green and pigs can't fly. He took it for what it was, and then went right back to playing.

It sounds trivial, but instances like this one get me all juiced up with excitement. Pure honesty, curiosity, and open-mindedness. It was an opportunity for this kid to gain perspective. I am not saying that right there on the spot he became accepting and understanding of all people different than him. But next time, I like to think that he might feel comfortable enough to at least start the conversation without a buffer.

That night, Red had to eat dinner with his wife, who'd just got home from work, and we used his house's inaccessibility as a solid excuse to get the night started without him. Mulling over the hassle to get Jimmy's chair in the van, carry him in, carry him out—a process that we were going to have to do at night anyway, we begrudgingly said it would probably be best if we headed to the bar.

The first spot he recommended didn't work out. There was a step to get inside, making it inaccessible. It would have been manageable had I asked a couple guys in there for help, but when I offered that option to Jimmy he turned it down. He had looked inside and saw a dive bar with a sparse crowd, and was hoping for something better.

So we continued down the street, but we only came across one other bar. The door was propped open, so before we were even inside we knew the hole in the wall we were walking into. It looked like the kind of place where the Chicago Ditka fans from SNL would have hung out, unchanged from 1980. It was smoky, with old décor, and had a ragtag group of middle-aged and older individuals sitting around the bar. There were two guys who looked about our age playing pool and a lone female bartender. I never got her name, but we can refer to her as Bozo.*

We considered going back to the first bar, as this place didn't look much more appealing. But we were already there and we didn't see any other options nearby, so we decided to head inside. I sat down at the bar and moved a stool for Jimmy so he could park next to me. The bartender came over. Usually it is just a formality when I ask Jimmy if he wants a vodka-Sprite, as it's rare for him to go for anything else. I guess all the traveling and

---

* There were plenty of other four letter names I would have preferred to use in reference to her, but Jimmy reminded me that she is just another person who didn't mean the harm she caused. No one ever knows how ignorant they truly are, because after all, that's what ignorance is. At the risk of sounding ignorant myself, I think I am being extremely gracious in this nickname.

business had him mindful of money, however, and he asked the bartender if there were any specials. Before I could even turn my head from Jimmy to the bartender for an answer, she had a conniption.

"No way I am serving him! NO, NO, NO. No way. He is too sick. No!"

Jimmy and I look at each other in shock. She continued yelling, saying that he is "too sick to drink" in a thick Eastern European accent. I tried to protest, but she wasn't hearing any of it. She went from zero to a hundred real quick, and kept getting angrier and angrier as she walked up and down the bar. I was a little disappointed in myself when it took Jimmy's suggestion to record it for me to get my camera out. I am that annoying friend that wants to video anything and everything, and couldn't believe I was letting such an entertaining scene slip by.

I whipped out my phone as fast as possible. The actual conversation was a fast paced argument with a lot of talking over each other, but the following is the transcript of the video I captured*:

Me: He's not sick, he's just disabled.

Bozo the Bartender: Ok I'm sorry I told you I can't do it.

Me: Why not?

Bozo the Bartender: Because I say so.

Me: There's absolutely nothing—

Bozo the Bartender: Ok, then go someplace else.

[she walks to the other end of the bar to serve other customers]

Jimmy: I can't believe that, I never had that happen. I've never had that happen before.

Me: Excuse me, miss?

Bozo the Bartender: Yes?

---

* Full video on YouTube, titled "Bartender in Chicago Not Disabling Limits"

Me: How is that different than anybody else here?

Bozo the Bartender: Uhhhh, it's different because, they're not…

Me: Just because he looks different?

Bozo the Bartender: No—

Me: He's not sick—

Bozo the Bartender: I know, but he cannot walk, and can't talk—

Me: Well, I mean—

Bozo the Bartender: And I cannot serve, ok! Don't give me hard time, go 'cross the street!

Me: I don't—

Guy playing pool: Do you have an ID on you?

Me: Yea he has an ID! This kid—

Jimmy: Yeah!

Guy playing pool: Well if he has an ID . . .

Me [to Bozo]: He has an ID!

Bozo the Bartender: I told you so, that's it!

[She storms away. Jimmy and I laugh in disbelief]

Guy playing pool: She sounds like an asshole.

Me: Oh my gosh, this is just blatant discrimination.

Jimmy: Oh my goodness.

Bozo the Bartender: If he gonna pass out, whose gonna be responsible? You or me?

Me: You can say that about anybody at the bar.

Bozo the Bartender: No, no, I am not serving alcohol.

Me: If anyone passes out you can say that.

Bozo the Bartender: No, no I tell you [inaudible blabbering as she storms off]

Me: I just can't believe this.

Jimmy: Me neither.

Me: You wanna leave?

Jimmy: Not yet.

Me: Not yet? [laughs] Alright. [To the bartender] Well can I at least have a drink?

Bozo the Bartender: Alright [inaudible rambling]

Jimmy: Whoaa!

Bozo the Bartender: Why can't you go 'cross the street?

Me: Why can't I just have a drink?

Bozo the Bartender: Ok I am done, you want me to call cops?

Me: Yeah, I would love you to call the cops because you're the one breaking the law here—

Bozo the Bartender: Yeah, sure.

Me: You're discriminating against somebody.

Bozo the Bartender: I'm not so sure.

Me: You are! You are discriminating against somebody just because he is in a wheelchair.

Bozo the Bartender: Ok, then why don't you go—

Me: So please call the cops—

Bozo the Bartender: Ok.

Me: Can I have a drink?

Jimmy: Eddie, whoa whoa, wait.

Bozo the Bartender: Yeah, show me your ID.

Jimmy: NO! Don't give her your money.

Me: What's that?

Jimmy: Don't give her money.

Me (to bartender): Oh, never mind, I'm sorry

Bozo the Bartender: Ok.

Me: He told me not to give you money because you're being obviously—

Bozo the Bartender: I don't—

Me: —discriminatory.

Bozo the Bartender: I don't want it, just, you want a drink, show me your ID and I'll serve you a drink.

Me: For free?

Bozo the Bartender: NOO, you crazy?!

Me: Right, well that's what I just said!

[Bozo marches away]

Jimmy: Wait, Eddie . . . order it . . . and then you give it to me.

Me: Order it and then give it to you? She'll definitely kick us out.

Jimmy told me he has never been questioned or denied service before, and in the five years I spent going to bars, clubs, and restaurants with him since he turned twenty-one, there was only one instance where I remember a bartender asking me personally if he was ok to drink. It was at a college bar, the bartender was young, and when I told him it was fine, Jimmy was served and that was that.

The way I see it, when you don't have experience with something, the only stupid question is the one that isn't asked. When I was a college sophomore, underage and living in the dorms, I wasn't the first in line to give someone with a disability who I didn't know a drink. Alcohol has a physical effect, so it is fair to wonder how it may affect someone who is physically different. Bozo's problem wasn't that she was ignorant to the fact that Jimmy could drink; her problem was that she already made up her mind about something she didn't know anything about.

I was livid. Shit, I was more pissed than Jimmy was. Not long after I stopped recording did we get up and leave. I was running my mouth to the bartender on the way out, and continued my rant to Jimmy when we stepped outside. He was in-between being in total shock and trying to calm me down.

The two guys playing pool had walked out after us, telling us, "Fuck that place, it's just some old shitty neighborhood dive anyway."

But it wasn't enough for me to know it was a shitty dive bar with an idiot bartender. I wanted everyone in there to know it was a shitty dive bar with an idiot bartender. I was too fired up not to have the last word. I would regret this later, but I grabbed a stack of [dis]ABLE flyers that Jimmy always carried around, and despite him telling me to let it go, headed back inside. I gave one to every single last person in that bar. I had envisioned tossing the rest of the stack across the room, creating confetti out of [dis]ABLE info cards, but chickened out and settled for sliding them across the bar. My tirade came to a brief halt when I noticed how gracefully the stack slid and spread out, like I was a professional card dealer with a fresh deck on smooth green felt.

I snapped back to reality, and explained to everyone in there, in the nicest tone my anger would allow, that the bartender was full of complete shit. I told them that what just happened here was not right, and that they should go the website on the flyer I gave them, and see who Jimmy really is. I told them that he started a business on the side of his full time job in order to combat this very thing, and that even though people like Bozo may be hopeless, maybe everyone else in there could actually learn something from this exchange. In retrospect, I realize how pointless and ridiculous my display must have been, but at the time, I didn't give a fuck. I was pissed.

When I finished my rant, there was a guy sitting by the door who waved me over. When I stepped to him, I could see Jimmy again. He had not come back into the bar with me when I went on my mini-crusade. Instead, he stayed on the sidewalk, and he seemed to have moved on from the incident already, as he was in a friendly conversation with passersby. The guy who called me over told me he "kind of works for the bar"—I am guessing that means he was some degenerate that drinks for free in exchange for doing little things around the place. His All-American insight to my address was: "I know the owner, and I know he has specifically said he doesn't want handicapped people around here." In time, we would learn exactly the kind of person the owner was.

Over the next couple of days, we shared the video with a couple of friends, and there were numerous suggestions that we reach out to the news to share the story. I sent it to a couple of Chicago stations, and within a few hours got a call from a producer who was absolutely appalled at what she saw. She set us up with a reporter, Craig, and we Skyped into an interview with him. Jimmy and I were pretty happy with how it went. We thought he was asking real questions—questions he would ask anyone—rather than sugarcoating things just because Jimmy was in a chair. The story was set to air on the 9 o'clock news.

We were able to stream the broadcast online. We were excited to be the first story, but our optimism stopped there. The report opened with "a man *suffering* from muscular dystrophy . . ." Jimmy hated that. He knew right away Craig had missed the point. In our long conversation with him, Jimmy tried to convey his outlook on life—that his disability wasn't disabling. In this entire ordeal, what bothered Jimmy most was that he was perceived and portrayed on the news as one who was "suffering."

We were about to witness some bush league reporting. I get that the news needs to present both sides, and be fair, and make a story—but damn it, the story should make sense. The bartender's defense was that we refused to show IDs.

I am in my late twenties. I still get carded most of the time. I kind of like it when it happens—it makes me feel like my receding hairline isn't as noticeable as I think it is. If that were the case—that we refused to show IDs, this shouldn't have been a story. It's the way bars work—people get carded. With both of us having valid identification showing that we were over twenty-one, there was no reason we wouldn't have presented them. Not only did this reporter let that bullshit excuse slide, but he edited our video in the news segment, cutting out the part where we tell the bartender that we have IDs.

In retrospect, there were clear signs during our interview that it was amateur hour. When we first connected on Skype, we asked how we looked on his screen. I was proud of myself, using the on-set skills I had learned in my past to create solid lighting in Jimmy's apartment (really, all it meant was that I closed the blinds and moved a lamp behind the computer). Craig said it looked great, and "it is obvious you guys have done this sort of thing before." This guy had us pegged as issue agitators from jump street.

I'll be the first to admit, from a newsperson's perspective, me leaving those flyers didn't look good. Had I the smallest inkling that going to the news would even be the slightest possibility, I wouldn't have done it. At the time, though, it was the only way my frustration saw possible to fight the bullshit that was happening right in front of me—without being destructive.

It also bothered me that the issue was presented as a controversial thing: to serve or not to serve, and not as the blatant discrimination that it was. We did the math. Between bars, clubs, and restaurants, Jimmy made an extremely conservative estimate that he has ordered a drink at least three different days each week since he was twenty-one. That meant in over 780 instances, nothing like this had ever happened before. Again, in another part of the video Craig edited out, Bozo offered me service after refusing Jimmy. That's a fucking textbook definition of discrimination.

What bothered me most about the whole scenario, however, was the owner. The way I see it, the bartender is a lost cause. To have such an instant and passionate reaction just from the sight of Jimmy—I don't think people like that have a chance of changing. As for the reporter, he is just some guy who isn't particularly good at his job. Sure, that job entails spreading information to an entire city, and there is a lot of responsibility and power that comes with that, but I am not going to lose sleep at night because he isn't the next Bob Woodward. Maybe he had an off day.

The owner, though—I just can't wrap my head around his response. He wasn't there when the event unfolded, and of course he has to defend his bar and his business. I get that. I can even get passed him being so simple-minded that he tried to vindicate himself by saying, on a phone interview that he knew was going to be broadcasted to all of Chicago, "In fact, I have a regular customer in a wheelchair." I can write that off as ignorance, albeit very absurd ignorance. It reminded me of when people try to excuse their racist comments by saying, "but I have a [insert race] friend." What I can't understand is that, even after being told by the reporter that Jimmy's condition does not prevent him from drinking, that he is perfectly fine and capable to do so, and has done so in the past, the bar owner said, "As far as I'm concerned, I would have wanted her [the bartender] to do it exactly the way she did it."

The older I get, the more I see this insanity. I don't know if it's pure stupidity, not being able to make simple connections—or if it is a hubris that blinds one to the evidence right in front of their face. Maybe it is simply vanity, not wanting to admit wrongdoing. Regardless, an enormous frustration comes over me as I think about the world of people touting their open-mindedness and willingness to learn, but are too afraid of judgment to recognize that maybe, just maybe, there was something they didn't know. Without the possibility of change, there is no hope.

That night in Chicago, after what happened in Bozo's bar, Jimmy and I started walking, looking for another spot. We had no other choice but to move on. I had been on a rant since we left, and eventually Jimmy started to calm me down. It was our last night in Chicago, The Kid was flying in, and Red and his wife were meeting us out—we couldn't let some Bozo ruin the night. He reminded me for the millionth time, that just like the people who give him unwarranted compliments, or thank me for hanging out with Jimmy, Bozo just didn't know what she was doing. It is times like these I wish people could see the man Jimmy is, and what he brings to our friendship. That kind of confidence and patience is contagious, and his perception and insight, priceless.

Eventually, after a decent walk, we found another bar, The Anthem. In the same exact sequence of events, Jimmy and I find a seat. The waitress comes to our table. I ask Jimmy if he wants a vodka-Sprite. Jimmy asks the waitress if there are any specials. Then . . . what do you know, the waitress tells us Margarita pitchers are five dollars. So we ordered a margarita pitcher. When the waitress came back and kindly poured our drinks, I thanked her for serving us without a hassle and relayed our recent debacle.

She was appalled. She had never heard of anything like that. She said to Jimmy, "Sure, you look different, but it's your prerogative to drink or not, just like anyone else."

Before long, Red, his wife, and The Kid arrived at the bar, and as usual, we turned a casual, low-key Wednesday night into a party. We were obviously the waitress's favorite table, and in no time, she was hunched over, leaning on Jimmy's armrest, giving him her life story. She had mentioned what had happened to us to her coworkers, and before the night was over it seemed like everyone in that place had stopped by to say how ridiculous it was for Jimmy to be treated like that. Even the manager came out, and offered us a round of shots on the house, to which Jimmy replied, "Only if our waitress gets one too." She thought that was so sweet and funny. If she was lured in before, now she was hooked.

The manager took a liking to us as well, and even though Jimmy and the waitress were doing their own thing to the side, he hung out for quite a bit. He was in disbelief about that bartender. According to him, what that woman did was so incredibly illegal. In fact, he explained that it is even illegal to deny service to a woman who is pregnant—the courts have ruled that to be discrimination.

The law allows for bartenders to deny service if a patron appears visibly intoxicated. All other judgements have no bearing—otherwise, he explained, the bartender is left with too much power. It could leave the door open to deny service to someone who they don't think is smart enough, or even go so far as to deny food to someone overweight.

After another round of drinks from the manager, and a temporary break in his new love connection when the waitress had to go check on her other tables, Jimmy had to use the bathroom. As it goes, when we were in the stall, a stranger walked into the restroom. Jimmy started to say the kind of things that would leave the stranger to believe we were having sex behind the closed door ("Grab hold of it and put it in!" . . . "Oh, this feels so good" . . . "Almost there, almost there, ahhhh") . . . and as it goes, I played along.

The stranger left the bathroom before we came out of the stall. As I washed my hands, I looked over at Jimmy staring at himself in the mirror.

"Damn, I look good tonight. Perfect hair day, too. Perfect."

I just shook my head.

"Eddie." Jimmy jolted back from the mirror and squared up to me. His look changed. Nothing but pure seriousness consumed his entire being.

This had to be it—the moment his confidence would break. I was ready to finally be there for him the way he was always there for me. I was ready to tell him that I have hard time understanding this world, and the people in it, as well. I was going to be a friend. I was going to have his back. I had a feeling there would eventually be a time when he would falter—finally succumbing to the weight of the world bearing down on him and his disability. After not being able to go into that first bar because the world wasn't designed for people like him. After being denied service just because of the way he looks. After being screamed at before getting a chance to speak, and after being told he looks too sick to do what anyone else can. I was ready to console him, to pick him up after he fell down.

With the utmost sincerity, Jimmy looked me in the eye, and said, "Do you think Red would be pissed if I brought the waitress back to his place?"

I couldn't even bring myself to respond. I could only shake my head and laugh as I opened the bathroom door and we headed back into the bar.

46

The Lady at the Rest Stop in Missouri

On the way to our next event, we made a pit stop at rest area in the middle of Missouri. We had been driving through farmlands for hours, and it seemed like we were a world away from any type of city or town. The Kid and I got out to stretch our legs, and Jimmy's door was swung open to get him some fresh air. We noticed a middle-aged woman checking us out. She looked very curious, and eventually came over to the [dis]ABLE mobile.

Peering into the van, she asked, "Is that Abdul?"

"Huh?" I said.

"Abdul? Abdul Patel?"

Jimmy, The Kid, and I looked at each other, confused. I may be the number one offender of mistaking a person for someone else, but I've never mixed up skin color.

"Uhhh . . . no. That's Jimmy."

"Oh my goodness . . . he looks just like my neighbor. He is in a chair just like that." Though just a tad bit ignorant, this lady had that Midwestern kindness that you can't get mad at.

"Ah, classic mix up," I said, turning to Jimmy, with a shit-eating grin on my face. "All y'all look alike."

"Well," the lady continued, "I think it's super nice of you to hang out with him."

By this point, I've heard this comment, or a variation of it, so many times I can receive it in a way Jimmy would want me to. "Nah," I deferred. "If anything, he's nice to hang out with me. Someone's got to keep me in line when I get hammered." That had become my go-to line in dealing with these empty compliments.

This lady seemed a little surprised at my comment. After a pause, she said, "Well, people like that," nodding towards Jimmy, "they know."

"Know what?" I asked. I was having a ball with this sweet ol' thing.

"Know when you've had too much to drink."

"That's true," I said, turning to Jimmy, who was also trying to contain his laughter. We looked at each other like, *What in God's name is this lady talking about?* "That's very true."

Back on the road, we talked about how blind the wheelchair can make people. Don't get me wrong, I realize I am completely assuming what Abdul looks like. I know I can't say for sure people with certain names have certain skin colors. Shit, I've always thought I would name my kids Jamal, Zhang, Pablo, and Raj just to keep them on their toes. I figure it would encourage them and everyone they ever interact with to have an open mind, and, more importantly, provide me with lifelong entertainment. So, we admitted, there is a small chance Abdul could very well have actually looked like Jimmy. We had a strong feeling, though, that this lady wouldn't mistake Jimmy for Abdul if they weren't both in wheelchairs.

"You know how everyone always assumes you're my brother, Eddie?"

"Yeah."

"Well, they assume that with everyone."

"Yeah, I've heard that."

"No, I mean everyone. Like there have been people that asked me if Allen, Mark, and John were my brothers."

"Bullshit." I couldn't believe that.

"I'm serious. It's happened multiple times." Allen, Mark, and John are black. "I mean, I know there's a million different ways that a family could look . . ."

"But no one naturally assumes people with different skin colors are siblings. That's pretty funny, Abdul."

47

Or vs. And

The [dis]ABLE team consisted of Jimmy and me, and The Kid, who we consider our first employee—even though he hired himself and doesn't get paid. The [dis]ABLE-mobile was a dark blue Honda Odyssey that was converted to an accessible van. The Kid wasn't able to join us for the entire trip, and flew into Chicago to meet us on our last night there before heading to the annual SMA Conference, which took place in Kansas City. It was a running joke that The Kid had taken a flight into one of the coolest cities in the world only to drive across cornfields and cow farms to go to some whack city we knew nothing about.

The only excitement during that ride was a thunderstorm, which broke up eight hours of nothing. I swear I only saw one hill. Our GPS said we were twenty minutes away from our destination in downtown Kansas City, but it still looked like we were in the sticks. We were nervous—twenty minutes outside of Center City Philadelphia still feels like the city, but here we could've counted on our hands the number of houses in sight. The only thing we knew about Kansas City was that the Chiefs played there—we didn't even know it wasn't in Kansas. An uneasy feeling filled the [dis]ABLE mobile, all of us thinking to ourselves something along the lines of, *What the hell are we doing with our lives?*

Just as I was about to apologize for suggesting this trip, we came around a turn to see something that would put the Emerald City to shame. Lit up against the dark night was a beautiful skyline. We couldn't believe what we were seeing, plopped right in the middle of nowhere.

The Kid did a quick google search of Kansas City nightlife, and we learned that Howl at the Moon—a popular piano bar chain and one of our go-to spots in Philly—was two blocks from our hotel. It was destiny.

We had an early wake-up for the conference the next day, so I thought it was fair when I suggested that if we wanted to go out that night, we could take shifts manning the table the next day, or we could even skip going out altogether. I said it might be a good idea to do one or the other—it would be tough to go out hard tonight and work all day tomorrow.

"Eddie," Jimmy said, in a disappointed tone. "We aren't 'or' guys. We are 'and' guys."

The next forty-eight hours were pure greatness. Not only could we park for free on the street outside our hotel, right in the middle of downtown, but the hotel valet was the one who made that suggestion (neither would ever happen in Philadelphia). The unique, Midwestern kindness continued when the hotel staff upgraded us to a penthouse suite when we asked if they had any handicap accessible rooms available. They also gave us handfuls of free drink tickets and suggested where we should go.

Turns out their recommendation was where Howl at the Moon was located—a giant venue called Kansas City Live. We were familiar with and enjoyed XFINITY Live! in Philly, but the one in Kansas City blew it out of the water. It was after midnight on a Thursday, and the place was still popping. The Kid walked up to the first group he saw and said, "Kansas City is crushing it, and the entire Northeast has absolutely no idea about it!" Naturally, that group took us in, because—well, it's Kansas City. Nothing goes wrong there.

Our thrill ride continued the next day at the conference, as we got to meet a ton of awesome people and connect with folks from so many different parts of the country. What I found particularly interesting was the number of children in wheelchairs, and even more so, my reaction to them.

Before I started going to all of these different events, and even before I hung out with Jimmy, like most people, I felt terrible when I saw a kid in a wheelchair. It was one of those things that didn't make sense to me, a real-life tragedy in front of my eyes.

I noticed at this conference, however, I didn't have that reaction. I saw them simply as kids. If a girl was rolling her eyes at her Dad, I would think it was funny. If a boy was whining and complaining I would think he's a brat. If a person in a wheelchair was in my way, instead of taking a ridiculously long, roundabout route, I would simply ask him to move. I am not making the argument that being in a wheelchair is not significant, or that it is a nonissue to have SMA—not in the slightest. All I am saying is, for the first time, I saw strangers as strangers, not as people in wheelchairs, and certainly not as charity cases. That, I'm pretty sure, is a great thing.

That night, we hit our last outing in Kansas City hard, and the next day, we continued to crush it at the conference. After saying goodbye to our new friends in hopes of linking up with them next year, we packed up the [dis]ABLE mobile and started to mentally prepare ourselves for the trek back to Philly.

Before we left the city, we stopped for dinner at a Chipotle. Jimmy is a sucker for burrito bowls. Jimmy and The Kid were still inside as I was waiting by the van—wanting to be outside as much as possible before being on the road for the next eighteen hours. I was thinking about how much fun it was working with those two—making decisions and making mistakes, experiencing successes and rebounding from failures. I thought about how fun it was to check the Kickstarter email account together, seeing if we had any new backers. It made me realize that in all the Kansas City excitement, we hadn't checked in a while. There was a good chance we had gained at least a couple of backers. I thought I would wait for Jimmy and The Kid to come back out so we could enjoy checking it together.

Then a couple seconds passed and my impatience set in. I thought, *Nah. Forget them.*

I refreshed my email, and much to my surprise, the inbox was flooded with Kickstarter notifications. One of them looked different, and said "Congratulations." Just as Jimmy and

The Kid came out, I clicked it. I didn't think it could have happened so soon, but sure enough, we had hit our goal. I didn't say anything to Jimmy and simply put my phone on his lap for him to see for himself.

As he read the email, a middle-aged man approached us with some sap story about how his phone died and he needed money to buy minutes to call his daughter, who was in the emergency room across town.

I interrupted that bullshit, as I usually do, by telling him there was no shot we are giving him any money. We did, however, have a couple of pre-made boxed lunches that the conference gave us, and offered one to him. There was also an unopened fifth of Burnett's that I got at a gas station when we first arrived into town (there was a two-for-one deal . . . again, only in Kansas City), and since we didn't want a glass liquor bottle floating around the car on our ride home, we offered that to him as well. I think his heart may have skipped a beat.

I wanted to get a picture with Jimmy commemorating the moment we found out we hit our goal, and invited the stranger to join in for the hell of it. After The Kid snapped a couple pictures (Jimmy always needs multiple options to choose from), we thought the guy would go on his way, until . . .

"Yo, let me get them Ruffles."

"Huh?"

"The Ruffles." He was pointing at the stack of lunches in the van. "The box you gave me has plain chips. That box has Ruffles. Let me get them, too."

"Are you being serious?" Despite his bullshit emergency room story, we had just given this guy a full meal and enough booze to kill a small animal, and he was asking for more? The Kid, much more patient than me, grabbed the bag of chips and gave it to him, just to get him out of our hair.

I couldn't believe it. Lord knows, this stranger could have every excuse in the entire world to be in the position he is— but at the end of the day they are just excuses. Here he is trying to squeeze three people he never met before for an extra bag of potato chips. And in that very same parking lot, at the same point in time, is a guy who can't even brush his own teeth but created a company on the side of his full-time job and just met his goal on Kickstarter.

I'll never know why some people turn out the way they do—why some people succumb and others survive, why some feel responsible and others feel entitled. Thanks to Jimmy, though, I do know this:

As we drove through downtown Kansas City on our way out of town, with a "came, saw, conquered" feeling filling the [dis]ABLE mobile, Jimmy said, "We aren't even 'and' guys. We're 'comma' guys."

48

The Most Beautiful Person in the Room

One night, Jimmy and I headed out before the rest of the crew. I was standing in front and to the left of Jimmy at the counter, waiting to get the bartenders attention and Jimmy was talking to someone he'd just met on his right. I noticed some Drunk Asshole turn from the conversation he was in and place his drink on Jimmy's left armrest, as if it was just another piece of furniture in the bar.

"YO!" Like anyone from Philly, I have learned to use that word to communicate a million different messages. This "YO!" was, "Hey buddy, pick your damn drink up off the armrest." He understood immediately, picked it up and went back to his conversation, as I turned back to the bar.

Just then, a girl walked up next to me at the bar, and if she was not the best-looking person in the room, then one-legged ducks don't swim in circles. She was the kind of beautiful that catches attention. I could notice the guys across the room sneaking glances, and even staring.

Now, a wise man would use this as an opportunity to offer to buy her a drink, but I am no wise man. The way I see it is that there are many women who look like that who make it their mission to walk up to some sucker at the bar in hopes of getting a free drink. Little did she know, I am no sucker. After a few minutes of waiting for the bartender, to no avail, I said, "I bet you shots he takes my drink order before he takes yours."

"You're on," she said, extending her hand for a shake. She then fluffed up her hair and adjusted her shirt and did whatever else it is that women do in order to look more presentable even though they look exactly the same after doing it, and I took out a wad of bills—making sure the twenties were in front of all the smaller bills, and held it just high enough above the counter for the bartender to see I was ready to pay.

I always thought it was an interesting thing to see a bartender operate behind a packed bar. He has to make decisions that will maximize his tips, but also keep all customers happy. Long story short, I was banking on the fact that the bartender would be the one guy in the room that would care more about me than her, as long as he thought I had a lot of cash and was ready to spend.

The bartender finally comes to our side of the bar, scans from left to right, and then points and nods at me, asking for my order. Victory.

Now, a wise man would use this as an opportunity to tell the girl not to worry about the bet, and then buy her a drink. Well, I was still not a wise man. I ordered drinks for Jimmy and me, and silently enjoyed the puzzled look and brief silence from the beautiful girl when I didn't get her a drink anyway.

As I waited for my order, I looked back at Jimmy to tell him our drinks were finally on the way. He was still talking to someone on his right, but I noticed that Drunk Asshole's drink found a way back onto Jimmy's left armrest. I waved to get his attention and said, "YO!" pointing to his drink. This "YO!" was more of a "this is your last fucking warning, dickhead."

My drinks came, and the bartender asked the beautiful girl for her order. She conveniently "forgot" about our bet.

"Whoa, don't forget about the shots!" I said. She said it was an honest mistake, but I think she was trying to skip out on what she owed. It's not my fault that I believe in equality for the sexes. I know a lot of guys think I am crazy for this, but I ain't apologizing for shit. I would have delivered if I had lost, and if it was a dude I had bet, I wouldn't think twice about making him own up to his end of it. It's not my fault that I respect her and her decision-making. If I were to let her skate on her end of the bargain, I would be singlehandedly setting the entire female gender back forty years.

As she waited for the shots, I turned to give Jimmy his drink. Drunken Asshole was now leaning against Jimmy's chair. "Dude, this is the last time I'm going to warn you. Get away from his chair."

He offered a drunken apology as Jimmy took a sip. I was still holding Jimmy's glass as I am telling him why I have a shot on the way, when, in his drunk antics, Drunken Asshole stumbled into me, knocking my arm and sending the drink flying. This was more than a typical accident at the bar . . . this was an exclamation point after the guy had been using Jimmy's chair as his own personal furniture for the last ten minutes.

With Jimmy's drink completely spilled, some on me, and some on Jimmy, I was close to losing it. I looked at this guy—he was probably in his thirties, dressed professionally, nice haircut, and I even noticed a wedding ring on his finger—and for some reason, it felt as though it would be pointless to say or do the hostile things I wanted. There was something about seeing a guy, who at first glance looks as though he has it all together, trying so hard, at that kind of bar full of twenty-somethings, that just seemed so incredibly pathetic to me.

"Look dude, just buy him a new drink, and we are cool." I was pissed, but I concealed my anger as best I could and delivered it in cordial, albeit firm, manner. I think the sympathy I had for this guy played a major part in why I handled the situation so delicately. I like to believe, though, there was a part of me that finally realized meeting ignorance with anger is futile. In all honesty, I was pretty surprised that I didn't escalate it to a place it didn't need to go. Put me in that same situation a few years ago, and I think I would have handled it a lot differently. Jimmy was watching me, and though he didn't say it, I knew I finally acted the way he would have encouraged me to.

He became so apologetic it was uncomfortable. He asked me if he could talk to Jimmy. Usually I think it's stupid when people ask me for permission to talk to him, but this time, I was glad he did. When Jimmy heard his request, his eyes got wide and, looking at me, decisively shook his head no. "Sorry man," I said to the guy, who was in the middle of another apology. "He's talking with someone else. Just grab him the drink you spilled and we're cool."

Jimmy went back to his conversation, as I went back to the bar for the shots. Despite her looks suggesting otherwise, this chick was actually pretty cool. We were getting a pretty solid conversation going, when there was a tap on my shoulder. It was the Drunken Asshole.

"Hey, can I show him a picture?" he asked, pointing to Jimmy.

"No." I turned back to the girl and continued the conversation, hoping he would go away.

He didn't. After a few seconds, I felt another tap.

"It's a picture of someone I know in a wheelchair. I think he would like it."

Why the fuck would you think that? And why do you keep coming to me, asking me? And why do you think it's ok to just interrupt my conversation, in hopes of interrupting Jimmy's conversation?

"No, dude, seriously, we are all good. Just let it go."

Fortunately, that was it for that drunken asshole, and I was able to rejoin the conversation with the girl. It was going great, until Jimmy came over to join us.

"Lauren, this is Jimmy, Jimmy, this is Lauren." I said, introducing the two.

As Jimmy said, "Hello," she looked at him, and then back at me, and said, "ALS?"

"What?" I heard the sounds her mouth had made, but it didn't register until after I asked her to repeat herself. As she started to answer, I was praying to heaven that she wasn't one of *those.*

"Is it ALS?" She was. Fuck. All the hopes and dreams I had about this chick who was way out of my league were dashed in that instant. Who the fuck would start a conversation like that upon first meeting someone else?

I don't even think the part that pissed me off the most was that the question was in her head. It's a reasonable question, coming from understandable curiosity. And I wasn't most mad at the tone, either, even though she was asking if Jimmy had a terminal disease as nonchalantly as someone would ask if they had gotten pepperoni on their pizza. I know Jimmy has had people ask him similar questions in similar situations, and he understands. What I couldn't believe was that this very personal question about Jimmy, was being asked *in front* of Jimmy, but directed *at me*. I know she could have very well have had the best intentions in the world, but I had seen this scenario play out too many times. I knew a person like that was going to subtract from our night much more than she was going to add to it . . . no matter how good-looking she was.

Despite that, I tried to give her an out, brushing off the question and changing the subject. But she eventually brought it back, pressing me hard as to why Jimmy was in a wheelchair.

As I answered her question, I could see Jimmy rolling his eyes and shaking his head. It's not like he is ashamed about it. Shit, that's a big part of his story. It was just very unsettling, the way it was brought up, her intentions behind asking the question (who the hell knows what they were), and most importantly, how she was asking me as if he wasn't there. We were out at the bar, trying to have a good time—I just don't understand why she wanted to know so badly.

Eventually, our other friends arrived at the bar, and we parted ways with that pretty woman. As always, Jimmy was undeterred in his own pursuit of a good time, and a girl he had been chasing since college coincidentally showed up at that same bar.

He was on the dance floor with her for quite some time, and I went to tell him we were about to get one more drink and then bounce.

"Go ahead without me," Jimmy said, confidently. "I'm good."

Standing at the bar with friends, finishing my last drink, I could still see Jimmy across the room, having a ball with that girl from college. "I don't know how he does it," a friend said, noticing the same thing. I just shook my head in agreement.

I'm a confident guy, and I'm not one to worry too much about the clothes I am wearing or the way my hair looks when I go out. But if I get one comment from a female friend saying that I need to shave, or a buddy telling me that he wore a similar outfit to a middle-school dance,* I do tend to give up on the possibility of any sort of romantic interaction that night. It's not

---

*I fully intend on rocking polos, jeans, and Iversons until the day I die.

in a sulking sort of way, but more of a, "hey, this is the way I chose to present myself, these are the consequences" sort of way. Jimmy, though—he just doesn't have that in his DNA. He could literally start his night hearing that asinine comment from that girl, and go on undeterred.

As I finished my thought, and drink to go with it, I turned to the bar to pay my tab when I felt a tap on the shoulder. It was the girl Jimmy was dancing with.

"Uh . . . Jimmy says he needs to go the bathroom."

I laughed a little to myself. "Alright," I said

I found Jimmy on the dance floor. "Do you really have to go, or was that just a ploy to get her alone?"

"No, I have to go!"

"Seriously? The bar is closing in ten minutes, you can just do it at your place." It would have been a lot easier. It is kind of ironic that our favorite bar in the city does not have the best accessibility.

"Eddie, I really have to go!"

"Alright." I didn't believe him, but we headed back to the bathroom anyway. As I held him over the toilet, waiting . . . and waiting . . . and waiting for him to start going, he finally let out the littlest spritz and started to laugh.

"Fuck," he said. "I really thought it would finally be the night with her. You can put me back in the chair."

"I fucking knew it!" I exclaimed, relieved I could finally set him down. "I can't lie though . . . I'm impressed with the follow through just to save face."

"Looks matter, Eddie. Perception is everything."

"Just when I thought I couldn't like you any less, here you go getting philosophical on me with your dick out. Spectacular."

The next morning, we grabbed some breakfast, and started to recap the night. We wondered about the thought process that goes through people's head when they say things like, "Let me show him a picture of someone in a wheelchair," or when they open a conversation with the question "ALS?"

"Dude, the second she started with "ALS," I apologized to Jimmy, "I should have just ended the conversation there. My bad."

"It's all good."

"She was just so freakin' hot."

"She was, she was."

As I cut up his food, we both retreated into our own thoughts. Jimmy finally cut into the silence.

"Is that all they see in me?" He wondered aloud. His question was not in a sad tone, but rather, an objective bewilderment. "It's like . . ." his voice trailed, before he could finally put into words what he was thinking . . . "Is my condition all that they think I am?"

49

Running into Gloria

Another year passed, and with it, another cycle of the Jimmy and Gloria merry-go-round. After running around on Boyfriend No. 2 for a couple of months, she eventually called that off, and was back to spending all of her time with Jimmy. And, as history tends to repeat itself, Jimmy wanted commitment, and she wouldn't give it. Jimmy started to distance himself, and Gloria started seeing someone else. Jimmy told her to leave him alone, but she continued to insert herself into his life when she could sneak around Boyfriend No. 3—everything from daily texts to weekend-long sleepovers. Eventually, Jimmy started to hate seeing her, realizing the insecurity and mistrust that festered with every get together. But he couldn't resist. He wanted her to love him, to accept him, so badly.

Finally, Jimmy received help from the most unexpected of sources.

"You know how you are always telling me it's unbelievable how I can hit people with my chair, only to have them apologize to me?" He asked me one day. "Well, you will never guess who just reached out to me."

Out of nowhere, Boyfriend No. 2 had messaged Jimmy on social media. Like all exes in the twenty-first century, they knew of each other, even though they didn't know each other. Jimmy was shocked when he saw his name pop up on the message screen.

Boyfriend No. 2 wanted to reach out, just to say hello. He wanted to clear the air—he had heard a lot of things about Jimmy, and assumed Jimmy heard a lot of things about him. The two talked and exchanged stories about Gloria and her wicked ways. Jimmy learned that all of the bullshit she had pulled on him—well, she did all of the same things to Boyfriend No. 2. He was always unsure if Gloria treated him like that because of who he was, or because of who *she* was. He finally found the answer.

"And guess what . . . he wants to buy a shirt."

Jimmy literally slept with this dude's girlfriend, and told him about it, only to have said dude message him to say he respects him, *and* buy a shirt from him.

After that, it was easier for Jimmy to exclude Gloria from his life. He didn't want that kind of person around, no matter how much he still loved her. He wasn't going to invest any more energy until she was ready to invest it in him.

By the time the summer came back around, and with it, another seasonal rental down the shore, Jimmy had totally cut her off. After a prolonged period of ignoring her texts and calls, he took another step in blocking her number, social media accounts, and deleting every picture or text or any other possible reminder or connection he could have with her. He told me he was worried about running into her down the shore by chance, as he knew she still spent many weekends in the small vacation town. If that was the case, he just hoped he would handle himself in the right way, or would be tipsy enough to not care about handling himself the wrong way. Knowing Jimmy, one of those two options becoming a reality was all but a guarantee.

Eventually, one day down the shore, our paths would indeed cross at happy hour. As usual, Jimmy was inside on the dance floor, next to the blaring speakers, listening to a cover band, with girls dancing all around and on his chair. And, as usual, I was outside with friends, where I could actually hear myself think. Across the patio, I saw her.

"Ah shit," I said out loud, thinking about Jimmy inside. "This could get ugly."

A lot people have asked me what I think about Gloria—Jimmy probably the number one repeat offender. To me, the answer is simple: when he likes her, I like her. When he doesn't like her, I don't like her. He's my friend—if something or someone makes him happy, it makes me happy. All that said, I had gotten to know her well enough in the time the two spent together that I would have felt rude if I didn't say hi. More importantly, I wanted to look out for my boy.

I walked across the bar to say hello. She greeted me, introduced me to her friend, and then asked, "Where's Jimmy? I have been texting him and that asshole isn't responding."

"I'll be honest," I laughed, "I don't think I'm supposed to answer that."

"He blocked me, didn't he?"

I was silent.

"I knew it! He's such a dick!"

"Yeah, yeah." The two of them had that weird play-fight aspect of their relationship, and I knew these insults were her own special way of saying she misses him.

Standing there at that bar, with her pressing me for his location, and Jimmy right inside—I felt like it was time I finally said something. I knew if he saw her, no matter how it turned out, it would tear his heart apart. I had seen the effect she had on him—how terrible she could make him feel. It was as if she was the only one in the world that could convince him he wasn't good enough. Every time she led him on, only to leave him, it screamed to him how worthless she thought he was. I wanted that to end. I wanted to do something. I knew Jimmy would do it for me—he had stuck up for me in any and every situation I ever got myself into. It was my turn now.

I asked Gloria why she kept putting on this charade. It was obvious to everyone that she loved him, that she was happiest with him. Her friend even nodded her head in agreement. "You don't leave an engagement, then another boyfriend, and cheat on a third for a guy you don't care about. No matter what, you keep coming back to him, only to constantly deny yourself something that makes you so happy. Was it what other people thought? Was that it? That's not going to help you sleep at night when the day comes that it is too late and you missed your chance."

"That's exactly it, Eddie." She started tearing up, holding her neon plastic drink cup, in the midst of a crowd of young men and women in tank tops and bathing suits showing off their arms and legs and chests, looking for love at a beach bar happy hour.

"What is?" *I know you're prone to the dramatic, but damn Gloria, are these tears necessary?*

"How one day, that time is going to come."

"Huh?" *What the hell is she talking about?*

"Then it really will be too late."

Wait. What did she think I meant when I said she is going to miss her chance? She knows I was talking about Jimmy moving on, right?

"I think about that all the time."

"Think about what?"

"You know . . . when he . . ."

"When he what?"

She didn't say anything, and just looked down into her cup.

"Are you talking about him dying?!"

"It's all I ever worry about."

"Seriously?" *What in the fuck just happened here?*

"Yes, and I tell him that all the time."

"You do?"

"I'm *always* thinking about it."

"Well that's fucking morbid." I was so shocked at where this conversation went, I didn't really have time handle it delicately. Through her tears, she explained to me that the thought of Jimmy dying consumes her—she can't think about any sort of future with him without picturing him passing.

In that moment, I could have pointed to countless tales that everyone has heard about doctors being wrong when they give someone a certain amount of time that they have left, but I didn't. I don't think it would have been anything she didn't know. I could have told her that there was a man with the same exact condition as Jimmy who lived to be seventy, but I didn't. I could have even told her that there is a chance she dies before Jimmy, or how every day medicine and science evolves, but I didn't. I don't look for comfort in mere possibilities. I find comfort with certainty.

And I was certain when I told her she was being fucking stupid. I couldn't understand it. Everybody is going to die—it's just another part of life. It made me wonder how much life is lost because people are stuck tormenting themselves with things that have yet to come to existence, and sometimes never will. It was a rare feeling that overcame me, but in that moment, I felt sorry for her. I was looking at someone who had the chance to get exactly what she wanted simply by making a decision—but was too afraid to take the leap.

Later that night, back at our house, I told Jimmy I saw her. It was a Saturday night in Sea Isle, and after a day of partying he was running on emotion and instinct. I barely finished my sentence before he whipped his chair around and hightailed it back to the bar, looking for her. He found her, and she was happy he did. The two had a wonderful time together, and he brought her back to our house. She stayed over that night, and the two holed up in the bedroom well into the next morning. Eventually, she left, and their merry-go-round was set in motion once again.

And, once again, Jimmy wanted a commitment from her that she just wouldn't give. She was back in his life for a couple of weeks before Jimmy started asking again what was holding her back. She would beat around the bush, telling him how important he is to her, but never telling Jimmy exactly why she still wouldn't commit to him. This confused Jimmy as much as it hurt him, and he started to distance himself as best he could from her.

Eventually, I told Jimmy what she said to me that day at the bar. He had been vocalizing his confusion for a while, but I had been holding off telling him. I wasn't excited to tell my friend that the main reason the girl he loves wouldn't be with him was because she expected him to die soon.

"It doesn't make any sense to me," Jimmy said, after I shared what she had said. He sounded weak—he sounded small. "If she is going to be sad when I go, why wouldn't she want to spend even more time with me now?"

I didn't know what to say. Who would? I just started rambling—I didn't like seeing him like this. I told him I didn't understand Gloria, either. I don't understand how people always focus on the end, and never think about what it took to get there. Just like how people only see the championship trophy, or the million-dollar house, and they don't see the beautiful struggle of the hours and weeks and years of blood, sweat, and tears it took to get to that glorious end. Gloria only saw a heartbroken end, and didn't see all the beautiful moments she had—and could continue to have—with Jimmy that would make that ending so sad.

It is the kind of thinking that encourages people to do nothing, for the only certainty in this life is that one day, whether it be a career, a relationship . . . life itself . . . the only certainty is that it will end. All we can really do is take it step by step, as best we can, and try to enjoy the journey as much as possible. Otherwise, we'll end up with a past built upon worry and fear, leaving us filled with nothing but regret and the tragic thoughts of *what if* and *what could have been.*

I told him that I wish there was something that could be done to show Gloria that, but it was out of our control.

Jimmy was in rare form following that conversation. I had never before seen the man so down, so dejected, so hopeless.

A couple days later, I was playing around on the [dis]ABLE website, when I noticed a blog post of Jimmy's, written over a year prior. I had never seen it before. It was titled "When Time Expires," and it was about an event that Jimmy had never mentioned to me. It read:

I'm a light-hearted guy. I don't take many things too seriously, and I don't take offense when people make silly comments about being in a wheelchair. But recently when one of my friends who had a disability passed away, someone made a comment that bothered me. This person, who will remain anonymous, made a post on social media that a mutual friend "lost their battle" with their disability.

I feel like this is the line you hear after so many people with a disability pass away, but it's unfair to say. First of all, it's not right for someone to make a judgment about whether or not another person won or lost against their disability. And personally, I wouldn't even consider living with a disability a "battle." This is just my life, and like everyone else, I have obstacles I have to overcome. But if you want to make a judgment about whether or not a person won against their disability, shouldn't you make that judgment based on how that person lived their life each and every day they were alive? We all die in the end, but when my game clock expires, nobody is going to say I lost.

It had to be fate that I would come across it at the time I did. I immediately copied, pasted, and sent the post to Jimmy. I figured it there was anybody in the world that could talk Jimmy out of his slump, it was himself.

I told him that I never bought into the whole handicapped inspiration stuff. I told him I don't have the slightest bit of respect, or sympathy, for his wheelchair or anything that came with it. What made him so attractive—what made so many people want to be around him, and have fun with him, and trust him, and confide in him—was the way he conducted himself. Every day, he chooses to take it for the gift that it is, undeterred by the doubt and disbelief of those around him, undaunted by the fear of failure and rejection.

And that is why I love Jimmy.

Afterword

One cold, rainy winter night, Jimmy and I were freezing our asses off waiting for a bus, just off Temple's campus in North Philadelphia.

A young man in ragged, dirty clothes approached us. Everything about the situation told me this man was going to ask for money. I had been asked for money by people that looked exactly like this guy hundreds of times, on that exact corner, throughout my college career. At this point, I didn't even think I was being stereotypical—it was a fact.

"Hey, how you guys doing," he started. My defenses were up, waiting for him to ask for something from me. "I just got off work, and I was meeting my wife and daughter for a quick bite," he said, pointing to a young woman and a stroller just inside the glass door of a fast food place. "I'm thinking the rain might stop by the time we are done eating." Looking at Jimmy, "You can have my umbrella if you want."

I have never been so happy to be wrong. It may seem trivial, but this was one of the best moments of my entire life, and I know it is all because of Jimmy.

The thing is, more than anyone else, I know my heart. I know how I feel about people, whether it is based on gender, age, race, socioeconomic status—whatever. I don't worry about an accusation of an "-ism"—classism, sexism, racism—because I know the truth about how I feel. I truly believe that when people so quickly throw those terms around, it is usually more of a reflection of their own bias, not of how they are being treated. I also don't have too many qualms about stereotypes, or making assumptions. It's a necessary thing, to guess, in order to make it through this crazy world of ours. And I'll be honest, put me back on that same corner, and have the same kind of guy approach, I would be lying if I said I wouldn't expect the same thing as before.

What struck me about the guy with the umbrella, however, was no matter how valid, or fair, or justified an assumption can be—it is never certain. It made me wonder how much life I had missed, how much beauty was in the world that I didn't see, because I had already made up my mind.

It also made me think that here was a generous, caring individual that, had I not been with Jimmy, I would have never encountered.

Had I not been with Jimmy at that bus stop—or the park, or the restaurants, or the dorms, or the bars, or the beach, or the basketball games—I wouldn't have seen the extreme and simple kindness that people from all different walks of life display on a daily basis. Without Jimmy, I would never see the most impatient line calm when he exits the bathroom, or a testosterone-filled man unclench his fist after turning to find it was Jimmy who bumped into him. I wouldn't get to see how quickly it's possible for someone to open up and trust a stranger, and I would never get to see the length people would go to help someone in need.

I have witnessed a man show understanding and empathy to the guy his girlfriend cheated with and I have seen complete strangers take someone they didn't know to the bathroom.

I got to see a kindness I would not have known was there had I not been with Jimmy—a thoughtfulness that doesn't seem to exist in normal interactions, an uncommon compassion in a world full of disregard and disdain. It is the most beautiful thing—and also, the most tragic. When I dwell on it too long, I can't help but lose a little bit of faith in humanity. I see an indescribable and unlimited goodness in people when they interact with Jimmy, yet it is invisible in the way they so often treat others.

I tell this to Jimmy often, and I tell him that I wish people could realize he is just like everyone else. This is not a wish for him; not a hope for him to be treated the way others are—this is a hope for others to be treated the way Jimmy is.

People see him and they want to help because they think his image is evidence of a struggle or a pain. What people forget is that there is a Jimmy in all of us. There is struggle and pain and confusion in everyone—that's part of the human experience. I wish people could see that in others when they are faced with a choice to forgive, or to be patient, or kind, or caring. I know they have it in them, I have seen them use it with Jimmy.

I think about these things, and it brings me down. It is the saddest thing in the world—when you have the ability to do good and instead, choose otherwise. Jimmy is always there to stop those thoughts, to tell me it's not true, that it is up to me to decide what I am seeing. He says it is a rare and pathetic person who actually intends to bring someone else down. Instead, the bad things people do are not personal—they are simply the result of people wrapped up in their own world, trying to make sense of their own problems, their own worries, their own fears. He has the most persistent and convicted belief in people's kindness—in their willingness to help.

He always reminds me there can be a lot of good in the world, a lot of beauty in people, if you just look at them the right way.

At the time of this publication…

Jimmy Curran lives and works full-time as a market analyst at an insurance company in downtown Philadelphia. He is still operating [dis]ABLE, which he views as a multifaceted platform of fashion, speaking engagements, and literature that is changing the perception of what it means to be "disabled." He recently published his first book, a children's book about overcoming adversity, inclusion, and acceptance, titled "Will The One-Winged Eagle." For more information on his book or how to schedule a speaking engagement, check out disablethebrand.com, and follow him on social media @disablethebrand. Jimmy still proudly owns and wears those Gucci Shoes.

Eddie Doyle also lives in the Philadelphia area . . . in Delco, specifically (if you have been there, no explanation is necessary, and if you haven't, no explanation will suffice). He recently appointed himself as Philly's favorite Uber and Lyft Driver, though no one listened. For more of his work, you can follow his blog at ihatejimmy.com, or check out his Youtube Channel: The Driver Ed Show. Eddie still tells Jimmy he hates him . . . but we all know the truth.

Acknowledgements

In truth, I was and still am pretty conflicted in how to handle this section. On one hand, I have always found acknowledgement pages somewhat excessive and obnoxious, a mix of humble brags and ass kissing. On the other hand, the amount of gratitude I have in my heart for those who have influenced this project is too much to go unmentioned, but at the same time, I fear a page or two in the back of the book would not do it justice. And on the third hand, the unoriginality of the previous sentence has the cynic in me firing on all cylinders.

If I did decide to include an acknowledgements page, I am tormented by the question, who do I thank? The first two people that instantly come to my mind are my Mommom and Poppop, even though I am not even sure if they knew I was writing this, and to be honest, I would be more than happy if my Mommom, who quite possibly may be an actual Angel, didn't read some of the stories in here. But the influence and inspiration that they have both had on me, and the entire Doyle family, is unmistakable. But if I thank them, I know I will bring upon myself the inevitable label of "brown-noser" that I am sure at least three of my aunts will mark me with, complete with the closed-fist-around-the-nose motion that, now that I know it's significance, find it kind of absurd I was introduced to it as a toddler. But once I realize that I can stomach the teasing, especially if it helps solidify my claim as the second favorite grandchild, I would feel the need to mention that I have always thought that Doyle family gatherings was where I first experienced the power of, and where I first fell in love with, good storytelling. But is that really something specifically related to this book? Of course I would thank Laura and Stephanie for editing the book, as well as those who read the earlier drafts. And of course I would include the obligatory comment about how those drafts were absolutely awful (which they were). But should I include those readers' names? What if I leave out someone who may have only read parts of it but provided great feedback, but included someone like Calvin, who read it all but didn't really give me any feedback even though he drank the beer I promised him for reading it? Seems a little unfair. I feel like I should thank Chris, who has been beyond helpful with design, but what about all the people who helped with the little things, like which font I should use? I should probably thank Martin, who spent countless lunches at Lil' Pete's sharing his marketing expertise with me, but do I include my appreciation for Lil Pete himself for having had the best lunchtime special in Philly? Without that gigantic porkroll and cheese on Kaiser, steak fries, chicken noodle soup, and unlimited coffee, all for under $7, I don't know if I would have been so dedicated to making those meetings. Do I thank Mike, whose influence extended well beyond this book, offering by far and away the best writing advice I have ever received? Or do I save that appreciation for a different work, perhaps an embarrassing attempt to rip-off Kerouac? Or what about Sean, who made me believe that I have some sort of artist buried somewhere inside of me, even though I am pretty sure the true artist in him would find the attention unwanted and this section superfluous? Do I thank all of those people who doubted me, who judged me for taking a different path, who made those terrible and insulting comments? "All those who said I couldn't," so to speak? Though I hate giving that crowd any sort of attention, every single one of those instances either motivated or amused me. Do I wait until this book is a commercial success in order to stick it to them, otherwise they will think that they were right in their doubting? Or do I include it anyway, because the goal was never that, but only to do something I'm passionate about, and tell this story the best I could? Do I thank my parents, who raised me to not get hung up on what other people say, be it good or bad, but to do what I think is right? Seems a little cliché to go that route. Or what about my Grandmom? Knowing her, she would probably get upset whether I include her or not. "I'm already in the book!" if I do, "Why didn't I get acknowledged?!" if I don't. I wonder if I should thank my brother for telling me he didn't want to read my early drafts. Would people realize that I truly did appreciate that, and saw it as a sign of him taking my writing seriously, which he always has, and that the people who offered to help not out of interest, but out of politeness, were one of the most difficult obstacles during this project? I'd feel the need to shout out my friends who are in these stories, as well as those that aren't, but should I thank all those people who caused the difficulties as well? Without all of them, I wouldn't be where I am now. Undoubtedly, I would have to mention The Kid, who was beyond helpful in so many stages of the game. But should I also thank him for all the other things he does too, like being the voice of reason when Jimmy and I celebrate a bit too much, or are in one of our famous disagreements? And then there's Jimmy. Do I really need to thank him for helping me, going over each and every line, helping me ensure everything is as accurate as possible? From supporting me from Day 1 of this project? I mean, I just wrote a whole damn book about our friendship that culminated in me saying that I love him, which I'll admit, made me somewhat uncomfortable. Almost had to throw a "no homo" in the footnotes there. I feel like any more positivity toward Jimmy would be so beyond excessive it would borderline inappropriate.

In considering all of this, to sum it up, I guess I would just like to acknowledge that I was pretty surprised at the negativity I got from so many people during this endeavor. From people I thought I knew well, to strangers in my Uber, the amount of people that had an opinion on my life was surprising. On one hand, my near-delusional confidence and positivity found it somewhat endearing. I had no idea that some of these people even knew what I was doing, let alone cared enough to form an opinion on it. "The opposite of love is not hate, it's indifference" sort of thinking.

On the other hand, it made me extremely appreciative of the people who demonstrated the opposite. From people I know well, to strangers in my Uber, I held on to even the smallest and quietest words of kindness and encouragement from you, even when it was not specific to this project. Not only did your words, actions, and attitudes motivate me, but I am sure it is more reflective of who you are as a person and how you choose to interact with the world around you, rather than who I am and how you chose to interact with me. And that, as per the afterword of this book, truly inspires me.